TRIBAL SOCIETY IN INDIA

TRIBAL SOCIETY IN INDIA

An Anthropo-historical Perspective

K. S. SINGH

MANOHAR
2026

First published 1985
Reprinted 2026

ISBN 978-93-88540-85-8

Published by
Ajay Kumar Jain *for*
Manohar Publishers & Distributors
4753/23 Ansari Road, Daryaganj
New Delhi 110 002

Printed and bound in India

To
My Mother

Preface

The tribal world of India is an area of study which has been intensively researched, if not critically investigated. For over two hundred years, administrators, ethnographers, missionaries, census authorities, anthropologists, sociologists and historians have been at work in it, fascinated by tribal ways. A view, consistently projected over this span of time, has been that the tribal people are waiting to be absorbed and swallowed up by the tide of culture rising from the "cradle of Indian civilization" and by its economic and political systems There are many variants of this model which do not quite fit in with the concept of the autonomy of social formations in various regions—the rise of which could be seen in time—the pluralistic character of our society, the many streams of culture, the cluster of communities with their distinct life-styles that make up the people of India, a pattern in which the communities known as tribes also seem to fit. Each has contributed to make, what India is, today. It is equally true that overarching this there has been a cultural ethos, a commonality of symbols and idioms for the vast majority of people, a sharing of ideals and dreams that India has come to represent through ages. These structures and values and dominant modes of production have influenced social formations both at the core and on the periphery. Various communities have retained their identity, the consciousness of which has, if anything, been accentuated, particularly of those who have been guaranteed certain privileges, though for a limited period, under the Constitution of India. Generally, the communities have not been swept off their feet by winds of change, but have gained in an awareness of their identity.

Of the many streams which have contributed to the study of the tribes, anthropology is the best known, followed by history. The relationship between history and anthropology has been consistently explored in the past two decades, more by anthropologists than by historians. In our country the implications of this relationship in regard to the tribal factor have only just begun to be understood. Ethnographers and anthropologists attempted the reconstruction of tribal history as they understood it. In the monographs on tribes some of them displayed a marked degree of sensitivity to historical dimensions. However, the treatment of history or pre-history in tribal monographs remained, by and large, an exercise in speculation. Little attempt was made to separate history from myth, verify oral tradition and integrate it with archaeology for the writing of pre-history and history of the tribes. For long anthropologists desisted from an analysis of the process of change in time because the influence of the 'functionalist' was hostile to history. During the past two decades, however, descriptive tribal studies have been followed up by interpretative studies of tribal communities, and the functional approach to tribal and rural studies has been supplemented by cultural-historical lines of inquiry.

Historians have compiled accounts of Indian tribes both ancient and modern, and applied anthropological concepts to the organization of historicai material to explain social formations. Historians of ancient history have described the extension of brahminical influence into hilly areas through land grants, acculturation of tribal communities, proliferation of castes and incorporation of new tribes and castes within the emerging production system. They have explored the processes of state formation in tribal societies in the tracts extending from the Himalayan foothills to the Vindhyan mountains, and of the emergence of rural foci of political power led by the autochthonous chieftains in the medieval period. In the area of modern Indian history, a few studies have appeared in the political history of the tribes, particularly of their movements. A great deal however, remains to be done in the way of the reconstruction of their political and social history, and therefore for some years to come the major thrust of research in this field has to be of an exploratory nature. It is often stated that the data-base for the historical study of such non-literate societies is limited. This can be augmented by the use of anthropological literature and through field-study of the living communities, of the structure and function of their social system, and of their oral traditions that reflect their perception of social formations in time. A major problem therefore is to evolve a combined methodology of historical reasearch and anthropological field-study. Field-study is even otherwise important because a good deal of history survives in the day-to-day life of the people. A social historian, no matter what the period of his research might be, should expose himself to the contemporary social situation by studying the structure and function of the society he wishes to study in time, and thus of necessity familiarise himself with the tools of field investigation.

II

Over the past twenty-five years, I have worked in the area of anthropo-historical research relating to tribal society. This was because I spent a good many years of the formative phase of my career serving the tribal people in a part of middle India, Chotanagpur. Many streams including administrative experience have contributed to the development of anthropological and historical literature in our country. It would be idle to pretend that a public servant today has the leisure, the opportunity and the resources to cultivate the disciplines as did the administrators in the expansive pre-1920 phase of modern Indian history, when they collected basic information about the country and its people, when they made use of their long grass-roots level experience and familiarity with local conditions to write local histories and accounts, and when a furlough would enable the more enterprising among them to visit the centres of learning in their home country to keep themselves abreast of the theoretical developments in the fields of their disciplines, many of which were in their infancy. Times have changed a great deal. The cultivation of a discipline now requires single-minded application, and the rapidity with which each discipline is generating and discarding its theoretical models makes one a little confused. And yet participant observation provides an insight into the working of a system and constitutes an element in the passage from the present to the past, which is complementary, in the words of historian E.H. Carr, to the historical method, the movement from the past to the present, both being essential to the study of the social system, of tribe and non-tribe.

Like many administrators I too started my career in a tribal area with a dichotomous perspective on tribe and non-tribe. Fed on such of the anthropological literature as was available to us we tended to treat the tribals as isolates. Only a few months' study in the tribal areas was sufficient to convince one of the fallacy of such ideas. Administration and more so economy tended to bring tribals and non-tribals together. The pattern of their interaction could be seen in areas as far apart as the emergence of a common language or a mode of communication, religion, magic and witchcraft, diversification of economy and rise of settled agriculture. Many of these processes could be seen at work in time, and I tried to investigate them in the 1960s in the course of researches relating to state formation, tribal movements, and the impact of the national movement on tribes.

This was the point of investigation at which I stood in 1970. My study of tribal affairs had reached a critical stage at which I wished to stretch the canvas of my study and to test the hypotheses concerning the nature and processes of social change through the interaction of the tribals and non-tribals and under the impact of other exogenous forces. This revolved round the following set of questions:

1. Whether the conceptual frame for the study of tribal history, which held sway, was adequate for the understanding of tribal society?
2. What was it really that triggered off the process of change in tribal society—a simple case of hinduization as held by ethnographers or a change in the mode of production brought about by state formation in tribal regions?
3. What was the nature of colonial impact on the tribal society?
4. What were the consequences of the colonial encounter in terms of the uprisings, movements and revolts which suggested both tribal participation in the freedom struggle (I was fascinated by Mahatma Gandhi's impact on some sections of the tribes and their folklore) and their own movements to preserve their identity?

5. What has the post-colonial transformation of tribal society been like?

The focus of this inquiry into tribal society was middle India though it often narrowed down to Chotanagpur in order to highlight the processes of change and development at the micro-level. However, the scope of inquiry at times embraced all-India perspectives.

The chapters that follow are organized around these issues. We start with the conceptual framework of the colonial transformation of tribal society in middle India. The roots of change go back to the pre-colonial processes such as state formation even though it antedates colonialism. Alongside state formation, transfer of technology from peasant and artisan to tribe emerges as an important historical process, both in the pre-colonial and the colonial context. This presentation is followed up with the exploration of the processes of the integration of tribe with the cultural system of jati, economic organization and agrarian structure. The tribals as a dominant community in some regions set the model for emulation by others too. Anthropology is a child of colonialism, a historical experience that sensitized administration to the problems of primitive communities. Anthroplogists played a key role in the formulation of colonial policies on tribal people, some of the elements of which still persist. Colonialism introduced far-reaching changes in the tribal society in middle India, further opened it up to colonization by non-tribal communities, instituted a peasant mode of production and brought the tribes within the ambit of established administration. This resulted in a series of movements which could be periodized in ideological and structural terms. Tribals participated in the freedom struggle and also engaged in various forms of struggle that articulated their search for identity. In this connection Mahatma Gandhi's influence on tribal movements and sanskritization processes deserves particular notice. The post-colonial scenario represents a radical transformation of the tribal society.

The tribal society we propose to study consisted of the communities which were labelled as tribes and sought to be enclaved as such by the colonial system. This was because they rebelled often or were otherwise prone to "give trouble" in the regions considered strategic to colonial interests. Their society has been generally described as peripheral to larger formations but in many ways it is one of the matrices of the Indian social system, the study of which provides an insight into its evolution and functioning.

I acknowledge with thanks the permission given by the Nehru Memorial Museum and Library to reproduce my paper, "Freedom movement and Tribal sub-movements 1920-47" published in *Essays in Modern History* and by the Indian Institute of Advanced Studies to reproduce the paper, "From Ethinicity to Regionalism: A Study in Tribal politics and movements in Chotanagpur from 1900 to 1975", published in *Dissent, Protest and Reform in Indian Civilization*. I also thank the National Museum and Rashtriya Manav Sangrahalaya for making available the photographs of Santal artifacts reproduced in this book which show the vibrancy of tribal life and tribals' perception of themselves in a fast-changing world. One of them, forming the design on the jacket was suggested by Prof. Sankho Chaudhury for which I thank him.

All papers incorporated in this book were written as part of the project on tribal society taken up under Jawaharlal Nehru Fellowship, over a number of years. Therefore, there has been a certain amount of repetition in the later chapters. Many of these, already published, have now been revised and updated, wherever possible. The views expressed in this study are those of of the author, and the Jawaharlal Nehru Memorial Fund bears no responsibility towards them or for such commissions or omissions of facts as might have occurred.

Contents

1

History, Anthropology and Colonial Transformation

Two sets of assumptions have generally governed the historical writings on the tribes. The first could be set forth in terms of the conceptual framework developed by the British administrators-turned-ethnographers and anthropologists, which was inspired by the then prevailing model in anthropology. Tribal communities were treated as isolates, tribals as Noble Savages, and the primitive condition was described as a state of Arcadian simplicity. The deterioration of tribal communities was attributed to the sanskritization of the semi-tribal chiefs and to the vulnerability of tribal character. History, as we understand it today, was not a strong point of these scholars though some of them were sensitive to the historical dimension, and economics was seldom the strong point of the scholarship in this area. These scholars overlooked the operation of the historical processes that led to the formation of the state, the emergence of a complex regional system in the wake of the migration of non-tribal communities and functional castes and the penetration of cultural influences. It is evident that in the semi-exposed tribal regions the portrayal of a tribal as a Noble Savage, innocent of the operation of the historical processes, was both naive and untenable, but this led to the build-up of a myth that has bedevilled all historical writings on Chotanagpur and inspired all tribal movements. This simplistic model also served to justify the presence of the raj and the role of the missionaries as the protectors of the tribals against non-tribals.[1]

The second set of assumptions postulated that the tribes were a sub-system of the Hindu system and that they were being absorbed into the Hindu society.[2] The Hindu mode of absorption was spelt out by an anthropologist in terms of their integration into the economic organization of the caste.[3] There was very little Hindu about this mode of absorption. The tribes were, in fact, getting integrated into a secular system of production, a market system, as it was extended to the tribal region.

History and Anthropology

These assumptions raise the question of the relationship of history and anthropology. On the face of it, history and anthropology are opposite disciplines. History is one of the oldest disciplines, while anthropology is a child of the Age of Reason. History is a dialogue with the past while anthropology is concerned with the immediate present, existing institutions, values and ideas and their interrelationships. A measure of historical bias could be discerned in the works of the two schools of anthropologists: the Evolutionists who regarded mankind as one, used the comparative method, underlined the process of unilinear evolution from savagery to civilization; and the Diffusionists who stressed the transmission of cultural elements as the most important factor in cultural development. The historians dismissed the historical content of their writings as much too speculative. The functionalists, who followed, studied society as a whole at a point of time. They were ahistorical and dismissed history as irrelevant.

In our country, the dichotomy between history and anthropology was not very evident in the beginning. Indology and ethnology or even ethnography developed hand in hand. Some historians used ethnographic data. Sarat Chandra Roy was the first secretary of the Bihar and Orissa Research Society, and his association with it as such was as symbolic as was his break with it a few years later. Roy continued to display a keen historical sense in his contributions to the study of the agrarian system and tribal movements. He was the first and the only anthropologist to have recognized the usefulness of the archival material as a source of ethnography. Later, he turned to functionalism, and Indian anthropology since has not been, generally, able to overcome the functionalists' hostility to history.

From the early 1960s there has developed a wide awareness of the limitations of the functionalists' approach to the study of society. The social anthropologists in the west, in Africa and Latin America have moved back in time to study the process of change, into the arena of contemporary and even modern history, analysing and examining archival data, family history, census reports, etc. In a perceptive paper on the relationship of social anthropology and social history, E.E. Evans-Pritchard has observed :

> So, I may as well oblige my critics by confessing that I can see no vital difference between sociological history and what some anthropologists like to call social dynamics or diachronic sociology or the study of social change or processual (sic) analysis. Indeed, in a broad sense, I would say that social anthropology and history are both branches of social sciences, or social studies, and that consequently there is an overlap of relevance between them and each can learn much from the other . . . anthropology must choose between being history and being nothing . . . history must choose between being social anthropology or being nothing.[4]

If social anthropology is moving closer to history, social history is also moving closer to social anthropology, albeit slowly. The social historians have once again turned to the study of regional and local systems and institutions, and simple and complex communities. They are using the archival data at the district and village level, studying family history and even interviewing people who are either directly involved in historical movements or remotely associated with them. An oral history project is under way.[5] The researches being conducted now differ from the ethnographic and historical studies of castes, regions and villages in the past. Young scholars are now engaged in writing history of local institutions, movements and processes of social change at the micro-level in terms of ecology, demography, settlement patterns, interaction of groups and communities, etc. This shows the profound influence that social sciences are exercising over historical studies. From this vantage point, it is only another step to participant observation. There is no reason why a field study should not be undertaken by all researchers and why a historian, particularly a town-based one, should shy away from using the living material, critically exploiting the oral tradition and participating in some aspects of folk/rural life, and thus gain an insight into the contemporary situation and institutions, which may help him in understanding the past. A historian should take note of yet another strong point of anthropology, its conceptual framework, the holistic concept which stresses not only wholeness but the interrelatedness of aspects of social formation i.e., ecology, economy, legal and political system, kinship organization, religion, etc.

Many developments in recent times have helped anthropology transcend its traditional boundaries and move closer to history and other disciplines. One which deserves to be mentioned particularly is the rise of the school of Marxist anthropology in the West.[6] So far, most of the social anthropologists had held the view that Marxist anthropology was irrelevant to the history of anthropological theory, and that cultural anthropology had developed independently of the ideas of Karl Marx. The larger availability of the Manuscript of 1857-8 dealing with pre-capitalist formations of many types in the process of transition of feudalism kindled interest in the possibilities of the application of Marxist theories to the primitive societies. While it is admitted that the ethnographic data available at the time of Karl Marx was inadequate and fragmentary and that his treatment of evolution of the primitive societies to feudalism was superficial, it is nevertheless recognized that his studies provide a brilliant insight into the transformation of the communal mode of production and the processes of transition from status to contract. These seminal ideas seeped through the writings of H. S. Maine and B. H. Baden-Powell. Nor could Marx's influence on the school of cultural materialism be underestimated. All this is history.

The rise of the school of Marxist anthropology, which has been recognized as one of the four contemporary schools[7] reflects the recognition of the limitations of traditional economic anthropology and even social anthropology. The traditional economic anthropology concerned itself with the organization of production, distribution and consumption; with market, capital formation, land-ownership, circulation of goods, etc. It did not recognize the relevance of production relations. The traditional description of the primitive societies as non-acquisitive, non-monetary and non-machine is no longer entirely accepted. A new merit has thus been discovered in Marxist theories.

> What Marx's theories offer to social anthropology is a set of hypotheses about social relations and especially about social change. Marx's insights—about the basic significance of economic factors, especially production relations; their relation to structure of power; the formation of classes and the opposition of their interest; the socially relative character of ideologies; the conditioning force of a system upon individual members of it—embody propositions which must be taken for critical scrutiny into the body of our science.[8]

The French Marxist anthropologists go a step further. They seek a return not to Marx and resumption and defence of his ideas about primitive society and the beginning of class society; they go even beyond the literal Marx.

> Unlike the Marxism which is usually practised, a Marxism which soon turns to vulgar materialism, we maintain that Marx—in characterising infrastructure and superstructure and stating that the profound logic of societies and their history depended in the last analysis on changes in their infrastructure—did nothing less than bring to light for the first time a hierarchy of functional distinctions and structural causalities, without in any way prejudicing the nature of structures, which in every case perform these functions (kinship, politics, religion...) nor the number of functions which a structure may support. In order to arrive at this profound logic we must go further than a structural analysis of forms of social relations and modes of thought and try to decipher the 'effects' of structures on each other through the various processes of social practice and place them in the hierarchy of causes determining the functioning and reproduction of economic and social formations.[9]

It is not necessary at this stage to go into the various aspects of the debate concerning the infrastructure and superstructure, primacy of relations of production against relations of exchange or technology of production, mode of production against mode of exploitation, unilinear versus multilinear processes of development, etc., and whether the primitive society should be labelled feudal or pre-capitalist or whether it had its own mode of production. Suffice it to say that caution is required in the collection and processing of data, and the temptation to fit them to certain stereotypes must be resisted as much as the reluctance to see them in perspective and to generalize from them.

We may consider another concept, development of underdevelopment,[10] based on the Latin American experience, which is now being extended to Africa and other parts of the developing world[11] and which has great possibilities for the study of social formation in the tribal regions. Briefly stated, it assumes that development and underdevelopment are interrelated, that underdevelopment is a result of the historical process of the capitalist development over the past centuries, and that there is a continuing trend towards evergrowing development and growing underdevelopment. Of late, a number of models have been generated by economists to explicate the pattern of development in many parts of the developing world.[12] What interests us in these exercises is the fact that some of these theoretical models are being extrapolated backward in time to explain historical situations.

Anthropology and Colonialism

We will now touch upon some aspects of the interrelationship of anthropology and colonialism. As the colonial system has disintegrated, an acrimonious debate is developing over the nature and function of anthropologica research in the former colonial societies and the extent of collaboration between anthropologists and colonial administrators.[13] On the one hand, anthropology has been labelled as a child of imperialism,[14] while on the other it has been stated that anthropology is not "a bastard of imperialism but the legitimate child of the Enlightenment",[15] a full-fledged discipline which has developed its own autonomy and is now an art and a science. No doubt, ethnography had its roots in the administration's need to collect information about the people, which made for efficient governance. In this sense, anthropology developed as a part of the colonial system. Some of the anthropologists turned out to be the apologists of the colonial regime, which was projected as the protector of the minorities, while others criticized the disruptive effects of the colonial system on the small, encysted communities which they were allowed to study in some countries. The anthropologists were also charged by the nationalists with having destroyed national identity, created a social category called a 'tribe' for which there was no word in many native languages, introduced alien concepts, and supported the obscurantist chiefs and indirect rule. There was also the other side of the picture. The collection of data at the grassroot level resulted in a radical orientation of politics. Certain ideological trends in anthropology supported anti-colonial movements. Anthropology also stressed the role and function of ethnicity and diversity in the formation of a nation-state.

In India,[16] most of those trends could be witnessed. There was, however, one difference. It was not the anthropologist but the colonial officer who played the key role as an adviser, researcher and administrator in tribal affairs. There was one exception to this. Sarat Chandra Roy became the spokesman of the tribal interests in the Bihar and Orissa Legislative Council, and later emerged as the ideologue of the separatist movement in Chotanagpur. The colonial administrators working in the tribal regions sought to influence the debates preceding the drafting of the Government of India Bill of 1935, and argued in favour of the total exclusion of the tribal regions from the ambit of constitutional reforms. They even suggested that if this was not done, the Congress movement would sweep the tribal regions like wild fire.

Precolonial Situation

The precolonial situation has, generally, been described by ethnographers as static. Historical evidence, however, suggests at least three major trends. First, there was colonization and establishment of settlements (*bhum*) by peasant castes, who were encouraged by the Mughal rulers and zamindars to reclaim land and offered various incentives for this purpose, or by other categories of immigrants. Trade or strategic routes passing through the jungle regions acquired a new significance. The Jharkhand[17] and Gondwana emerged as historical regions in the medieval period. Secondly, many tribes, such as the Bhils, Minas, Kolis and Gonds were recognized as dominant communities by the Mughal empire. Thirdly, and most important of all the region witnessed the rise of the state either out of the tribal matrix as in the case of the Gonds and Cheros or as a result of the imposition on the tribal system of the authority of the Rajputs and other castes which established their power, in the highlands of Orissa, central India, Gujarat and Rajasthan.

The phenomenon of state formation has been extensively investigated in the two Americas by anthropologists, archaeologists and historians and has emerged as a major theoretical concern. Karl Wittfogel's theory that large-scale protective irrigation works led to the rise of the state has now been questioned. Two supplementary hypotheses have been postulated concerning growth of population and multi-variable emphasis in regard to state formation based on recent anthropological and reinterpreted ethno-historical evidence. In India, the interest in this phenomenon has developed only recently.[18]

A crucial precondition of the formation of the state in middle India was the extension of cultivation through the reclamation of land and the introduction of a new agricultural technology by the peasantry from plains. The Gond, Nagbansi and Chero chiefs encouraged the settlement of non-tribal peasant communities such as the Kurmis, Koeris and Kunbis who, with their superior agricultural technology, alone could generate the agricultural surplus that the new states required. A new mode of production thus emerged. A consequence of the imposition of the feudal superstructure on the tribal society was its breakdown and fragmentation into distinct social strata based on corresponding distribution of power and economic interest in land and defined in terms of ritual status. The new states acted as the agents of sanskritization but they also strengthened the sense of tribal identity. State-formation stimulated commercial activities, developed trade routes and promoted small-scale urbanism. A variety of castes ranging from the brahmins who were tempted by generous grants of land to the artisan communities flocked to the new fort-cities. All in all, a complex social economic system had emerged in certain parts of tribal middle India even before the colonial system was established there.

Political System and the Concept of Protection

The political system of tribal India was based on the concept of direct rule. Unlike Africa which adopted the system of indirect rule, namely, rule through the traditional chiefs in many territories, a large part of the tribal region and most of the tribal population were integrated within the administration of the provinces of British India or within that of the Indian states where the British Resident kept a watch on the tribal situation and, in some cases, even acted as the agent for the tribal regions. However, there were areas of tribal concentration which were enclaved to 'reclaim to civilisation' the tribes who had often rebelled or were difficult to pacify. It was in these enclaves that the concept of protection of the tribes as an ethnic community developed in stages. Its main features were (a) the paternalistic rule of the district officers—the tribes needed a government by men and not by a system; (b) keeping tribal areas out of the operation of the regulations, laws, etc., which were alien to tribal ethos and undermined it; (c) laying down a set of simple rules to settle disputes, restriction of the jurisdiction of the courts which enforced normal laws, and exclusion of the lawyers from courts; (d) special agrarian laws; (e) regulation of the entry of the aliens into tribal areas; and (f) strengthening tribal institutions and traditional leadership.

The Agency system established with the objective of quelling rebellions was the earliest mode of protective administration. One agency was set up to pacify the Bhils (1825), another in Chotanagpur, the South-West Frontier Agency (1833), a third in the Meriah tract (1839-65) to abolish the practice of human sacrifice, and the fourth one in Ganjam (1839), which has survived longest. The first three were wound up as soon as the objective for which they were formed was achieved. The Agency settled tribes, opened up the tribal world, laid lines of communication, established *chatties* along highways to supply the army which brought in merchants, traders and peddlers and which developed into markets later, and set up cantonments and centres of administration and trade. The pace of urbanization gradually went up. The British historians built up the 'founders'—Augustus Cleveland, James Outram and Thomas Wilkinson—into legends. However, within a few decades, Cleveland's Paharias were impoverished and decimated, and the Bhils and Chotanagpur tribes repeatedly rose in rebellions. With the establishment of regular administration the pace of the colonization of the tribal regions, which had begun in the medieval period, as mentioned earlier, was accelerated. In Chotanagpur alone, for instance, between 1871 and 1931, the incidence of immigration rose from 96,000 to 307,000.

Thus the colonial system ended the relative isolation of the tribal society; brought it into the mainstream of the new administrative set-up, policy and programmes; put an end to the political dominance of the tribes in the region; and roped the tribal communities which had been spared the strain of surplus generation into a new system of production relations. The colonial system, as elsewhere, followed the dual policy of strengthening the feudal crust of the tribal society, formed by the rajas, chiefs and zamindars and simultaneously creating conditions in which their economy and political system were undermined by the rampaging market forces.

The principle that the normal laws should not automatically apply to tribal areas underlay the passage of the Scheduled Districts Act (1874) and the concept of the backward areas in the Government of India Act of 1919. Whether or not this principle should continue to be applied was a matter that figured in a most lively debate in the early 1930s. While one school contended that the aborigines formed a distinct element and should be placed in charge of the British Government, the nationalists saw in this proposition the continuation of the imperial policy of divide and rule. However, the tribal and non-tribal areas were both partly and fully "excluded" in the Government of India Act of 1935. The need to provide adequate safeguards for the tribals was again extensively discussed in the Constituent Assembly, and the nationalist opinion favoured incorporation of far more radical provisions for the safeguard of the tribals' interests in the form of the Fifth and Sixth Schedules of the Indian Constitution. This was an index of the profound change that had come over nationalist opinion in regard to the tribal question owing to the efforts of Mahatma Gandhi, Thakkar Bapa[19] and Rajendra Prasad, the unfolding of the humanism of the freedom movement, and the liberalism of the tribal leaders themselves. This appreciation of the uniqueness of tribal factors within the framework of Indian nationalism and the extension of political rights to tribals were beyond the expectations of the colonial administrators and anthropologists.

Agrarian Restructuring, Economic Transformation and Mode of Exploitation

It is only now that anthropologists have taken up the study of the agrarian processes of social change that cut across the traditional boundaries of kinship and ethnicity. It is an area in which the historians have been more active, and the scope of collaboration between the two streams is wide.

The land system in the tribal area was integrated within the two broad categories of land tenure—the zamindari and the ryotwari. The tribal regions in Bihar, Bengal and eastern parts of the Central Provinces belonged to the first, and those in Bombay, Gujarat and the western parts of the Central Provinces to the second category. Tribal or non-tribal chiefs in the tribal regions were recognized as zamindars/*malgujars*; *ghatwals*, the guardians of passes and wardens of marches (Bengal, Bihar, Berar); *bissoyies* and *muttadars*, as landlords, and the other classes of tribals were occupancy tenants or sub-tenants. In both systems there were primeval survivals of the communal mode of production: the *khuntkatti* tenure in Chotanagpur and Angul, and the special tenures related to communal ownership of land in the Bombay Presidency. The institution of village headman who was the representative of the relatively intact tribal village community, the Munda-Manki system of Chotanagpur and the Manjhi-Parganait system of the Santal Pargana were strengthened, and written into law.

The tribal land laws, framed in the background of the rebellions, incorporated new agrarian concepts. For instance, the idea of the prevention of alienation of tenure/land could be traced to the Wilkinson Rules (1833). The provision against usury appeared in the Santal Pargana Regulation of 1873, and this was further strengthened through a series of Acts to regulate moneylending. The Chotanagpur Tenancy Act (1908) innovated many provisions to give protection to the aboriginal tenants and became a piece of model legislation. The Punjab Land Alienation Act (1900) inspired the Central Provinces' legislation (1916), even though the region was contiguous to Chotanagpur. While these laws did give a measure of protection, they could not prevent, as a Chotanagpur survey in the 1920s showed, either alienation or usury on a large scale.

The most striking feature of this period was the breakdown of the communal mode of production and the emergence of private right in land.[20] The first was generally related to the technology of hunting and food-gathering, the slash-and-burn cultivation, which were, again, associated with the system of communal ownership/control of land and use of collective labour. To facilitate commercial exploitation of forest shifting cultivation was forbidden in many areas. The pressure of population increased and the carrying capacity of land diminished. The peasantry coming up from the plains introduced, as mentioned above, the concept of agricultural season and new crops, implements and practices[21] related to both wet and dry land farming. The tribes had already taken to terrace and wet cultivation, and developed an excellent indigenous technology suited for them on both communal and private family land. The new technology helped them to extend cultivation. Thus they were transformed from the reclaimers of land into peasant cultivators, largely living off the land. Multi-caste and multi-ethnic village settlements came into existence underlining the cooperation among peasants and artisans and other functional castes in the process of production.[22] The transition from the tribal to the peasant system was however neither uniform nor complete. Dependence on forests as a source of food, shelter and occupation was still crucial in many ways. By and large, all major tribes in the nineteenth century were emerging as a community of peasants while the minor tribes still depended on the forest.

A further stage in the development of the peasant system was the penetration of tribal economy by market forces. The colonial system created a demand for money in non-money economies to pay land revenue and other levies, to defray expenditure of various kinds, and to buy necessities. The traditional form of barter exchange died away. There was evidence that sections of the tribes took to commodity production on a limited scale. It was not so much the grain as minor forest produce such as lac that brought the tribals into contact with the market. Fluctuations in the international price of lac impoverished them and boosted their income by turn. Even the most primitive economies came gradually within the operation of the market system. There is evidence that coerced cash cropping in cotton and sugarcane was resorted to in parts of western India, and the tribals were evicted from lands which were brought under it.

With the market came the middle men, merchants and moneylenders. The concept of *diku*, the aliens, becomes crucial to the understanding of agrarian relations. A *diku* was the creature of the colonial system who performed a variety of functions as a middle man in administrative matters, as a moneylender, as a trader who controlled production of foodgrain through the system of advance credit, and as a landgrabber.

The processes of 'peasantization' and, 'depeasantization' were at work simultaneously. The latter could be seen in large-scale incidence of alienation of land from tribals to non-tribals. The tribal handicrafts declined. Emigration from Chotanagpur alone was 3,30,000 in 1891, 7,07,000 in 1911 and 9,47,000 in 1921. Tribals went out to work in the tea gardens, on plantations, as industrial labour, and as share-croppers and labourers in the regions peripheral to their homeland. Had this vast number remained at home, the process of depeasantization would have been much faster in Chotanagpur and other tribal areas. This may be seen in the context of and as an example of the development of under development at the micro-level, while the development industries based on forests and minerals made tribal areas forge of ahead in terms of the indicators of modern development.

Social Stratification, Sanskritization and Christianity

There existed within a tribe a measure of distinction between the high and the low in terms of social and physical distance, notion of purity and pollution, prestige and status, habits and customs, etc. The colonial system created and strengthened a threefold division with the feudatory chiefs/zamindars at the top, the well-to-do headmen in the middle and the general mass at the bottom. A class of insider *diku* and professional tribal money-lenders also grew up as the unintended result of the anti-land alienation laws, which restricted transfer of land from tribals to non-tribals. A rich stratum of tribal buyers of land emerged as suggested by the data on transactions in land and moneylending in the district settlement reports. There were also reports of conflicts between the secular and religious leadership though these did not seem to have any enduring consequence.

But this internal differentiation did not grow to a point of complete alienation of one stratum from another. The bonds of kinship and ethnicity and the appreciation of the political advantages of the continuation of the tribe as an entity after 1920 became stronger. This inhibited the development of intra-tribe contradiction, which was also overshadowed by the confrontation between tribals and non-tribals.

The foregoing analysis shows that the tribal society was moving closer to the peasant/caste system. This brings us to sanskritization, the process of upward mobility, which had been restricted to a family or a group of persons in the pre-colonial situation. Under the colonial impact, sanskritization became a movement encompassing tribes and sub-tribes. The Santals put on the sacred thread and claimed the status of the ksatriya; the Mahtos of Chotanagpur got themselves descheduled as a tribe in 1931 and tried to establish a pan-Indian identity. A Gond chief in the 1930s requested the Rajput Mahasabha to confer the status of a ksatriya on him, a request which was refused; he took recourse to the traditional method of seeking elevation: he married into a Rajput family and got a family history written; he was finally accepted as a Nagbansi ksatriya. A rigorous analysis of the census reports of the pre-1941 period at the district level—unfortunately most of them have perished—would show the extent of the success achieved by various communities seeking higher status, and the reflection of it in the accretion of strength to higher castes.

We may now turn to an evaluation of the role of Christianity as an ideology in the colonial context, particularly in the tribal regions.[23] Such an evaluation has necessarily to base itself on the missionary records made available to the researchers so far and the study of the impact of Christianity on the tribal population; it will not be appropriate here to consider the modernizing role of the Christian missions and the participation of the Christians, alongside other sections of our people in the freedom struggle.

There always existed a close link between Christianity and colonialism. As the colonies were conquered, Christianity moved in to "civilize" the aboriginal races. The Aborigines' Protection Society, established in 1836, exercised a powerful influence on the colonial policy and administration. It should, however, be noted that the Christian missions in India did not emerge as agrarian institutions, though they did engage in activities of an economic nature such as introduction of trade, new techiniques and methods of agriculture on a small scale, and employment of labour on extensive building activities, which made them an economic asset. This was in contrast to the developments of a radical nature that occurred in Latin America, where the missionaries were transformed from the apostles who had earlier preached the tenets of racial equality and defended the Indians against the settlers into builders of great estates from the 16th century onwards.[24] The temporal power of the church was eventually equalled only by its spiritual power. In India the missions did acquire land or small zamindaris by way of gift or purchase, but they tended to depend more on the contributions raised for their support and the annual subventions from the central funds released by their parent organizations situated abroad, which in size were probably next only to the direct investment of foreign capital in India.

At the political level, the missionaries, in close collaboration with the colonial administrators, rationalized the raj, and sought to create a new bastion of support for it among the backward communities of India. The Christians, they contended, were loyal subjects, the *bhai-bahen* of the British crown, and, as such, they were entitled to receive certain privileges. The Indian Mutiny constituted a set-back to evangelization; but after 1860 it was taken up with renewed vigour. The official policy of social neutrality and non-interference in religious matters as proclaimed on November 1, 1858, was not always acted upon. Many of the district officers felt that this policy did not apply to the non-Aryan population of India, and, therefore, they supported the missionaries in their activities. A distinguished administrator, Sir Richard Temple, observed:

> I may remind you of the fortunate fact that in India out of 200 million British subjects (exclusive of native stock) 18 million are of aboriginal races, and 9 million of no caste at all. Thus 27 million are beyond the pale of the principal oriental religions and their minds present a tabula rasa on which Christianity may work.

Sir Richard was not alone. There were others who were more vocal and active in their support. Some of them even endowed the missions.

In the early phases, the missionary activities were disruptive of the tribal system. Evangelization was inherently ethnocentric. The missionary imposed a puritanical ethic on the permissive tribal society, though the approaches of various denominations to social questions markedly varied depending on the exigencies of the situation. The strategy of proselytization was carefully worked out to cover the distant and sensitive regions, major tribal communities and particularly their upper strata. Elsewhere outside middle India, the missionaries concentrated on the communities other than the tribes.

The missionaries also produced an ideology for the peasant system emerging in the tribal region. They grafted the notion of private property in land on to the communal mode of production; articulated the demands of tribals as peasant proprietors for the restoration of land, regulation of rent, and abolition of feudal dues; led and guided peasant struggles against the indigo planters in Bengal and the zamindars of Chotanagpur; worked for the passage of agrarian laws, and set up peasant organizations. They gave a new sense of self-respect to the tribal peasants and sought to create a separate identity for them. Here is a piece of the mission historiography dealing with the origin of the tribes of India:

> Now after the event of the Tower of Babel or confusion of speech, the descendants of Japeth settled in western and central Asia. The descendants of Cham or Ham also on receiving diverse tongues scattered, and they occupied better and warmer parts of the old world...of whom came the Negroes and other aboriginals of Africa... The descendants of Chanann...were known by the names of the Minoans, the Pelasgians and the Etruscans. The ancestors of the Dravidians belonged to Chanannites. The Proto-Australoids, who came to India after the Austries or the Kherwars belonged to the Chanannites of Palestine...The present Munda speaking Adivasis such as the Santals, the Mundas, the Hos and others, are the descendants of these Austrics or Kharwars.[26]

Having established the Biblical origin of the Mundas, the problem was how to bring them through Persia and Afghanistan to India. Sarat Chandra Roy noted the local Christian historical tradition introduced by the missionaries, which traced the migration of the tribes from the northwest to their present habitat:

> If we follow the order indicated in this tradition the Mundas would have appeared to have migrated from Northern India southwards to modern Bundelkhand and Central India, thence across eastern Rajputana, thence again to north western India and thence through modern Rohilkhand and to Bihar and finally to Chotanagpur.[27]

Roy was inclined to accept this local tradition even though he admitted that the circuitous route appeared to be "strange and perplexing". It went against all history and logic but it served to generate a sense of pan-Christian solidarity.

Tribal Movements

The colonial system bore harshly on the tribal communities who with a sensitivity born of isolation and with a relatively intact mechanism of social control revolted more often and far more violently than any other community including peasants in India.

The official records, scattered over a wide spectrum, refer to the acts of depredation, disturbances, outbreaks of violence and riots, rebellions and uprisings, raids and expeditions of pacification—the character of which has yet to be ascertained. These are generally described as incidents and episodes, whereas they have to be studied as movements, as a part of the social system.

Since the Second World War, there has been an upsurge of interest in tribal movements.[28] The movements in Africa, Oceania and in the Americas have inspired new conceptual and methodological leads by the French, Italian and German historians of religion and anthropologists. Comprehensive studies of the messianic movements have been brought out. Vittorio Lanternari's *The Religions of the Oppressed* (1963) is a masterly study of modern messianic cults by a historian, but it excludes from its purview the Indian movements. Peasant movements have also been intensively and critically studied. An attempt has been made to formulate the laws and processes of tribal revitalization movements and the pattern of their leadership in terms of the concepts evolved in the context of the study of Amerindian and African movements, and their applicability to the Indian situation has to be critically examined.

In our country historian-administrators and social workers took a lead in the study of tribal movements. In 1945, appeared[29] a descriptive account of some of the movements. The Santal, Kol and Bhumij, and Munda movements have been studied[30]. The officially sponsored studies in the freedom movement and the Indian Mutiny dealt with tribal movements as a part of the national struggle.

It is only recently that a determined effort is being made by historians, archivists, anthropologists and sociologists to study the rich Indian material on tribal and peasant movements in their contemporary and historical setting.[31] This underlines the need for inter-disciplinary cooperation. A historian has not only to draw on the archival material, particularly that lying in the mission archives, but also the private papers and documents devoutly preserved by many tribal people, and study in collaboration with the anthropologists the social structure of the movement, the sects thrown up by it, and its oral traditions consisting of the magical formulae, incantations and folklore, which reflect people's perception and involvements. He has also to keep in mind the time-frame of the movements because there is a tendency not only to regard all tribal movements as of a piece but also to see the shadow of a movement behind every act of conflict or incidence of excitement. As the structure of the tribal society has changed, so, too, has the character of the tribal movement. We will therefore attempt, briefly, a periodization of tribal movements, while stressing the fact that the chronological frame has to be kept flexible in view of the wide range of variations in local situation and social structure, and the fact that many movements tend to overlap it.

The first phase (1795-1860) of the tribal movements coincided with the rise, expansion and the establishment of the British Empire. It saw the rise of what we may call the primary resistance movements. Resistance is inherent in all movements but during this phase it was spontaneous, elemental and widespread involving not only one tribe but many. The tribes played a dominant but by no means an exclusive role in it; there were large sections of the non-tribals who also joined hands, lending the movements the character of a regional upsurge. It was led by the traditional chiefs and their subordinates, who had been dispossessed of their property and thrown out of their occupation by the new system. It was resistance to the new system and to the new classes of the people who were inducted by it, namely, the system of local administration and taxation, evangelization and humanitarian measures, the new landlords, moneylenders, and government officials, all of whom were to be thrown out in a violent upsurge. This formulation generally applies to all the movements of this period; the Chuar rebellions (1795-1800), the uprisings of Chero zamindars and disturbances in Chotanagpur in 1820, the Kol and Bhumij insurrections, the resistance offered by Gond zamindars in 1819 and 1842 ,and the Khonds' resistance to the abolition of the Meriah sacrifice from the mid-1830s. This phase culminated in the Indian Mutiny of 1857, which saw the Chero and Gond zamindars revolt, while many other tribes kept out of it.

We have deliberately excluded from this scheme the Santal insurrection (1855-56) about which much fresh material has been discovered making a fresh study necessary. It represented a transitional phase and partook of the characteristics of both resistance and agrarian-cum-revivalistic movements of the second phase.

The second phase (1860-1920) coincided with the intensive phase of colonialism, which saw a much deeper penetration of tribal and peasant economies by merchant capital, higher incidence of rent, etc. All gains registered during the first phase of the movements were washed away. Not only those who had been expelled came back but many more also came, intensifying the exploitation of tribes. As a result of this, there were not only a larger number of movements, represented by such evocative native terms as *mulkui larai*, *fituri*, *meli*, *ulgulan* and *bhumakal*, involving many tribes but also a far more complex type of movements, a curious mix of agrarian, religious and political issues.

Let us, first, untangle the agrarian stand. The basic issues were high incidence of rent, commutation of rent, abolition of forced labour and praedial conditions, the issues that affected the peasants who were particularly aggrieved against the zamindars and favourably inclined towards the distant government. There were complaints regarding erosion of traditional rights in forest, restriction on shifting cultivation, and exploitation by the local functionaries. In this respect the agrarian movements among the tribes and peasants had many points of similarity. There was a typical ambivalence towards a moneylender: his records could be burnt but his life was spared. In fact, there was little blood-spilling in the agrarian movements, though the covert acts of violence were many.

Unlike the peasant movements, the tribal movements developed a religious and political overtone. The failure of the first phase of the movements had made the tribes look inward. They sought to restructure the entire social system; this was the beginning of revitalization movements. All major uprisings of the first phase were followed by socio-cultural movements, the Santal insurrection by the Kharwar movement (1871-80) and the Munda-Oraon Sardar movement (1869-1895) by Birsa Munda's and Tanabhagats' reformative stir (1895-1921), which threw up the charismatic and "divinely-inspired" brand of leadership such as Birsa Munda among the Mundas (1895-1901), Sidhu, Kanhu, Bhagirath and Dubu Gossain among the Santals (1855-56, 1871-90), Jatra Oraon among the Oraons (1915-22), Govind Giri among the Bhils. They organized and led social and political action for the restoration of their people's rights and "kingdom", founded cults and expressed through borrowed Hindu and Christian idioms their urge for freedom. All ended in violent clashes with the authorities. A few rebellions during this period also resulted from the disturbance of the traditional relationship of the tribes with their rulers in Keonjhar and Bastar. However, behind this ostensible cause there was the set of factors mentioned above.

The leadership of the movements emerged from the ranks of the peasants, educated tribals or was offered by those outsiders who had gained a footing among the tribes. The tribes most involved were the Bhils, Santals, Mundas. Oraon and Khonds—all settled communities.

The third phase (1920-1947) saw the rise of the movement of a secular and political nature even though movements of the type mentioned above continued to occur on a smaller scale. The first involved (a) participation of the tribes in the national and agrarian movements and (b) emergence of a separatist movement in Chotanagpur.

The influence of Mahatma Gandhi in the process of the mobilization of the tribals during the freedom struggle[32] could be seen at two levels. First, the Mahatma, his personality and his message seemed to carry forward and deepen the process of sanskritization started by the tribal bhagats in the latter half of the nineteenth century. In fact, it is among the members of the bhagat sects, already sensitized to Vaishnavism, that Gandhiji made the greatest impact. *Chelas* of the Mahatma sprang up among the Bhils, Gonds and Hos. The Bhil bhagats, the Tana bhagats, and Sapha Hors among Santals, and the Haribaba movement saw in the freedom movement led by Gandhiji an opportunity for the recovery of their raj and their rights as agrarian communities which they had lost, for continuing social reforms such as temperance, purification and education, and for seeking social uplift and establishing an equation with peasant castes. Most of these bhagat sects in their origin antedated the freedom movement. They received a fresh lease of life through Gandhiji's reconstruction programme.[33]

At another level, the Gandhian reconstruction programme started the process of the politicization of the tribals, nurtured a generation of tribal leaders, and provided a common political platform for the tribals and non-tribals, thus bringing the first into the mainstream of national politics. Evidence of tribals' participation in the local level action organized by the Congress came in from Bihar, Central Provinces and Bombay.

The Koyas and Jatapus participated in the guerilla warfare waged by Sitaram Raju in the Rampa country (1922-24) for the attainment of a political goal: the independence of the country with the support of the upper crust of the tribal society: the *doras*. There were not many agrarian issues involved, and the targets of attack were the British officers.

The Prajamandal and Kisan sabha also mobilized tribals over agrarian issues. The agrarian struggle in Bengal, 1946-47, was marked by the participation of the Santal peasants.[34] The Warlis of Thane were very effectively organiezd to demand the redress of their grievances in the mid-1940s.[35] However, the efforts of Swami Sahajanand Saraswati to extend the Kisan movement to Chotanagpur did not succeed because there the payment of rent in kind (*bhaoli*) was not a burning issue, the tribals enjoyed far more rights than the peasants elsewhere in Bihar, and a movement of political separatism was developing, which put the agrarian issues in the shade.

Behind the separatist movement in Chotanagpur there were influences of many kinds: a high level of literacy and political consciousness, the role of the Christian missions, Bengali-Bihari controversy over employment, and Muslim League politics. The Chotanagpur Improvement Society formed in 1916 demanded employment for educated tribals, reservation in the services and legislative bodies and the formation of a sub-state joined to Bengal or Orissa. In 1938, a militant phase started with the formation of the Adivasi Mahasabha, which demanded not the formation of a sub-state but complete separation from Bihar. But by 1947 militancy had failed. The Sabha was routed by the Congress in the first elections held in 1946. The link with the Muslim League was broken, and the Bengali-Bihari controversy tapered off. This movement also stimulated a mini-renaissance among the Chotanagpur tribes; discovering or inventing scripts, revival of the forms of art and literature were all part of a movement to define and assert tribal identity.

To conclude tribal society lost its pristine character. Like other segments of Indian society, it, too, was transformed by colonialism but in a far more profound sense than has been understood so far. The uneven impact of colonialism could be understood with reference to the specifics of the local situations and structures including the tribal.

There is a whole range of possibilities of research in the tribal history of modern India, which is relatively little researched, in collaboration with the anthropologists. Interdisciplinary collaboration of this nature does not imply that history should cease to be history but that it should imbibe the insights offered by other disciplines. It means that while fully and critically exploiting the documentary material, a historian should not hesitate to go beyond the written word and use other source material to reconstruct the history of non-literate societies. After all, the function of a historian is to illuminate the process of social transformation, and to aid it.

Notes and References

Based on the author's Presidential Address to the Modern History Session, of the Indian History Congress, held at Bhubaneswar, December 26-28, 1977, later published under the litle "Colonial Transformation of Tribal Society in middle India", in *Economic and Political Weekly* July 29, 1978.

1. K.S. Singh "State formation in Tribal Society: Some Preliminary Observations", *Journal of the Indian Anthropological Society*, vol. 6. no. 2, October 1971.
2. G.S. Ghurye, *The Aborigines-so-called-and Their Future.*
3. N.K. Bose, "Hindu mode of tribal absorption", *Cultural Anthropology and Other Essays.*
4. E.E. Evans-Pritchard, *Anthropology and History.*
5. This project had been sponsored by the Nehru Memorial Museum and Library, New Delhi.
6. Marvin Harris, *The Rise of Anth-opological Theory, a history of Theories of Culture*, pp. 217-49.

The seventy-sixth annual meeting of the American Anthropological Association held from 29 November to 3 December 1977 devoted two sessions to the discussion of "Current issues in British Marxist Anthropology" and "Class and class conflict in agrarian societies".

7. Edmund Leach, *Social Anthropology: A Natural Science of Society.*
8. Raymond Firth, "The Sceptical Anthropologist: Social Anthropology and Marxist Views on Society", in Maurice Bloch (ed), *Marxist Analyses and Social Anthropology, ASA Studies*, 2.
9. Maurice Godelier, *Perspectives in Marxist Anthropology*, pp. 2-3.
10. Andre Gunder Frank, *Capitalism and Underdevelopment in Latin America*, ; *Latin America : Underdevelopment or Revolution*, and *On Capitalist Underdevelopment.*
11. For the African studies, see Samir Amin, *Unequal Development* and E.A. Brett, *Colonialism and Underdevelopment in East Africa.*
12. Kamal Narayan Kabra, "Notes Towards a Theory of Indicators of Development", in *The Indian Journal of Public Administration*, Special Number, Development of Backward Areas, vol. XXIII, no. 3, July 1971.
13. Talal Asad, (ed), *Anthropology and the Colonial Encounter.*
14. Kathleen Gough, "Anthropology : Child of Imperialism", *Monthly Review*, April, 1968; also see "New Proposals for Anthropology", *Current Anthropology*, vol. 9, 1968.
15. Raymond Firth, op. cit.
16. The Indian perspective is presented through an account of the life and activities of Sir Alfred Lyall, which is by no means representative. See Roger Owen, "Imperial Policy and Theories of Social Change: Sir Alfred Lyall in India" in Talal Asad, op. cit.

17. Probably the first reference to the Jharkhand could be traced to a copper-plate inscription of the 13th century, See N.N. Vasu, 'Copperplate Inscription of Nrsimhadeva II", *Journal of the Asiatic Society of Bengal*, vol. XVI, 1869, pp. 256-7.

18. Surajit Sinha, "State Formation and Rajput Myth in Central India", *Man in India*, vol.42, no. 2, 1961: A. Guha, "Ahom Migration: Its Impact on Rice Economy of Medieval Assam", *Arth Vijnana*. vol. 9, no. 2, June 1967, p. 145; K.S. Singh, "State Formation in Tribal Society: Some Preliminary Observations", *op. cit.* An earlier and shorter version of the paper (1967) appeared under the title "A Study in State Formation among Tribal Communities" in R.S. Sharma, and V. Jha (eds), *Indian Society; Historical Probings in memory of D.D. Kosambi.*

19. K.S. Singh, "Mahatma Gandhi and the Adivasis" *Man in India*, vol. 50, no. 1, Jan-March 1970.

20. For a graphic description see J. Reid, *Final Report on the Survey and Settlement Operations in the District of Ranchi* 1902-10 ; also see K.S. Singh, "Tribal Land Organisation in Chhotanagpur and its Development", in *Trends of Socio-Economic Change in India, 1871-1961, Transactions of the Indian Institute of Advanced Study*, vol. 7.

21. K.S. Singh, "Pattern of Agricultural Changes in Tribal Chhotanagpur".

22. See for a study of the contemporary situation, K.S. Singh, "Tribal Economy in India", in Traditional Institutions in the Process Modernisation of Society: Independent India and Soviet Central Asia, Indo-Soviet Symposium in Social Sciences, February 22-26, 1977, Visva-Bharati, Shantiniketan.

23. See for instance, S.C. Roy, "The Effects on the Aborigines of Chotanagpur of their Contact with Western Civilisation", *Journal of the Bihar and Orissa Research Society*, vol. xvii, part iv, 1931; Suresh Singh, *The Dust-Storm and the Hanging Mist: A Study of Birsa Munda and his Movement in Chhotanagpur, 1874-1901*, pp. 13-31: Also see the second edition of the book, *Birsa Munda and His Movement* 1874-1901, and K.N. Sahay, *Under the Shadow of the Cross: A Study of the Nature and Processes of Christianization among the Uraon of Central India.*

24. Francois Chevalier, *Land and Society in Colonial Mexico.*

25. *Objections to the Missionary Work in India Considered and Answered: A Speech Delivered at a Meeting of the SPG in Foreign Parts*, (November 7, 1881), The Christian Missionary Society, London.

26. Timothy Tilkai Murmu, *The Adivasis, Past and Present: That is a History of the Indian Aborigines from the Earliest Time to the Present day.*

27. Sarat Chandra Roy, *The Mundas and their Country*, (rep) p. 20.

28. To cite a few studies, see I.G. Jarvie, *The Revolution in Anthropology*; Rodoflo Stavenhagen (ed), *Agrarian and Peasant Movements in Latin*

Amertca; Peter Worsley, *The Trumpet Shall Sound* and E.J. Hobsbawm, *Primitive Rebels.*

29. *Man in India, Rebellion Number*, vol. 25 (1945).

30. K.K. Datta, *Anti:British Plots and Movements Before 1857*; J. C. Jha *The Kol Insurrection of Chotanagpur*; *Bhumij Revolt* 1832-33; Suresh Singh, *The Dust-Storm and the Hanging Mist.* A number of dissertations on tribal movements have appeared.

31. For studies by social workers see V. Raghavaiah, *Tribal Revolts* and Godavari Parulekar, *Adivasis Revolt.*

See for the anthropologists' contributions, Surajit Sinha, "Tribal Solidarity Movements in India: A Review", and L.K. Mahapatra, "Social Movements Among the Tribes in India", in K.S. Singh (ed) *Tribal Situation in India.* The Indian Institute of Advance Study has brought out a volume reflecting an inter-disciplinary collection; S.C. Malik (*ed*). *Dissent, Protest and Reform in Indian Civilisation*" The All-India Sociological Conference at Chandigarh (1976) devoted a session to the social movements. An ambitious study in agrarian structure, tensions, movements and peasant organization in India has been jointly sponsored by the Indian Council of Historical Research, the National Institute of Labour, and the Indian Council of Social Science Research.

32. For further details about tribal participation in national movements and tribal separatism see Chapter 10 of this book and "From Ethnicity to Regionalism: A Study, in Tribal Politics and Movements in Chotanagpur from 1900 to 1975", in S.C. Malik (ed) *Dissent, Protest and Reform in Indian Civilisation.*

33. See Chapter 8.

34. Sunil Sen, *Agrarian Struggle in Bengal, 1946-47*, p. 84.

35. Godavari Parulekar, op. cit.

2

State Formation

Study of state formation in tribal society, a relatively uncharted area of anthropo-historical research, is crucial to the understanding of many contemporary processes such as the relationship of tribal and non-tribal communities, development of agriculture, emergence of stratification, interaction of the Great and Little traditions—all that has contributed towards the formation of complex regional systems in the exposed zones of tribal India. Such a study should help to put in perspective the development of these processes, set right the existing conceptual framework of study, and place the dynamics of state formation instead of the sanskritization of tribal chiefs, which is just a cultural aspect or consequence of the former, at the centre of the developments. While this phenomenon can be observed throughout Indian history, it can be noticed particularly in respect to the tribal communities spread over the entire tribal region from Assam to middle India in the medieval period. Again, while some documentation concerning the Ahoms and the Gonds exists, there is need for sustained interdisciplinary effort towards further exploration and evaluation of this phenomenon. The present paper deals with the Cheros in some depth at the micro level and then seeks to generalize the process in a wider frame of reference.[1]

I

Following the eclipse of the Gupta empire, the wide eastern tract extending from the Himalayan foothills to the Vindhya mountains (Kaimur range) witnessed the emergence of the rural foci of political power, led by autochthonous chieftains who acted as champions of neo-brahminism. Such communities as Doms, Bhars and Cheros in south Bihar, Kharwars in the Sone-Damodar valley, Gonds and Rakshels in the Chattisgarh region and the

Bhumij in the Jungle Mahals of Bengal filled the vacuum in the countryside in the medieval period. The Doms[2] founded kingdoms at the Himalayan foothills; in the 13th century one of their princes ruled at Ayodhya. The Bhars occupied a large area extending from Bundelkhand and Sagar to the eastern districts of Uttar Pradesh[3] and Bihar as far as Bhagalpur and Tirhut. Numerous place-names associated with these tribes indicate their widespread influence in the region. The ruins of their forts and tanks (*suryabhedi*) are scattered far and wide, and their legends and folklore point probably to their first experiment with state formation. At first they were a "God-neglecting and caste-disregarding"[4] race who wiped out centres of brahminism and violated brahmin girls with the result that these girls became *sati* and the presiding deities at the fairs still held in this region.[5] But after a period of initial resistance to brahminism they became hinduized and emerged as its enthusiastic champions. They were elevated to the ranks of the ksatriyas. The acculturated groups were now called Raj Gonds, Raj Bhars, and Chyavanabansi Cheros (Cheros descended from rishi Chyavana). To the following period may also be assigned the beginning of the hinduization of the tribes living in Jharkhand or Chotanagpur and also of the Mongoloid Tharus.[6] The emergence of autochthons as kingdom-builders and agents of culture change is climaxed and illustrated by the formation of states among the Mongoloid Ahoms in upper Assam[7] (1228-1819), by the Gonds in central India[8] (15th-18th centuries), by the Nagbansis in Chotanagpur[9] and by the Cheros in south Bihar (Shahabad and Palamau).

The history of state formation among the Cheros cannot in its early stages be based solely on the indigenous source materials, which consist of the highly brahminized accounts of the origin and growth of the Chero power. The monuments and mounds scattered in the eastern region traditionally associated with them may shed light on their material culture, but these are yet to be excavated. So are the massive ruins in Chotanagpur of the temples which represent early centres of Hindu influence in the region. Medieval chronicles revel in accounts of the invasions of Palamau; there is little else in them. Some inscriptions and *firmans* (imperial regulations) yield important information on the extent of acculturation and the feudal organization under the later Cheros. The earliest British accounts of the land system and jagirdaris in the latter half of the 18th century, towards the end of the Chero kingdom, help to unravel and analyse the different strands of the process of state formation. This exercise has to be supplemented by a study of the existing social structure of the Cheros, their village organization and economic system, which bear, despite the cataclysmic changes of the modern and recent periods, the marks of state formation.

The term Chero is derived from the word *chera*, a snake, and the Cheros claim descent from the historical Dravidian Nagas, who were a considerable power in central and eastern India.[10] According to their legends, they migrated from western India along the Himalayan foothills (Morung), swung to the south along the Gandak river and spread over the adjoining regions.[11] The Cherapadas are mentioned in the *Aitareya Aranyaka*[12] along with the tribes which disregarded Vedic sacrifices. From the Gandak region the Cheros and other tribes migrated southward and founded their settlements in the Karusa territory (now known as Shahabad) and along the Sone river as far as modern Patna, and for some centuries they remained locked up in intertribal warfare.[13] The fertile land mass, availability of iron in the Kaimur hill ranges and contact with new forces in the cradle of Aryan culture and brahminical Hinduism considerably contributed to their transformation into agricultural communities. The legend preserved by the Oraons mentions their settlement as agriculturists and landowners in the Karusa region.[14] The process was facilitated by an extension of the knowledge of agricultural seasons (*naksatras*) and of agricultural implements and practices carried by migrating hinduized communities into Jharkhand, which is in progress even today. Closely connected with this development was the spread of brahminical Hinduism into the tribal belt, attested by the discovery of temples on the periphery and in the heart of the region.[15] The grant of lands to brahmins in tribal areas, from the Gupta period onwards, as part of an emerging feudal system, which involved not only transfer of all sources of revenue but also surrender of police and administrative functions[16] helped this process and led, as the subsequent influx of brahmins showed, to colonization **and** the extension of agriculture.[17]

From about the 12th century the Cheros were an established rural power, masters of the Gangetic plains. A Chero chief killed the defiant son of a Sufi saint in southern Muzaffarpur.[18] Four Chero kingdoms sprang into existence in Shahabad. They collected one-fourth of the crop produce and one-eighth of the forest produce, including *mahua* flower.[19] They adopted Hindu and Buddhist images, worshipped them and also their traditional deity, *devi*. They claimed descent from Chyavana *rishi* which indicates their brahminization. When Buchanan visited the Cheros in 1812, he found that they used to "eat with Rajputs and wear thread".[20] The migration and thrust of the Ujjainia Rajputs into the fertile Gangetic belt from Buxar to Bihia brought them face to face with the Cheros. The confrontation between the two passed through two important phases, from 1333 to 1484 and from 1584 to 1611. The Cheros also came into conflict with Shershah and Malik Baya.[21] Ultimately the Chero rulers rallied their people in a last-ditch battle with the migrant Rajputs in 1611, but they were completely routed. When their power in Shahabad was destroyed, they migrated to Palamau, as some of them had probably done earlier. This migration marked yet another phase in their state formation.

A scion of the Chainpur line of the Chero chiefs of Shahabad, Raja Bhagwant Rai, overthrew in or about 1572 the ruling Rakshel chiefs who belonged to a hinduized tribe and were joined by the Surwar tribe (the ancestors of the present Rajput Thakurais). But it was not just the conquest by a minority, the seven clans of the Cheros (*barah hazari*), who subsequently founded their villages in Palamau, and the Kharwars (*atharah hazari*) participated in the conquest. Palamau was not a *terra incognita* at the time of the conquest. The Mars, another tribe, had introduced and extended agriculture by constructing water reservoirs and founded settlements in the area in which flourished centres of Buddhism and Hinduism.

Bhagwant Rai was succeeded by Anant Rai, whose reign witnessed two punitive invasions by the Mughal armies. Then came the golden age of the Chero rule under Medini Rai (1620-34), who not only extended the frontiers of the kingdom in all directions but also encouraged cultivation, improved irrigation facilities, settled tribals such as the Parahiyas and founded villages. During his reign "there was no house without a churner, without butter". He built a military fort near Daltonganj, where an inscription praises him as "effulgent like the moon on earth, equal to Indra, of renowned glory", etc.

Then followed three successive invasions by the Mughal armies in 1641-42, 1643 and 1660; the last invasion led to the conquest and annexation of the Chero kingdom, to the reduction of the status of Chero rajas to that of jagirdars of the Mughal empire, and to the creation of some jagirs independent of the Chero rulers. The Chero kingdom was further undermined by three successive invasions in 1720, 1730 and 1734, by internecine feuds between the Rajput Thakurais on the one hand and the Chero rajas on the other, and by a civil war which ravaged the country till the British appeared on the scene.

The British were not slow to recognize the strategic significance of the territory, of its forts and passes, against the Marathas from Nagpur (central India); important trade routes to central India and Uttar Pradesh lay through this region. The *casus belli* was provided by the need to protect the Chero raja Gopal Rai's interest against another Chero pretender, Jainath, supported by the Thakurais. The British forces marched into Palamau and captured the two forts in February-March 1771. There followed a brief civil war between the two parties (April-September 1772) at the end of which Jainath's supporters were put to rout. The following 40 years of confusion sapped the foundation of the Chero raj; the Thakurais built up their power particularly during 1783-86 under the Thakurai manager, Shiva Prasad Singh, who commenced the policy of commuting a portion of the rent payable by under-tenure holders to the raja in return for a lump sum, which reduced the raja's annual assets and revenue. The indiscriminate grant of jagirs through *firmans* by the later Chero rajas cut into the source of revenue; the emergence of powerful southern Chero jagirdars was registered at the expense of their kingdom. The financial bankruptcy of the kingdom was complete when Churaman Rai, the last raja, had to incur heavy expenditure in the Surguja expeditions. The jagirdars did not pay the revenue fully with the result that the Chero ruler could not pay off the government revenue, and this led to the sale of the kingdom in 1815.

The territory once ruled by the Cheros was handed over to the Rajput raja Ghanshyam Singh of Deo situated in the adjoining areas of Gaya. Numerous tenures of the Palamau jagirdars, mostly small, were sold for arrears of revenue. This led to the uprising of Palamau jagirdars, both Chero and native Rajputs, against the authorities in 1817; this was also an expression of the Cheros' pride which had been hurt at the fall of their raj. The territory passed under the direct administration of the East India Company.

The uprising of 1832 was more broadbased; the landlords and their raiyats, Chero and Kharwar jagirdars, rose against the Company, partly because the steep increase in revenue demand had hit them hard and partly because the property of jagirdars and under-tenure holders had been sold for arrears of revenue. A striking feature of the revolt was that Raja Ram Bahadur, the last representative of the former Chero raj, marched against his own people and fought bravely, even though deserted by his tribal followers: this illustrated the measure of alienation of the ruling family from the people. There was yet another aspect of the movement. Unlike the revolts of 1801 and 1817, it was also directed against the non-tribals who suffered and were killed on a large scale. The 1857 Mutiny was also an expression of the tribals' animosity towards the Rajput Thakurais. These successive uprisings, directed not only against the established authority but also against the non-tribals and those who had conspired against and destroyed the Chero kingdom, reflected an agrarian and political reality. The Cheros had been irretrievably replaced by the non-tribals, both indigenous and migrant, as dominant interests in the region.

This fact was brought out more unmistakably in 1895. The significance of some of these movements lay in the fact that they were fountain-springs of the later Chero revivalism, of which such Chero leaders as Jitu Singh (hero of the 1817 uprising) came to be regarded as culture heroes.

The Cheros did not depend on pillage and brigandage for building up their kingdom and keeping it going for well over two hundred years. Their two magnificent forts which survive (the later one is a fine piece of architecture) and their tributes to the Mughal emperor speak of a high stage of development and acculturation. They encouraged cultivation and settlements, particularly in the Oranga-Amanat valley which they opened up. Extension of cultivation and foundation of settlements were the two conditions laid down in the *sanads* granted by them. They constructed reservoirs (*ahars*) and were particularly good at constructing wells of large diameter and cylindrical shape, including underground wells (*baulis*), which still survive. The early accounts of Palamau in 1875 describe rich and fertile *tappas*, which constituted the main source of agricultural income mopped up by the Chero princes. As in Shahabad, they levied taxes at the rate of one-fourth of the crop produce and one-eighth of the forest produce. Moreover, the yields from *khas* villages (and these were largely intact under the Chero rulers till 1660) must have been substantial. There were also a levy of a few *cowries* (Chero currency and medium of exchange) on every village, the customary *mudud* (assistance) from the jagirdars and imposition of *abwabs* (miscellaneous dues) of various kinds. The Cheros also started *hats* and fairs, some of which may have developed from a tribal matrix. In any case these served as outlets for such products as cotton from the territories extending as far as Surguja and Mirzapur. The existence of a Chero township and of large colonies of traders and merchants points to significant commercial activities.

The immensely larger area of uplands *vis-a-vis* paddy lands (4 : 1 in Palamau) determined the character of land tenure, *pariadari*. It was based on an assessment of rice lands and the better part of the upland, the cultivators being free to cultivate without payment as much inferior upland as they chose; they were also entitled to a share in the forest produce such as *mahua* without further payment. The *paria* was divided into *pawa*. These tenures formed the basis of the organization of the village, *khuntkatti* (founded by clearers of the forest) or *khas* (in possession of the raja). On this village system was imposed a feudal superstructure in the form of jagirs and *ijaras*, and a web of rent and praedial conditions. Most villages founded by the migrant Cheros were organized around clans, though later they tended to become heterogeneous.

There is no evidence of grants of jagirs by the early Chero rulers up to 1685, which may lead one to infer that almost the entire Chero territory was probably administered as *khas*. From 1680 onwards under conditions of confusion and disintegration grants of jagirs progressively went up; the last Chero ruler (1784-1813) made as many as 37 grants of jagirs. The *sanads* composed in Magahi dialect, which was the court language, opened with a salutation to Kalanath,[22] to Lakshman Balaji or Balaji Lakshman and to Ramji. The maharajas were mentioned as endowed with great glory (*prabal pratap sampanna*), of rising glory (*udit pratap*), beloved of gods (*devadevanam*), etc., and the *sanads* were duly stamped with the royal seal.[23] In 1823 it was reported that the largest number of jagirs were related to military service and given to *Cherwan* and Kharwar Bhogtas (1,022½ villages), followed by other service jagirs (446¾) and maintenance grants to relations (*babuans*, 58 villages). All these records of title purport to everything that grows in the area such as trees and fruits (*gach*), fisheries (*mach*), produce of water (*jalkar*) and forest produce (*bankar*) in all directions. The grants are hereditary in some cases, though not in others. The rule of primogeniture and the right to resume jagirs on the death of male heirs were recognized. Another condition was the extension of cultivation, directly or indirectly, and rural settlement. There were in addition *ijara* tenures (lease or grant of *khas* villages), about 85 or 88 of them, and a large number of rent-free (*minhai*) jagirs. A copperplate grant (bearing Samvat 1753) mentions confirmation of the sale of two villages to two Panre brothers for a consideration of Rs. 601. The jagirdars, who were also called upon to render services, paid exceedingly small revenue in addition to large sums of *mudud* and *abwab* which were not mentioned in the *sanads*.

Repeated invasions of their territories and the compulsion to expand their kingdom led the Cheros to develop a sophisticated military machine. The remarkable contemporary painting showing Daud Khan's capture of Palamau fort (1661) throws light on their strategic fortification and troop formation. The old fort was a bustling town, with a street dividing two rows of shops and town dwellers' residences. The Chero cavalry under Palamau *kunwars* (scions of the ruling family) was armed with spears and shields, "a very respectable body, as well mounted as their foes", though diffident and purposelessly deployed. The Chero soldiery was a mixed group. It comprised a number of fair-complexioned and well dressed men showing that "in those days there was a considerable sprinkling of Aryans among the Palamau population". These could as well be mercenaries or Thakurais' men. But the bulk of the army was formed by the Cheros and Kharwar soldiers, "black, with only a loin cloth, bare heads and bare feet, bows with only one curve and plenty of arrows, besides which some had spears and some swords and shields". Both old and new forts were equipped with cannon. The latter was crowned with a big cannon (*dum dum*), though "the proportion of matchlock men to bowmen is small". The archers were recruited from every Chero and Kharwar family; in addition, the jagirdars helped with contingents of soldiers recruited or maintained by them.

The Chero territorial administrative divisions formed a four-tier system. At the apex came the pargana which was divided into *tappas*, the large territorial units at one time common to the regions comprising Shahabad and Palamau. Palamau pargana was divided into 22 *tappas*, each complete with its presiding deity and markets, but varying in cultivable area, population and number of villages. There is no evidence to establish that these *tappas* formed individual proprietary estates, though much later these were amalgamated to form police stations, the units of police and revenue administration. Within or cutting across *tappas* were *lats*, and there were 12 of them, given to a clan of the Cherowans each in recognition of its military service by the later Chero rajas. The *lats* were located at Rabda (clan Sawant), Betla (Sawant), Manasoti (Kunwar), Kurka (Mowar), Obra (Mowar), Lidki (Kunwar), Sildilia (Sawant), Khajuri (Sawant), Sua (Rautia), Chando (Mowar) and Mankeri (Mowar and Kunwar), Each *lat* consisted of several villages, and each village was broken up into *chatais* (hamlets).

The Cheros established almost complete social equation with other tribes. This is illustrated by the ease with which all the major tribes, Cheros, Kharwars and Rakshels, were absorbed into the Parahiyas' nature-spirit framework. Three Parahiya female deities were married to the male spirits of Rakshels, Kharwars and Chero tribes, each being assigned a region. The Parahiyas were treated well; their customary rights were recognized; they were required to contribute only broomstick and leaf-plates by way of tribute in return for their settlement in western and eastern regions. The Kharwars were granted jagirs and formed a part of the Chero soldiery.

II

The phenomenon of state formation among the tribal communities in India occurs particularly among the Dravidian tribes in the exposed central region and the Mongoloid Ahoms in Assam. The Kolarian tribes such as the Mundas in Ranchi (not the Bhumij, though they belonged to the same stock) with their communal agrarian organization borne out by their *khuntkatti* villages show little propensity towards the development of state. The view held by some that the Chotanagpur raj arose from the Munda culture matrix is bad history and poor ethnography. The Chotanagpur Nagbansi chiefs were the descendants of the historical Dravidian Nagas who ruled at Kawardha as late as the 14th century.[24] Other Dravidian tribes which witnessed the rise of states, apart from the Doms and the Bhars, were the Kharwars in the Sone-Damodar valley[25] and the Gonds of Garha, Mandla, Deoghar and Chanda. The Bhumijs no doubt form probably a solitary exception among the Kolarian groups,[26] but some of the Kolarian institutions such as *parhas* have to be investigated to find out whether they contain any Dravidian element.[27]

There were four preconditions for the formation of states among these communities. Settled agriculture and correspondingly organized tribal village community was one. The extension of cultivation through a network of irrigation schemes was necessary for building and sustaining states. The irrigated rice cultivation of some advanced sections of the Kachari tribe[28] led to early state formation in Assam. The migration of Ahoms[29] to Assam from the east in the 13th century and the subsequent expansion of their rule positively encouraged the extension of *sali* (wet land) cultivation and new transplantation techniques. They also built up with communal labour a system of massive dykes and embankments, unparalleled elsewhere. Lands were improved, and *dhu* (upland) and *bao* (broadcast rice) lands were made suitable for the *sali* crop in upper Assam, the cradle and core of the Ahom culture. There was also a variety of high-yielding Ahom seed, one of the dozens of *sali* varieties.[30] The Gond rajas also reclaimed wild forests and adorned their kingdoms with embankments and other irrigation schemes, "admirable works of engineering skill", and thus kept a "well-governed and contented kingdom".[31]

A second condition was acculturation. The long network of temples, bearing the imprint of Orissa architecture in the Bhumij region and extending to Panchpargana in Ranchi district in Chotanagpur, and the penetration of Kurmi peasantry from Bengal, explain the hinduization of Bhumij and other tribal masses long before the Bhumij kingdoms had taken shape.[32] The same is true of Assam, the seat of *tantric* Hinduism before the advent of the Ahoms.[33] The Gond territory of Andhra and Madhya Pradesh had been penetrated by Buddhist and Hindu influences.[34] The penetration of brahminism into the Sone valley is as old as the Tarachandi rock inscription of the Kharwar chief, Pratapadhavala Deva (V. S. 1225), who warned the people against forging land grants. The brahminical influence was also facilitated by land grants to the brahmins, which led to the extension of cultivation and rural settlement in eastern India, Orissa[35] and south Bihar.

A third factor was the role of a determined, acculturated, powerful tribal minority which tried to foist its rule on its people or on a new territory. The emergence of the Nagbansis as the head of the *parha* confederacy, which ultimately developed into a kingdom, is an instance in point.[36] The Ahom ruler Sukapa (1228-68) with the following of eight nobles subjugated the Nagas and laid the foundation of the kingdom;[37] so did the Cheros in Palamau. The Gond rulers of Garha Mandala probably imitated the Rajput princes who were established in Madhya Pradesh from the seventh century onwards.[38] The establishment of a minority rule in tribal communities should be distinguished from the imposition of the migrant Rajputs' rule on tribes in some hilly tracts of Orissa, Chattisgarh and south Bihar, which represented varying degrees of social equation with subjugated tribes, which were in some cases kept in good humour by being associated with the coronation ceremony.[39] Where there was no such imposition by an immigrant group, tribal or non-tribal, internal developments led to a "constructive coagulation of traditional socio-political units" into a state, as happened among the Bhumij.[40]

Fourthly, once these states had come into being, they were subjected to a spate of invasions from outside, which together with their own urge for expansion put a strain on their resources, feudalized their structure, weakened them and hastened their end. The Ahoms were locked in perpetual hostilities with the Kacharis, the Kochs, the Daflas and the Chutiyas;[41] they were engaged and invaded by Muslim armies from Bengal from 1615 to Mir Jumla's expeditions against them in 1662-63, which resulted in their subjugation to the Mughal empire. The creation of such gubernatorial posts as Bar Phukan and Bar Barua followed.[42] The Mughals conquered lower Assam in 1658.

The Gond dynasty of Garha was attacked and conquered by Asaf Khan in 1564, but it survived till the Marathas brought it to an end in 1780,[43] the kingdom of Chanda having fallen in 1749. The feudalization of the Chero political structure after 1660 is proved by an indiscriminate grant of jagirs under the later Chero rulers.

The imposition of a feudal superstructure resulted in the break-up of a tribe into distinct social categories. The Cheros separated into two groups, the *barah hazaris* and the *terah-hazaris* or *birhandhias*. The first, the elite, was a typical creation of the processes of state formation in Palamau to be found in villages around the seat of Chero power, the Palamau fort; it is not found elsewhere among the Cheros. The second group was "unclean, formed by the illegitimate offspring of the first", occupying within the *barah hazari* social framework or ordinary primitive Chero tribal community the lowest rung of the social and economic ladder. Within the first there are three distinct sections. The first section comprises the *babuans*, who are scions of the ruling families (of Nawa Jaipur, Bishrampur, Nawagarh, etc.), fully acculturated, intermarrying with the Rajputs and once in possession of large jagirs comprising more than a hundred villages. Once known as powerful southern Chero jagirdars, these *babuans*, builders of temples and shrines, deny indignantly their being Cheros, except when they have to seek votes during election and stipends for education of their wards for which only "tribals" are eligible. Over the years their 'marriage zones' have widened. The second section consists of the *Cherwans*, that is, the Chero soldiery who occupy the intermediate level. They are jagirdars holding villages, ranging from a *lat* or a cluster of 12 villages to one village. They intermarry among themselves, but have been thoroughly brahminized. The third group consists of "ordinary Chero" peasantry spread over a hundred villages which is partly brahminized and still a part of the tribal nature-spirit complex. The more the distance from the culture complex of Palamau, the less the hinduization. The Cheros on the periphery of the district or in Mirzapur are much less hinduized.

The aristocratic stratum that emerged in the once egalitarian tribal communities survived even when the political role of tribal states had been played out. The Bhumij also had a threefold or fourfold social stratification based on corresponding distribution of power and economic interest in land,[44] and defined in terms of "ritual status". The Ahoms had seven powerful clans (*satgharia*)[45] at the apex of their society.

The manufacture of a spurious genealogy involving the conferment of the status of ksatriya is an important indication of the sankritization of the tribes. There are two versions of the origin of the Cheros, both representing the widening social distance of the ruling group from its mores and its people. The first version, fairly well known, speaks of a Rajput raja of Bundelkhand who was blessed with only one daughter. The brahmin astrologer in the court prophesied that she would marry a *muni* (a mendicant); and so she did in the Morung country. The offspring of the Chyavana Rishi and the king's daughter were the Cheros, Chyavanvansi Rajputs (children of the moon), and there began a long line of rajas who moved from Morung to Kumaon, from Kumaon to Shahabad.[46] This legend was widespread in Shahabad when Buchanan visited the region in 1812. The second, a later version, emphasizes the more legitimate and pure ksatriya origin of the Cheros rather than the Rajput one, because they rebelled against the latter.[47] What is more interesting, even the Kayastha and Rajput families, anxious to establish their association with and to prove their loyalty to the Cheros (obviously to protect their jagirs in later times), built up and furnished to the government an equally spurious, brahminical version of their own origin and migration with the Cheros from Morung to Shahabad and Palamau.[48]

The rulers accelerated the reclamation and cultivation of lands through the construction of embankments and reservoirs which yielded the agricultural surplus necessary to support the governmental machinery. The land in *khas* or *khalisa* villages was cultivated through free plough and labour, and the rulers devised a set of *abwabs* which were commuted in tribal areas only a few decades ago. The system of *abwabs* prevailing in

Chotanagpur estate[49] in later times, from the raja down to his jagirdars, by and large represented such survival. There were 21 varieties. Some of these were: *dasai* (a contribution at the time of the Dusserah festival), *bhatta* (expenses of the landlord visiting a village); *neg* (customary payment on social occasions); *nawa kharni* (contribution of rice on an auspicious day); *bhandari dhani* (contribution to landlord's local agent or store house for the support of village shrine); *mahua behri* (contribution for extraction of *mahua* flower); *kathar behri* (contribution for using jack fruits); *brahmana niskar* (payment to brahmins at religious festivals); free plough or exaction of the best oxen from the villages, *begar* or free labour in the *khas* village comprising three days' ploughing, three days' digging, three days' planting or sowing, three days' cutting, one day's thrashing, one day's storing of grain and one or two days' carrying jagirdar's or landlord's burdens on his journey.

The formation of the state gave a fillip to commercial activities in fort-cities and encouraged artisans and traders. Trade routes were explored and developed. A trade route from Chanda through Chinnoor and Paloncha to Rajahmundry lay through the Gond territories. The Cheros controlled the route to Madhya Pradesh. They also helped the development of tribal *hats* and fairs.

There developed an administrative system with the raja at the top and a line of communications extending through a chain of forts (*garh*) under jagirdars or rajas' own men. The Ahoms[50] developed a powerful army and navy and built numerous strongholds, as did also the Gonds and the Cheros. The Ahoms perfected the technique of guerilla warfare, and introduced and conducted the census of their population to ensure the stability of their state. They were thus able to gauge their military strength and economic resources and to keep a watch on population, both indigenous and foreign. It will not be correct to assume that a centralized and bureaucratic machinery was imposed cutting across the principle of sub-infeudation in the Gond kingdoms of Garha and Chanda.[51] In fact, the set-up at the top was never fully centralized; the Ahom kings, with a few exceptions, always shared their power with the councillors of the state (*gohains*), just as the Cheros, for all the proclaimed divinity of their rulers, did with the jagirdars. The autonomous character of territorial divisions and social institutions remained intact under the Cheros. The introduction of the Rajput polity into tribal areas led to the "imposition of clan aristocracies on old and settled villages".[52] The practice of appointment of villages in units of 12 and 84 was noticed in Gujarat and in a ninth century Chalukya inscription. The practice seemed to be common all over tribal India, and it appeared to be a part of the clan-based territorial system. Among the Gonds, the territorial unit of *garh* was coterminous with the territorial unit of clan (*gotra*). The development of the original territorial group system into the *garh* system has been traced to the Rajput influence which should be investigated a little more critically.[53] In those areas where states did not emerge from the indigenous matrix this kind of development from the territorial system is not noticeable. The Cheros developed a different kind of four-tier territorial system with clan-based village as the unit above *chatai*. The Gond kingdom consisted of the two largest territorial units divided into 18 *garhs* (forts), sub-divided into units of 84 villages (*chaurasis*), which were broken up further into units of 12 villages (*barhots*).[54] Under the Cheros the *lats* were initially divided into units of 12 and five.

The rajas became the agents of sanskritic social change and its pace-setters to their people. Generous grants of lands tempted brahmins from upper and central India to settle in the new lands and oblige their masters with drawing up fabricated genealogies which established a link between the mythical heroes and the newly converted rulers. The striking similarities between the accounts of the origin of the Chotanagpur raj family[55] and Bhumij rulers of Barabhum given in the *Brahmanda* section of *Bhavisya Purana* illustrate that they did not even exercise elementary caution in avoiding a duplication. The brahmin chronicler of the Nagbansi annals also gave a brahminical account of the history of the Mundas through their patriarch, Madra Munda.[56] The Ahoms made generous grants of lands to temples and brahmins for charitable purposes. The brahmins expounded the Hindu law. The Ahom court patronized the translation of Sanskrit classics, epics and puranas, and their rajas claimed to be the votaries of the three major cults in the Brahmaputra valley: Shaivism, Shaktism and Vaishnavism. Their social institutions were partly Hinduized, though in the beginning they tried to stick to some elements of their tradition.[57]

The grant of service jagirs led to an influx of brahmins, Rajputs and other castes into the tribal region, which with the erosion of tribal power intensified the economic exploitation of tribals and hastened their retreat into the hills and forests, their present habitat. The brahmins performed ritual service, which replaced some of the old tribal practices; the Bhumij rulers gave up their connection with clan ossuaries. The brahmins introduced Vedic ceremonies in life-cycle functions, wearing of sacred thread, maintenance of Hindu idols, observance of food taboos, restriction on widow remarriage, child marriage, etc.

The brahmins also popularized first the ksatriya model and then the Rajput model of protection to cows and brahmins, valour and statesmanship. The ksatriya model remained untarnished among the Cheros and the Bhumij community; the later animosity between the Cheros and the Rajputs blurred the Rajput model for them. In earlier days the Rajput rajas were paragons of excellence for the aspiring tribal groups. But the tide has turned now because of the grant of stipends to tribal boys, legislative protection against alienation of land and the power of ballot in election which can upset the power structure in villages, and the tribals are recognizing the value of their old roots.

The tribal states performed, apart from the propagation and popularization of ritualistic brahminism, a cultural role. The rapid spread of epic traditions which resulted in the association of the tribal gods with Mahadeva and Parvati, Pandava heroes and Hanuman was an important aspect. The pradhans (bards) composed epics extolling the Gond rajas. The Chero folklore eulogize Ghughulia, a culture hero, now regarded as a Rajput, but whose real identity is betrayed by his name. In Bastar the cults of the tribals and of the rajas interacted, and the cult of Danteshwari spread over a wide region.[58] The converted tribal rulers proved zealous builders of temples and ponds; their inscriptions and seals, art and architecture speak of their new faith. But the little tradition did not disappear; it flourished under the great traditions which were imposed or borrowed. Both got mixed up. The brahminical liturgical rituals stopped short at a stage beyond which local rituals and ceremonies held sway. Temples were located in old sacred groves, many localized sacred groves were upgraded to higher levels in the Bhumij area, and thus the regional culture was "upgraded" and "universalized".[59] The male spirit of the Cheros became the presiding deity of the Durjag *tappa* where their capital was located; at the same time their female deity, *devi*, was identified with the mother goddess of the Vindhya cult.

We would like to revert to the first precondition of state formation in order to highlight an allied process. The chiefs of all these kingdoms in middle India, the Cheros, Nagbansis and Gonds invited non-tribal peasantry from the plains to settle and cultivate. The tribal people of their kingdoms were spared the strains of generating surplus which was done by the incomers with their superior agricultural technology. Virgin lands were brought under cultivation. The Cheros granted *sanads* which spelt out the twin conditions of settlement and cultivation as mentioned earlier. The Nagbansis brought in artisans and peasants. The Gonds invited the Kunbis from the south (the Maratha country). It was stated that during the reign of one of the Gond chiefs, Bakth Buland "the rich lands to the south of Deogarh, between the Wainganga and Kunhan rivers, were steadily developed. Hindu and Muhammadan cultivators were encouraged to settle in them on equal terms with Gonds, until this region became most prosperous". Moreover, "industrious settlers from all quarters were attracted to Gondwana, many towns and villages were founded, and agriculture manufactures, and even commerce made considerable advances".[60] An anthropologist has provided us with a graphic description of this process in the Dangs:

> According to local tradition, the Bhil Rajas had permitted Kunbi immigrants from the plains and neighbouring district of Nasik to settle in their domains. While the Kunbis brought bullocks and ploughs and introduced permanent cultivation into the hills, the Bhils persisted in their forest life. They levied taxes from the Kunbi settlers and sometimes a Raja or a chief would call his Kunbi ryots to cultivate his field for him, expecting them to bring their own ploughs and bullocks. In this way the two economies existed side by side, and though the Bhils might have benefited from the introduction of superior type of cultivation by their Kunbi ryots they took no steps to model their own agriculture on similar lines. The relation between the two peoples was one of the rulers and the ruled, and even today Kunbis would tell of the past oppressiveness of the Bhil chiefs who would come with their bowmen, take possession of Kunbi crops and cattle, demand supplies of food and on occasions even abduct Kunbi girls. On account of this, the Kunbi used to prefer to live in the thickest forest so as to escape from the eyes of the Bhil chiefs. . .However, the Kunbis maintained their own ritual superiority in terms of the Hindu caste hierarchy by refusing to accept food at the hands of the Bhil and of ex-communicating any Kunbi who had sexual relations with a Bhil, even though the Bhil Raja imposed no reciprocal rule on his own tribemen. As the Bhils had no inhibition in eating beef or buffalow meat, the Kunbis, who strictly abhorred beef maintained social and ritual separation from the Bhils. . .Despite the inequalities of ritual and political status, the Bhils and the Kunbis of the Dangs share in many respects a common culture pattern. Due to this, both of them are called by outsiders by a generic term 'Dangi'.
>
> The real unity of the Dangi Bhils and Kunbis is to be noted in their folktales and folk songs which tell them the glorious history of the Dangis. Their legends, from their very childhood make them aware that they are distributed on all the hills of the Dangs and in the past they were the exclusive owners of this land.[61]

We have described the endogenous processes of state formation whereby the tribes such as the Chero and Gond founded states. The Koli, too, established a state in northern Konkan, and the Bhils had their chieftains. There is also the exogenous model of state formation whereby "non-tribal" individuals, split off from their community, founded states in the tribal regions extending from Chotanagpur and Orissa (hilly region) to Rajasthan and Gujarat, either in collaboration with the tribes, which was institutionalised in the coronation ceremony that will be described later, or without it. A mythology of state formation developed.[62] Here is an example of how the "invaders" reached the "alpine region" of the Kamidi, Kalahandi and Jeypore on the border of Orissa and Andhra to set up states:

> A certain Rajah of Puri, named Pratap Rudra Devo, had one illegitimate, and eighteen legitimate sons. In obedience to a divine command, he nominated the bastard his heir; and this nomination being confirmed by sundry undeniable manifestations of the will of the gods, the legitimate sons dispersed in quest of new possessions,. One of these brothers, Bhimo Devo, was walking alone in his journey towards a second home, when a crow followed him flying round his head, and uttering certain auspicious words. A man was drawing toddy from a date tree, and hearing these words, came to the conclusion that a person of rank must be in the neighbourhood. Seeing the prince approach, he recognized him to be such from his demeanour, saluted him, and inquired the cause of his being alone. The prince replied that he was in distress, and in quest of some country over which he might become ruler. The man carried him on his shoulders until they came to a place where eight chieftains, desirous of a prince to rule over them, were assembled in council. He was gladly received and became the head of a small tract in Kamidi, designated the country of the "Eight Mallikas", the site of which is not known. While being carried on the man's shoulders, he made an inward vow to sacrifice him to some chosen goddess, if he obtained his wishes. The votary on being informed of his fate, cheerfully offered himself for immolation, but the affair was deferred, the prince being of the present perplexed as to his choice of a goddess. Meanwhile the wanderer carried his arms into the Kalahandi country ,and subdued it. The capital (a village which still bears the same name) was attacked, and the inhabitants forsook it. In it there was a Brahmini, a widow, who had an only daughter, whom she tenderly loved. But the girl had died, and the mother had formed an image from her jewels and golden ornaments. When the village was deserted, the widow fled and abandoned the image. In course of time the image became endowed with the gift of speech, when it gave out that the deceased girl had

> been deified, and was to be worshipped hereafter under the symbol of this jewelled image, and with the title of 'Manikeswari', or the 'Goddess of the jewels'. In her the prince found his '*Ishta Devi*', and to her sacrificed his victim; and when, resigning Kalahundy (Kalahandi) to his son-in-law, a scion of the Mago Bansa family, whom he established in Jeypore, he proceeded southwards to form a dynasty in Kamidi, he took the image with him and enshrined it in his new capital.[63]

Such legends have many facets. These are brahminical accounts which give a central role to the brahmins, either as one of the parents or as a deified person. The invader or the founder of the kingdom is a loner. He is received favourably by the people he is going to rule, who are, in fact described as looking forward to him. He is not averse to use force or a subterfuge to gain his end. Lastly, he adopts the local deity as his family deity to consolidate his acceptability among his people. Even though he later introduces the Jagannath cult and the Dusserah festival in which the tribals join, he adheres to the worship of the local deity, which he flaunts, among others, as the symbol of his symbiotic relationship with his people.

Both endogenous and exogenous models of state formation produced similar results. They spared the tribes the strain of generating agricultural surplus for the state and even treated some of them with a measure of respect by giving them a higher ritual status. The non-tribal peasantry moved in to produce the agricultural surplus for the new states. They set in motion the process of transfer of agricultural technology and the diffusion of a new culture (a form of sanskritization), that will be described in later chapters. Both types of states were also "feudalised". As the new states required many types of functions to be performed, a multi-caste, a multi-community pattern of settlement emerged, and economic interdependence between the tribe on one hand and non-tribal peasant and artisan on the other, came into existence. Many castes moved into the tribal areas and formed their settlements (*bhum*): Brahmanbhum, Gopabhum (founded by Sadgops) and Singhbhum, Manbhum, Barabum etc., named after Rajput lineages in parts of middle India. State formation thus produced far-reaching changes, and a complex social and economic system in the exposed tribal regions, particularly of middle India, gradually developed.

III

Memories of tribal states, among other factors, have inspired some of the revivalistic movements in recent times. The Ujani Ahom Rajya Parishad, organized by the Ahom-Tais of upper Assam, demands a separate state to be carved out of the districts of Dibrugarh, Lakhimpur and Jorhat, where the Ahom-Tais preponderate. The Parishad harks back to the past when the Ahoms ruled the Brahmaputra valley, but it ignores, in its demand for the division of Assam, the fact that the Ahom rulers had in fact unified Assam. The movement led by Kangla Manjhi, which has been simmering for about fifteen years, aims at the revival of the Gond raj, the Gondwana, which will comprise the districts of Jabalpur, Raipur, Mandla, Chhindwara, Durg, Balaghat and Bhandara. The Manjhi has set up a "parallel" but "invisible" adivasi government complete with the paraphernalia of an established authority: a seal with the inscription "Bharat-Gondwana", a cadre of khaki-clad volunteers and "officers" wearing the badge "Taj Hind", and a system of collection of revenue and imposition of fines. The Manjhi himself appears, so the legend says, on an elephant, to take the salute at the Independence Day at Durg (?). In July 1960 the Manjhi set up his headquarters at Donargarh (Durg), and eighty-four of his followers were rounded up for committing offences. By August 1962, the Manjhi cult had cast its net wider to include about one hundred thousand adivasis in its fold over an area extending up to the Bhandara district. Its slogans were typically revivalistic, the tribal women would not discard their traditional gear, and tribals would assert their rights over forests, land and lakes.[64] The movement appears to have petered out. Sporadic activities of the movement however are reported in the press: as late as July 10, 1971, *The Times of India* reported the arrest of the functionaries of a "parallel government".

Chero revivalism in the 1940s, led by the Chero peasantry, looked to the Palamau forts as the symbol of racial pride and achievement. The fact that the Chero raja and the *babuans* had broken away from the tribal matrix did not bother the votaries of the "Fort cult". But there was more to it. A Chero Sudhar Sabha (reform conference) met in July 1945 and laid down the guidelines to promote formation of caste panchayats, develop education, redeem debt through the organization of grain *golas*, and carry out social reforms such as the prohibition of child marriage and promotion of widow marriage.

In all the three cases cited above, we find that the past has been invoked to assert political identity (the Ahoms), to seek re-establishment of the old order (the Gonds), and to promote social reforms (the Cheros). In all the three cases it is not scientific history but myths which have been used to provide grist to the political mill. The means to the achievement of the objectives has been constitutional (participation in election) in the first case, subversion in a very naive way in the second, and persuasion in the third case. The first movement is active, the second has been driven underground and has largely lost its appeal, and the third has become extinct.

Notes and References

This is a revised version of two papers, one, "A Study of State-formation among Tribal Communities", R.S. Sharma and Vivekanand Jha (ed), *Indian Society: Historical Probings in memory of D.D. Kosambi*, the other an enlarged version of this paper, "State Formation in Tribal Society: Some preliminary discussions".

1. Based on the author's imcomplete manuscript: "Cheros: A Dynamic Study". The references to Cheros are extracted from this study of Bhumij from Surajit Sinha, "State Formation and Rajput Myth in Central India", *Man in India*, vol. xlii, No. 2, 1961; to Gonds from C. von Furer-Haimendorf, *Raj Gonds of Adilabad*; to Ahoms from E.A. Gait, *History of Assam* except where otherwise indicated; Surajit Sinha in his article has built up an interesting conceptual framework for such studies. However, some of the facts culled from secondary sources are open to question in the light of the findings of current historical research, which do not substantiate the theoretical framework of Sinha on several points.

2. Lala Sitaram, *Ayodhya Ka Itihas* (in Hindi), pp. 54-58.

3. B.H. Baden-Powell, "The Population of the Ganges Plain", in *The Indian Village Community*, pp. 105-10.

4. P. Carnegy, "The Bhars of Oudh and Benares", *JASB* (1876), pp. 297-98.

5. Suresh Singh, op. cit. These fairs are held at Dumraon and Barhampur.

6. S.K. Srivastav, *Tharus: A Study in Culture Dynamics*, pp. 15-17.

7. E.A. Gait, op. cit.

8. Furer-Haimendorf, op. cit.

9. R.D. Haldar, "An Abstract of the Annals of the Nagbansi Raj Family of Chotanagpur", *Man in India*, vol. VII, 1928.

10. T.V. Mahalingam, "The Naga in Indian History and Culture", *Journal of Indian History*, vol. XLII, Part. I April 1965.

11. The survival of the settlements of the Cheros on both banks of the Gandak river and in eastern UP and western Bihar in close proximity to those of the other allied Dravidian tribes such as Bhars and Suirs is a fact recorded in the Gazetteers of the districts of the region.

12. Suresh Singh, op. cit.

13. Ibid.

14. S.C. Roy, *The Oraons of Chotanagpur*, pp. 27-29.

15. D.P. Patil, *Antiquarian Remains in Bihar*. The temple remains at Manjhion (Ranchi) and Deogaon (Palamau) are significant.

16. R.S. Sharma, *Indian Feudalism*. We have no information whether the temples and monasteries in Palamau—and there are extensive ruins of these—belonged to any land-owning establishment. The Nalanda seal mentions that some five villages in Palamau were earmarked for the maintenance of the Nalanda University (D.P. Patil, op. cit., pp. 349-54).

17. R.S. Sharma, op. cit., p. 41.

18. S.H. Askari "A Shuttari Saint of North Bihar", *JBRS* (March-June 1951), pp. 75-76.

19. Tarikh-i-Ujjainia, ii (hereafter mentioned as TU),

20. C.E.A. W., Oldham (ed.), *Journal of Francis Buchanan*, 1812-13, pp. 1-4.

21. Suresh Singh. op. cit.

22. Kalanath was the disciple of Chetnath, founder of the Naga cult and of the ashram at Chandihar in Balia district; he became the preceptor of the families of Chero rulers and also Nagbansis in the 18th century.

23. The first complete record of these jagirs is available in 1828, i.e. 14 years after the fall of the dynasty when considerable erosion and disintegration of the Chero authority had taken place, and these too related only to Palamau pargana which was only a part of the Chero raj, The extant 200 *sanads* constitute only one-third of the total number of existing tenures.

24. Mahalingam, op. cit. E.T. Dalton mentions surviving colonies of Nagbansis in Jashpur which point to the probable route of migration of this tribe into Chotanagpur (*Descriptive Ethnology of Bengal*, pp. 131-32). The author has tried to establish the view that the Nagbansi of Kawardha overthrown by Gonds emigrated later to Chotanagpur; they shared the *phani* (cobra-hood) emblem with the Nagbansi of Chotanagpur.

25. Pratap Dhawal Deo is a Kharwar feudatory of Gahadaval kings. Kharwar Rajputs migrated from Palamau to Jashpur (Madhya Pradesh) and founded a raj there. The Ramgarh Kharwar Rajput family founded a kingdom in the Damodar valley (See W.W. Hunter, *A Statistical Account of Bengal, Hazaribagh and Lohardaga*, pp. 206, 117-19.

26. Surajit Sinha, op. cit.

27. *Pattis* rather than *parhas* appear to be the original Kolarian institutions in the Munda region of Ranchi district; the *parha* institution at Torpa (Ranchi) has been thoroughly Hinduized: the *parha* raja has become a maharaja. The interaction of the Oraons and the Mundas at Torpa deserves to be studied in depth.

28. A. Guha, "Ahom Migration: Its Impact"; "Rice Economy of Medieval Assam", *Artha Vijnana*, vol. IX, no. 2 June 1967, 145.

29. Ibid., pp. 139-40.

30. Ibid., pp. 150-53.

31. Quoted by Furer-Haimendorf, op. cit.

32. Surajit Sinha, op. cit.

33. Gait, op. cit., chap. IV.

34' Furer-Haimendorf, op. cit., pp. 6-12.

35. R.S. Sharma, op. cit., pp. 274-75, 285.

36. Haldar, op. cit., p. 79.

37. Gait, op. cit., p. 79

38. Furer-Haimendorf, op. cit.

39. E.T. Dalton, op. cit., p. 142. The Bhuiyas assert that the Raja (of Keonjhar, a Bhanj Deo) is "of their creation, and that the prerogative of installing every new Raja on his accession is theirs and theirs alone". See chapter 5.

40. Surajit Sinha, op. cit.

41. Gait, op. cit., chapters V-VI.

42. Ibid. p. 112.

43. Furer-Haimendorf, op. cit.

44. Surajit Sinha, op. cit.

45. Gait, op. cit., pp. 257-58.

46. L.R. Forbes, *Report on the Ryotwari Settlement of the Goverment farms in Palamau*, pp. 28-29.

47. The second version of the origin prevails in Bishrampur family.

48. See for instance the genealogies of these families maintained in the Record Room, Daltongani (Palamau).

49. J. Reid, *Final Report on Survey and Settlement Operations in the District of Ranchi* 1902-10.

50. Gait, op. cit., chapter IX.

51. Quoted by Surajit Sinha, op. cit.

52. R.S. Sharma, op. cit., pp. 106-7.

53. Quoted in Surajit Sinha, op. cit.

54. Ibid.

55. Haldar, op. cit.

56. Ibid. p. 269.

57. Gait, op. cit. chapter XIII.

58. Surajit Sinha, op. cit.

59. Ibid.

60. Quoted in and from Jadunath Sarkar, *A Short History of Aurangzeb*, p. 410.

61. R.B. Lal, "Soical and cultural life in the Dangs", *Adivasis Gujarat* (date not given).

62. K.S. Singh, "Chotanagpur Raj: Mythology, Structure and Ramification".

63. Carmichael, D.F. (ed) *Manual of the Distt. of the Vizagapatnam in the Presidency of Madras*, pp. 87-89.

64. G.S. Ghurye, *The Scheduled Tribes*, pp. 337, 374-5; also see for a detailed study later "The Gond Movements", the material for which was collected during the field study under the Jawaharlal Nehru Fellowhip, K.S. Singh, *Tribal Movments in India*, vol. 2.

3

Technology and Acculturation

The objective of this chapter is to examine the brahminical model of the diffusion of agricultural technology and culture change in tribal areas as canvassed by both historians and sociologists. Although it has been developed in the context of ancient and early medieval periods, its relevance to modern times has been stressed in such concepts as hinduization and sanskritization which were developed to explain social change in modern India. But we consider this model inadequate in the situations of continental diversity obtaining in our country, and hence suggest a multilinear alternative to explain the dynamism and complexity of social processes.

I

Historians have described the processes of the settlements of the brahmins who were induced either by land grants or otherwise influenced to emigrate to the forest regions peopled by tribes. The colonies established by them were stated to have acted as the centres of the diffusion of a new agricultural technology as also of a new culture among the tribes. D. D. Kosambi[1] tells us that the brahmins acted as pioneers in underdeveloped localities into which they introduced plough agriculture that replaced slash-and-burn cultivation or food-gathering. In fact, a whole new package was introduced by them with new inputs such as new crops, the knowledge of agricultural seasons (*naksatra*), and a network of markets, trade and settlements. As the brahmins preserved the local traits of jati, the tribes turned into a new peasant jati group. R. S. Sharma explains this process in the context of the early medieval period. He has brought in the fact of the land grants that encouraged the brahmins in large numbers to settle in tribal areas where they introduced the new agricultural technology. In his words:

> land grants served as an important means of bringing virgin soil under cultivation in Central India, Orissa and Eastern Bengal....Enterprising brahmanas were given useful employment in the backward, aboriginal tracts where they could spread new methods of cultivation. Some beliefs and rituals sponsored by the priests helped material progress among the tribal people. Thus the idea that the killing of a cow was as bad as homicide helped towards the preservation of cattle wealth, so essential for agriculture. The priests taught the primitive people not only the use of the plough and manure but also fostered agriculture by giving them the knowledge of seasons and planets, especially of the recurrence of the rains. The connections of various agricultural operations with different constellations (*naksatras*) were made widely known. Much of this knowledge was written down in the form of *Krsi-Parasara*, which seems to have been a product of this period.[2]

In his later work[3] Sharma highlights the process of culture change by citing the instance of the application of norms of brahminical society to the aborigines who were exhorted to practise nonviolence towards women, children and ascetics and to protect the cows and interests of brahmins.

The reconstruction of the evidence on the emigration of brahmins and other jatis, stimulated by land grants, into tribal areas is a construct of great significance for social scientists. The epigraphic evidence has to be carefully analysed to show the extent of such migration on the part of various jatis to different areas that fall within the tribal belt of India today. A thorough account of such an emigration and the functions that such communities performed in terms of the transfer of technology and culture change is very important. Fortunately this trend is being pursued and more and more evidence is coming in of reclamation of forest land by brahmin donees in the south, the extension of irrigation by excavation of tanks, the establishment of new villages, the institution of agricultural credit, the introduction of new crops such as sugarcane, betel leaves and arecanuts, fruits and plants.[4] Evidence has also been collected to suggest that such penetration was not a peaceful operation and that there were conflicts between the incoming brahmin jatis and the indigenous people over the extension of the forest boundary, collection of rent, sharing of water, etc. Such conflicts between the brahmins and local people appear to have been almost endemic. For example, in south Shahabad district of Bihar there are traditions of the occurrence of a violent conflict between a powerful brahmin zamindar who wanted to excavate a channel and the local people who resisted this. As a result of the conflict numerous brahmins were slain and a maund of sacred threads was collected from their dead bodies.[5]

That the penetration of brahmins and other jatis into such areas was not always a peaceful affair is further attested by sociologists. G.S. Ghurye tells us about the exploits of warrior saints such as Agastya and of warrior gods such as Skanda who acted as the agents of "Indian acculturation". That the ashrams situated in forests amid an alien population did not always practise non-violence but also occasionally acted as an arsenal is supported by him when he cites the example of Agastya presenting Rama with weapons at his ashram. The great sage in fact blessed Rama's mission to exterminate the *rakshasas* from the Dandakaranya, which the warrior from the north accomplished.[6] Ghurye, however, goes a step farther than historians inasmuch as he suggests that the brahmin prospectors also introduced the idea of endogamy and other elements of caste and that they applied schemes of occupational segregation and endogamy to various groups according to their respective abilities, though it seems they could not disturb the physical mixture of the region where they went. He thus concludes that caste in India is a brahminical child of the Indo-Aryan culture, cradled in the land of the Ganges and the Jamuna and thence transferred to other parts of the country.[7] There is nothing in anthropological literature to indicate that tribal endogamy did not have its roots in tribal society itself.

The facts regarding the influx of the brahmins and the diffusion of new agricultural technology and all that goes with it are indisputable, but there are also severe limitations to the application of the brahminization model to various regions of India, particularly tribal India. First, the epigraphic and other evidence relates not only to brahmins but also to other jatis. One of the possible lines of inquiry could be who were these jatis other than the brahmins and what was their role in the diffusion of the new agricultural technology and a new cultural system, and if there was one, what was the difference in the roles performed by them and the brahmins? Secondly, we have evidence that different jatis emigrated to tribal regions supported by land grants or without them. The influx of peasants to tribal areas to escape oppression is an admitted fact. Large-scale migrations of peasants to tribal areas in middle India, of the Kunbis in western parts and the Kurmis in eastern parts, Mahtos in the centre and the east, could be traced to the later medieval period. They went in search of land. Others went in search of adventure. Still others such as the Ahirs, a pastoral people, went in search of pastures and the Chamars to collect hides. Such communities naturally carried with them their own technology, their own ideology and their own world-view which were not all clothed in brahminical idioms. Thirdly, there were areas such as the heartland of Chotanagpur where land grants given to brahmins could be traced to a much later period. For example, the land grants given to brahmins in Ranchi have been traced to 1767. The *Chaitanyacharitamrit* refers to Shri Chaitanya's passage through Jharkhand where colonies of brahmins existed.[8] A study of such brahminical settlements as they exist today would show that they hardly perform any function in regard to the diffusion of technology or transmission of culture. In fact such functions are performed by the artisan communities and the peasants in the entire spectrum of middle India. The brahmin communities who have moved into middle India have taken to cultivation and moneylending and have developed an antagonistic form of relationship with local people. There is a saying in Chattisgarh that "if you see a snake and a brahmin, kill the brahmin first". Such antagonism is also expressed in folklores concerned with other groups of outsiders. Fourthly, next only to the peasants, the artisan communities, some of whom have been labelled arbitrarily as tribes, have played a role in the diffusion of technology, a subject to which we will revert later.

The question that arises at this stage is why and how in the face of such diversities and conflicts evident on the point of various kinds of interaction, the brahminical model could be developed. The ethnographers of the 19th century were not ignorant of the realities at the grassroots level and yet they put forward a theory of proselytizing brahminism which influenced and which continues to influence the whole genre of writings in indology, history and sociology.

The origin of the brahminical model could be traced to the efforts of the administrators and ethnographers of the 19th century to make out a case for the propagation of Christianity in India by presenting brahminism as a proselytizing religion. Sir John Campbell in his foreword to the report on Bengal in 1871-72 wrote:

> It is a great mistake to suppose that the Hindu religion is not proselytising; the system of caste gives room for the introduction of any number of outsiders. So long as people do not interfere with existing castes, they may form a new caste and call themselves Hindus; and the Brahmanas are always ready to receive all who will submit to them and pay them. The process of manufacturing Rajputs from ambitious aborigines goes on before our eyes.[9]

A classical formulation of views on similar lines exists in writings of Sir Alfred Lyall. Contesting the generally-held view supported by F. Max Muller, that brahminism was a "moribund non-missionary religion", he argued as follows:

> An eye-witness would still be justified in affirming that this religion (brahmanism) although powerfully affected by social and political changes so strong and sudden that they would try the constitution of any national creed, is nevertheless not yet dead, nor dying, nor even dangerously ill; and ,moreover ,that so far from it being a non-missionary religion, in the sense of a religion that admits no proselytes, one might safely aver that more persons in India become every year Brahmanists than all the converts to all the other religions in India put together. The first of these modes is the gradual Brahmanising of the aborigional, non-Aryan, or casteless tribes. The clans and races which inhabit the hill tracts, the outlying uplands, and the un-

cleared jungle districts of India, are melting into Hinduism, all over India by a process much more rapid and effective than individual conversions. Among all these aboriginal or non-Aryan communities a continued social change is going on; they alter their modes of life to suit improved conditions of existence; their languages decay, and they gradually go over to the dominant Aryan rituals.

The second mode by which I should affirm that Brahmanism proselyizes is by the working of the devotees and leaders who found new sects, and set up new lights in divine matters....These movements are now going all over India: some of them increase and take root, others wither and disappear; but it is impossible to describe as non-missionary a religion which permits and largely adopts all this wonderful diversity and intensity of religious propagation....Many of these teachers address themselves to every one without distinction of caste or of creed; they preach to low-caste men and to the aboriginal tribes who are just emerging, out of a nomad state into a settled low-caste element; in fact, they succeed largely in those ranks of the population which would lean towards Christianity and Mahomedanism if they were not drawn into Brahamanism by some local saint or devotee.

Thus Brahmanism all over India (is) a necessary first stage for the outlying tribes towards Indian civilisation, or admission to the citizenship of the great Hindu community; it very rarely implies any ethical change, or even a formal abandonment of one ritual for another; it is usually a rapid sliding into Hindu customs, and an attempt at social assimilation. But the complete process does necessitate a considerable change of worship and ways of life; for perhaps the surest sign of a family's reception into Brahmanism is, that whereas the Brahman formerly was never called in he is latterly found officiating at domestic epochs and ceremonies of birth, marriage, or death. This implies conformity to Brahmanic rules of eating, inter-marriage and the evolution of a caste or subcaste. If the converted families are of standing among their own people, the Brahman, for a consideration proportionate to the emergency or complexity of the case, will usually discover for them a decent Hindu pedigree, or (what is much easier) a miraculous incident, which proves a half savage chief or rich outcaste to be really allied to one of the recognised castes. We know how readily the gods have always intervened to explain every awkward incident of birth, and to provide a great man of humble origin with a parentage better suited to his success in after life.[10]

The reasons for the resounding success of Brahminism, according to Sir Alfred, are:

(a) That it is indigenous, the produce of the soil and of an environment that still exists.
(b) That it is a social system, and a very elastic one; while the people in India, as a body, still need a religion which, like Brahminism, provides them with special rules, with laws of custom as well as of conduct.
(c) That it encourages and is nourished by a constant miraculous agency working at full pressure, and by relays of divine embodiments; while, in the present intellectual state of the population in India, no religion will be widely embraced without visible miraculous credentials.

These views on the aggressive and sweeping nature of brahminism have been cited in extenso, because these were substantially taken over by the census authorities, both administrators and ethnographers and explored in the context of regional situations. H.H. Risley[11] carried forward Sir Alfred's views on the brahminization of the "aboriginal non-Aryans or casteless tribes" in the eastern Indian situation and worked out a fourfold catagorization of this process as follows:

(1) The leading men of an aboriginal tribe, having somehow got on in the world and become independent landed proprietors, manage to enrol themselves in one of the leading castes. They usually set up as Rajputs; their first step being to start a brahmin priest who invents for them a mythical ancestor, supplies them with a family mirade connected with the locality where their tribe is settled, and discovers that they belong to some hitherto unheard-of clan of the great Rajput community.

(2) A number of aborigines embrace the tenets of a Hindu religious sect losing thereby tribal name and becoming Vaishnabs, Romayats, and the like.

(3) A whole tribe of aborigines, or large members of a tribe, caste, which though claiming an origin of remote antiquity, is

readily distinguishable by its name from any of the standard and recognized castes.

(4) A whole tribe of aborigines, or a section of a tribe becomes gradually converted to Hinduism without, like the Rajbansis, abandoning their tribal designation.

Such hypotheses about brahminization deeply influenced both historians and sociologists. In the process such terms as "Arayanization", "hinduization" and "sanskritization" were played about. Even when "non-brahminical" concepts such as hinduization or Aryanization were used, emphasis was on the core of brahminical values. Sanskritization as a concept emerged in the early 1950s. The first scholar to have used it as a concept was Suniti Kumar Chatterji (1951)[12] who described progressive sanskritization of various elements of the population in India, particularly in the north-east. He observed:

> The subsequent history of civilisation in India is the expansion and elaboration of this Sanskrit culture and its slow but inevitable acceptance by all the various peoples of India. And this went on hand in hand with the spread of Sanskrit or Indian culture in lands outside India (Ceylon; Afghanistan and Eastern Iran; Central Asia or Serindia; Tibet, Mongolia; Indo-China: Malaya and Indonesia, which were lands of a Greater India; as well as China and its cultural dependencies Korea, Japan and Vietnam). The progressive Sanskritisation of the various pre-Aryan or non-Aryan peoples in their culture, their outlook and their ways of life forms the keynote of India through the ages. And in the course of this Sanskritisation the affected peoples also brought their own spiritual and material milieu to bear upon the Sanskrit and Sanskritic culture which they were adopting, and thus helped to modify and to enrich it in their own circles.
>
> This 'sanskritisation' would appear to have been opposed by the advent of a militant Islam and an aggressive Christianity in some parts of India. But in spite of an occasional set-back, the leaven has never been inactive.

Chatterji identified sanskritic elements in terms of patronage of brahmins and Hindu religion and identification of the gods and legends of the Indo-Mongoloid (*Kirat*) with those of the Hindus and the use of pan-Indian cultural and religious idioms in inscriptions and other materials.

Around this period M.N. Srinivas (1952) used the concept of sanskritization in a structural (or positional) sense rather than in only cultural terms as expounded by Suniti Kumar Chatterji. It was possible, as Srinivas argued, for a low-caste to rise to a higher position in the hierarchy by adopting vegetarianism and teetotalism and by sanskritizing his ritual and pantheon. sanskritization was essentially a brahminical process. As he explained:

> In short, it took over, as far as possible, the customs, rites and beliefs of the Brahmins and the adoption of the Brahminic way of life by a low caste seems to have been frequent, though theoretically forbidden. This process has been called 'Sanskritisation' in this book, in preference to 'Brahminisation', as certain Vedic rites are confined to Brahmins and the two other 'twice born' castes. The tendency of the lower castes to imitate the higher has been a powerful factor in the spread of Sanskritic ritual and customs, and in the achievement of a certain amount of cultural uniformity not only throughout the caste scale, but over the entire length and breadth of India.[13]

However there is a difference. Whereas the colonial ethnographers represented brahminization as an exogenous process, a function of cultural diffusion, Srinivas emphasized the internalization of the process, i.e. voluntary adoption of the norms or the mores of sanskritization by a community.

As social research highlighted diversities, the brahminical model of sanskritization came under attack, and Srinivas (1966)[14] admitted that he had unduly exaggerated the brahminical model of sanskritization and ignored the other models—ksatriya, vaishya and shudra, which are, of course, all varna categories. There was a further devaluation of this sanskritic model as researchers pointed to the role of the dominant caste or social group in a region/subregion which set the pattern of emulation for others. Emulation of the high by the low being a universal experience, it was easier to emulate the dominant group in the neighbourhood.

Few scholars, however, seriously considered the authenticity of the so-called brahminical elements in brahminization or sanskritization such as (a) vegetarianism and teetotalism, and (b) role of brahmins in rituals and pantheon in the course of the adoption of the brahminical way of life. The question is not whether the brahmins themselves all over the country practise vegetarianism and teetotalism, but whether these are only brahminical values or whether they relate to the non-brahminical system also. The Jains practised vegetarianism and teetotalism of the extreme kind at a time when the post-Vedic people indulged in large-scale sacrifices of animals. Buddhism registered a protest against this and permitted eating of flesh of dead animals. B.R. Ambedkar traces the origin of vegetarianism in India to the attempts made by the brahmins to outdo the Buddhists in vegetarianism.[15] However, the rise of vegetarianism followed the spread of Vaishnavism from the Gupta period onwards. The Krishna cult of the pastoral communities who showed reverence for cattle, their mainstay, stood at the centre of the Vaishnava movement. The Todas of the Nilgiris, the only pastoral tribe in south India, are strict vegetarians. The once pastoral communities such as the Gwalas, Ahirs and Jats are vegetarians. Vegetarianism thus was the food practice of cattle-rearing communities which was transformed into a tenet of Vaishnavism. A similar process could also be seen at work in regard to teetotalism. Even today we can observe the distinction between the highly ritualized vegetarianism and teetotalism of the brahmins in the south and the simple, natural vegetarianism of the Todas. The peasant jatis who went into tribal areas of middle India were mostly vegetarians. Similarly, the much talked about impact of the Great Traditions upon the Little Traditions has been re-evaluated by recent studies which show that far from submerging the latter the two have coexisted in a state of "moving" equilibrium, and that the distinction between sanskritic and non-sanskritic traditions is more functional than historical. Srinivas, therefore, moved farther from his position and admitted to the possiblity of the existence of variant models of sanskritic Hinduism as well as non- and anti-sanskritic models.[16]

II

We may consider the possibilities of the application of an alternative model of the diffusion of technology and culture change between the tribe and the peasant. We would like to argue that in many situations of culture contact the diffusion of technology is more a function of tribe and peasant interaction and tribe and artisan interaction rather than brahmin-tribe contact. The role of peddlers, merchants and mendicants in the diffusion of culture is well known in anthropological literature, a story which has its counterpart in our country also. Not so well known, however, is the role of the artisan communities in the diffusion of technology. Kosambi often used to tell me that the Asurs of Chotanagpur probably borrowed the Mauryan technology of iron smelting, which they surely could not have developed on their own. Agarias like the Asurs[17]—it is possible to trace a belt of primitive iron-smelters across the centre of India—also practised iron smelting. Both these communities, now labelled as tribals, introduced iron implements in tribal areas and raised the productivity of agriculture. It is likely that through them the Indian plough, known in Sanskrit as *langal,* which first spread through the Gangetic valley, was introduced later into the valleys of middle India, as borne out by various derivatives in both dialects and national languages for the word plough. The plough then travelled southward (in Telugu it is called *nagali*). The *langal* emerged as the symbol of technological diffusion throughout the country. There were also other artisan communities who struck up the *jajmanī* form of relationship with the tribals, supplied them with utensils, terracotta artifacts, ornaments and other wares. Two such communities could be mentioned. The Gharwas of Bastar produced bell metal wares for tribes and the master potters of the Bhil territory produced a splendid array of terracotta wares which are offered by the Bhils to their ancestors. In the process of producing these wares the artisans also transferred their concepts to the tribes. In fact they performed a dual role as the preserver and custodian of "tribal crafts" and as the agents of acculturation. The Jadupatuas, magician painters and brass workers of the

Santal Pargana (they were not tribal converts), painted scrolls for Santal tribals as well as for peasants. Their repertoire included Santal heroes and kings and also Hindu gods and Muslim pirs. They also painted *Jadupatas*, magical scrolls, for tribal Santals depicting the journey of the dead Santals through the 'devouring terror of the nether world' in deference to the Santal belief that their dead wandered blindly until the Jadupatua gave them eyesight by painting the pupils of the eyes into the portrait of the dead spirits.[18] Through such processes many of the ideas of sanskritic tradition were transmitted by the artisans to the tribals.

We now turn to the discussion of the tribe-peasant interaction in Chotanagpur which serves as a window on middle India. Many of the Chotanagpur tribes had the advantage of being exposed to the impact of the agricultural technology of the Gangetic valley. It is possible to argue that the Dravidian tribes such as the Oraons and Cheros acquired the characteristics of an agricultural community in the land of Karusa in the Gangetic valley and a measure of familiarity with iron implements. The expulsion of the Kolarian tribes by the prolific Dravidian tribes would also be ascribed to the superior technique of agricultural production, acquired by the latter. The transformation of the Mundas from a pastoral into an agricultural community is a story faintly recalled in their mini epic, *Sosobonga*. This book descibes the conflict between the Mundas and the Asurs and the triumph of the Munda god Singbonga, the Sun God, associated with agriculture.[19] Agriculture and astronomy being closely related, a knowledge of agriculture was reflected in the astronomy of the Mundas and their star myths. For example, like primitive people elsewhere, when they took to agriculture and the plough, they looked for its counterpart in the heavens. Thus the Sword and Belt of Orion was interpreted as the plough and ploughshare which their god first shaped in the heavens and then taught the use of it to his people on earth. The star Capella was called *Barai* (the celestial blacksmith) and the Kids (shaped like an isosceles triangle) the bellows and charcoal fire. The Great Bear was *Parkom Kumru Ipil* (lit. bedstead and thief-star) which represents the bed of Singbonga which was sought to be stolen by the thieves. The Milky Way was the *Gaihora*, the path of the cows which Singbonga led every day.[20] The year stood divided into three seasons, the summer, the rainy season and the cold season. There was very little of the brahminical influence in this. Nor did most of the tribals show respect for cows until recently. However, the Mundas seem to have absorbed the concept of agricultural seasons (*naksatras*) and the names of days and months. It was the use of iron implements and the plough that transformed them into a settled peasant community. This process was further aided by the imitation of the agricultural practices of such peasant communities as Bhogtas, Kurmis, Ahirs and Koeris who emigrated to Chotanagpur. The tribals were experts at reclaiming land from forest from before particularly in the valleys, and they had developed an irrigation system suitable for such incipient agriculture. Their implements were simple. They grew their own varieties of millets, upland paddy and pulses. As iron was introduced, agriculture improved; they started growing many strains of paddy, vegetables and fruits; they constructed tanks, dug wells and terraced their fields. A comparison of agricultural implements used by the tribals and those used by non-tribal peasant communities suggests the similarity and extent of exchange that had taken place. The non-Mundari and non-Oraon nomenclature of most of the implements shows the extent of transfer of technology from the peasants to tribes. Similarly the extent of transfer of technology in manufacture of cloth is attested by non-tribal names of implements such as *charkha* (spinning wheel), the cotton cleaner (*pisri*), thread-making shuttle (*dhere*). The same pattern of nomenclature applies to household wares such as utensils.

What is true of Chotanagpur is also true of tribal regions of Orissa and Madhya Pradesh. The transfer of technology imparted self-sufficiency to tribal economy and made it productive; it also provided a large economic base for the development of a composite culture in which there was a great deal of give and take. Unfortunately this story yet remains to be told. The persistence of the dichotomous categories of tribe and non-tribe in our studies, made worse by the exploitation of the tribals as a whole by non-tribals, do not help matters. Nevertheless the critical dimension of the economic interdependence of tribes[21] and non-tribes deserves to be highlighted.

First, there is the rise of a link language in this region called Sadani in Chotanagpur, Desi in Madhya Pradesh and the pidginised Assamese in the north-east which serves as the medium of communication between the tribals and non-tribals. Such link languages have been influenced by both tribal dialects and the Hindi language as spoken by the peasantry. Secondly, a whole corpus of local customs—*lokachara* and *desachara*, shared by both tribals and non-tribals—has come into existence. One of the questions being raised in this context is whether the ceremony regarding application of *sindur* as a symbol of marriage, restricted to the Hindus of eastern region, is not basically a Kolarian custom as practised by the Santals. The third is the role of emigrating peasantry in the spread of the epic traditions and Bhakti movement from the plains of the north to the hills of middle India which had always provided shelter for the peasantry and the untouchables. Carried by the peasantry the epic traditions were adopted and readapted by tribals who identified themselves with one or another of the epic heroes. The vitality of the epic traditions is attested by the fact that they, among other factors, inspired the rise of modern literature in many of the tribal languages. The tribals have not simply borrowed from the common sub-puranic and epic traditions but they have also re-created a good deal of them, and these recreations together with their own rich folklores formed part of what has been called an aboriginal purana.[22]

The Satnami movement was very strong among the untouchables in Chattisgarh. The Kabirpanth movement spread from Chattisgarh into Chotanagpur. The leaders of tribal revivalism borrowed their own notions of Hinduism not from the brahmins but from peasant and artisan communities coming to their land.[23] Probably the most articulate expression of the Bhakti movement influencing the tribals is provided by the poetry of Bhima Bhoi, the Khond mystic poet and one of the foremost exponents of Mahima cult in Orissa. Belief in one absolute God, anti-ritualism and anti-caste stance formed the core of this movement, started by

Guru Mahimaswami (1826-76), who had a Savara disciplc, Sadanand. The movement turned against the worship of the Jagannath. Bhima Bhoi's appeal cut across the tribes and peasants. A recent study of this cult shows that about two-thirds of its followers belonged to the Chasa (farmer) or allied castes (Kaibartha, etc), about eight per cent are tribals, and about four per cent are harijans.[24]

These influences also account for a good deal of similarity between the contents of the religion practised by the tribes and peasants. The primitive sections of the tribal communities and the ordinary peasants in villages share such features as worship of ancestral gods, a vague belief in Great God or Supreme Being, feasting, dancing and noisy processions as prominent features of ceremonial life, animal sacrifices and ritual offering, use of certain ritual objects such as red powdered grain, iron, peacock feathers and chains, a belief in reincarnation and more vaguely in *karma*, etc.[25]

In the north-east there is no evidence of the existence of any brahminical settlement that acted as a point of diffusion of technology.[26] Even otherwise the caste system was loose and the concept of *chaturvarnya* almost non-existent in the Brahmaputra valley. Spread of wet paddy cultivation and increasing use of the plough (its local nomenclature was derived from the Sanskrit word), under the impact of advanced peasant communities coming in to settle, were the key factors in the transformation of tribes into peasants in the Brahmaputra valley and on its periphery as also in the valleys of the north-eastern hills. With agricultural surplus, emerged differentiation, a form of caste system and the states. Vaishnavism provided ideological support for the political system. Shankar Dev preached against caste and advocated vegetarianism and teetotalism. Among his disciples were a Naga and a Garo and followers from all sections of the society. In spite of the extension of wet paddy cultivation and the rise of peasants, the slash-and-burn mode of cultivation persisted for a long period. Among the tribes of the north-east the Khasis extracted and smelted iron and forged iron implements. Among the Mizos one of the village officials is a blacksmith. The Apatani smith manufactures swords (*dao*) and knives. It is only in recent times that some of the tribes in the hills have started using the plough and are replacing their simple agricultural implements made of bamboo by iron implements. However within their eco-system they have developed their own technology of terrace cultivation and irrigation which are marvels by even present-day standards.[27]

To conclude, the present exercise is not meant either to deny or denigrate the brahminical model of technology transfer and dissemination of culture among tribal people—the model has held its field for long and been useful in organizing material as it turned up at the early stage—but only to point out its inadequacy and to suggest the possibilities of the application of other models to explain the complex process of change and development on the periphery of what is considered the core of Indian society. There is nothing in anthropological literature to suggest that the brahminical settlements are functioning as centres of diffusion of technology. Such functions were performed by peasants and artisans. The passage from a unilinear to a multilinear model of social change has been under way. Research should focus on the many dimensions of the interaction among various communities some which have been arbitrarily labelled as tribes, in terms of transfer of technology, rise of link languages, absorption and recreation of epic traditions, all within the framework of an autonomous social formation in a tribal region.

Notes and References

1. D.D. Kosambi, *The Culture and Civilization of Ancient India tn Historical Outline*, p. 172.
2. R.S. Sharma, *Indian Feudalism*, p. 222.
3. R.S. Sharma, *Material Culture and Social Formations in Ancient India*, pp. 146-47, 172.
4. R.N. Nandi, "Growth of Rural Economy in Early Feudal India", Presidential Address, Ancient India Section, Indian History Congress, forty-fifth session, 1984.
5. P.C. Ray Choudhary, *Gazetteer of India: Bihar, Shahabad*, pp. 802-3.
6. G.S. Ghurye, *Indian Acculturation: Agastya and Skanda*, pp. 43-44.
7. G.S. Ghurye, *Caste and Race in India*, p. 176. For further discussion of Ghurye's view on brahmin prospectors, see K.S. Singh, "Varna, Jati and

Jana, An Anthropo-historical Perspective", *Proceedings of the Indian History Congress*, Burdwan, 1983 and the next chapter.

8. K.S. Singh, "Tribal Medieval Bihar", *History of Bihar*, vol. II, pp. 257-59.

9. Quoted in Sir Alfred Lyall, *Asiatic Studies, Religious and Social.*

10. *Ibid.*, pp. 133-51.

11. H.H. Risley, *Tribes and Castes of Bengal*, vol I, pp. xvi-xviii.

12. S.K. Chatterji, *Kirata Jana-krti*, The *Indo-Mongoloids*, p. 3.

13. M.N., Srinivas, *Religion and Society among the Coorgs of South India*, 2nd edn, p. 30; Surendra Munshi, "Tribal Absorption and Sanskritisation in Hindu Society", *Contributions to Indian Sociology* (NS) vol. 13, no. 2, 1979.

14. M.N. Srinivas, *Social Change in Modern India*, p. 7.

15. B.R., Ambedkar, *The Untouchables*, p. 117.

16. M.N. Srinivas, Forward to Milton Singer, *When a Great Tradition Modernises*, p. ix.

17. See Verrier Elwin, *The Agaria* and K.K. Leuva, *The Asur.*

18. Pupul Jayakar, *The Earthen Drum*, p. 153.

19. K.S. Singh, "Pattern of Agricultural Changes in Tribal Chotanagpur", *Trends of Socio-Economic Change in India 1871-1961.*

20. M.B. Bhaduri, "The Astronomy of the Mundas and Their Star Myths", paper presented at Second Oriental Conference, Calcutta 1922.

21. K.S. Singh, (ed), *Economies of the Tribes and their Transformation.*

22. Verrier Elwin, Introduction to *Myths of Middle India*; also see T.B. Naik, "Ramakatha among the Primitive Tribes of India", *Bulletin of the Tribal Research Institute*, Chhidwara, MP, no. 3, vol. I, Oct. 1957.

23. K.S. Singh, *Birsa Munda and His Movement 1874-1901*, p. 41.

24. "Autochthonous Hindu Reform Movement", in Anncharlott, Eschmann, Hermann Kulke and Gayacharan Tripathi (ed), *The Cult of Jagannath and the Regional Tradition of Orissa.*

25. Surajit Sinha, "Tribe-Caste and Tribe-Peasant Continuation in Central India", *Man in India*, vol. 45, March 1965.

26. Based on discussion with T.C. Sharma, Department of Anthropology, Gauhati Unversity.

27. M.C. Goswami, "Tribe Peasant-Caste Relations in North-East India", Presidential Address, 98th Indian Science Congress, 1971.

4

Varna, Jati and Jana

The purpose of this chapter is to discuss the interplay of such concepts as varna, jati (caste) and jana (tribe), the assumptions underlying them, and the processes of the integration of jana with jati within the varna system or outside of it with the larger socio-economic formation. This exercise is attempted as an investigation of these processes explored by historians and sociologists to show how their research findings could be dovetailed to provide a complementary, if not a complete picture.

I

Few subjects have excited as much interest as the jati in all its ramifications. The process of the integration of jati into varna and of jana with jati has fascinated historians, sociologists and anthropologists. Social historians have, however, been preoccupied more with varna than with jati for the simple reason that the sources of ancient history have dealt more with varna and less with jati. The evolution of the *chaturvarnya* and the assimilation of various communities into this system through extension of agriculture and economic differentiation has been highlighted by historians.[1] Yet another trend that has been underlined is the proliferation of peasant castes including *sankirna* (mixed) jatis and swelling of their ranks through accretion from tribal communities. The sudras, out of whose ranks rose royalties, have been rightly described as the most dynamic social category. The ksatriya and sudra varnas have thus been constantly enlarging.[2] These findings are of significance for anthropologists who study the integration of tribe with caste in a contemporary setting.

While Indian anthropologists have studied the hierarchy of castes in its local setting and discussed mutual perception of castes, many of them have generally ignored the study of varna as an ideology. The sociologists like these anthropologists have been concerned far more with jati than with varna. However, unlike many anthropologists, sociologists have not ignored varna. Field studies have revealed the infinitely complex formations of jatis; their ranking differs from place to place; their world-views vary. The jatis cannot be straitjacketed into the varna scheme; there is an obvious lack of fit between the two. The conceptual framework of *chaturvarnya* has been found by sociologists to be too rigid, too 'amorphous' to fit the social realities of jatis which are far more dynamic, complex and wide-ranging. Even so the varna system provides a framework within which there have been attempts to rank jatis, and within which jatis from one region seek to relate themselves to those from another, similarly placed. The Bedas of Mysore who are peasants and shepherds call themselves Valmiki brahmins, and the smiths of south India describe themselves as Viswakarmas, thus seeking affinity with the artisan groups in north India. The Viswakarma *puja*—lustily celebrated now—has been declared a holiday in many states, and it has emerged as a major festival for artisan castes like the festival of Ravidas, the harijan saint, which has become popular as the occasion to unify sections of the harijan population. The varna system has thus come in handy for everybody "as a simple and clear scheme which is applicable to all parts of India...varna has provided a common social language which holds good, or is thought to hold good, for India as a whole. The sense of familiarity, even when it does not rest on facts, is conducive to unity".[3] However, the culmination of the varna system as an all-India frame of reference is a recent phenomenon.

For long the confusion between varna and jati persisted. At times they were used as interchangeable terms. This was particularly true of the early phases of ancient history. This confusion partly reflected the state of social situation which was in a flux. The forms of caste endogamy and clan exogamy as also the notions of purity and pollution had not acquired the rigidity that they did later in the "Kaliyuga" according to some puranas.

That the dividing line between various varnas was not sharply drawn was also underlined by the fact that the authors of the smritis recognized the forms of *anuloma* and *pratiloma* marriages even though a few of them later condemned *pratiloma* and recommended only *anuloma*.

This confusion could also be due to the fact that between varna and jatis, varna appears to have taken root earlier than the jatis when the *Brahmana* works were composed.[4] From a twofold categorization between Aryas and Dasyus or Dasas based on difference of colour and culture or classes (of masters and slaves as indicated by the Buddha) the varna system evolved into a fourfold categorization, a *chaturvarnya* stemming not only from a division of labour but also from a division of peoples. Compared to varna as a classificatory device, the concept of jati based on birth and occupation appears to have evolved slowly as economic functions differentiated. The use of the word jati in the sense of caste could be traced back to the time of the *Nirukta*. There are also references to *hina* or *nicha* jatis (despised castes). The fact remains that in early literature the two terms, varna and jati, were used interchangeably because they seemed to share the characteristics of divisions based on birth and occupation, though in later works varna and jati were sometimes made distinct. This distinction has become explicit in sociological literature in recent times[5] with varna being accepted conceptually as a hierarchical system within which jatis are suitably ranked, and both varna and jati being regarded as structural systems.[6]

The question whether the concept of varna was an ideological framework or whether it reflected social realities or whether it was both has been interminably discussed. Varna was no doubt an ideological weapon in the hands of both the brahmins and the Buddhists to establish the supremacy of the varna to which they belonged. It is also true that it gradually became the instrument for establishing and perpetuating brahminical supremacy. Manu[7] gave expression to a very arrogant form of brahminism in a crude way, though Yajnavalkya who came later was relatively liberal and recognized the sudra's right to make gift. This difference reflected the social processes of the periods of Manu and Yajnavalkya. One cannot escape forming the impression that Manu was trying to overstretch the *chaturvarnya* model to include and categorize all kinds of people—the proliferating jatis—and he mentions many such communities far and near, within it. Thus the people who were powerful but outside the framework of the brahminical religion were called degraded ksatriyas. Those who were within it but placed at a low level were called *sankirna* jatis. Miscegenation had no doubt occurred on a large scale as it also did later, as attested by institutions of *pratiloma* and *anuloma* relationships, *niyoga*, etc. But surely there were physical and geographical limits to this kind of miscegenation and all people could not be condemned as belonging to *sankirna* jatis, the progeny of *anuloma* or *pratiloma* relationship, by bringing in the notion of "bastardy".

The fact remains that the varna system which was formulated as an ideological framework upholding brahminical supremacy did reflect social realities. As P.V. Kane tells us, even in the ancient period it was not merely to be striven for as an ideal but had a depth of actuality that represented real division of society at least to a very great extent.[8] Subsequently even the cases of the families improvised into the ksatriyas continued to reflect the bias of brahminical supremacy. A new brahma-ksatriya category emerged.[9] The Chandelas were described as the progeny of the moon god and a brahmin girl, Hemawati, and the Nagbansis as the progeny of the serpentman and a brahmin girl, Parvati.

Recent field-studies show that most villagers accept the varna categorization as a primordial make-up of their society at least to fit local jatis and jati-clusters within it. However, there were communities and territories which stood outside the varna system. A distinction was made between those who were within the varna (*savarnas*) and those who stood outside it (*avarnas*). The untouchables and the tribals were *avarnas* who stood outside the varna system. Between the untouchables (harijans) and tribals, while the harijans are a part of the social and cultural system of jatis, even though they are outside the varna system, the tribals are neither part of the jati nor of the varna system, despite efforts now being made to bring the tribals and harijans together on a platform as a political force.

For long the varna system remained confined to the Aryavarta, its cradle. It was generally assumed that as the concept of varna spread to the south and the east, it shrank from the fourfold (*chaturvarnya*) to the twofold category. In fact it weakened, the jatis both in the south and in the east (as far as the Brahmaputra valley) showing little concern for it, developing no matter however vaguely and loosely, their own hierarchies or divisions, without any reference to the rigid varna framework. While the authors of the smritis continued to speak of the four varnas, there were, in fact two varnas—brahmins and the sudras—in the south and also in the east. Part of this assumption could be ascribed to the fact that with the establishment of brahminical supremacy after the fall of the Mauryas, the ksatriyas and vaisyas were not supposed to exist in the "Kaliyuga". The *Vishnu Purana* tells us that Mahapadma Nanda destroyed the ksatriya race as if he were another Parasurama and thereafter the sudras became the kings. When it is stated that there were no ksatriyas after the Nandas, one does not know whether the ksatriya is meant here as a jati or as a varna. If it is jati then there is no pure jati of ksatriyas; if it is varna, then there are jatis with this status. The assumption that the brahmins had legislated the ksatriyas out of existence has been questioned today not only by historians[10] but also by sociologists. The brahminical literature which describes many ruling families as sudras understandably suffers from a bias, and such textual references are not corroborated by the context and the actuality. There is a long martial tradition in the south of which we have a powerful evocation in art forms. The ruling lineages of the Nayars, Urs (Wadiyars), Coorgis, etc. have long considered themselves ksatriyas because they have been warriors and their claim, as Srinivas tells us,[11] has not been seriously disputed by anybody. The difference between the Rajputs, another warrior community and the warrior communities of the south, both being jatis, lies in the fact that while the Rajputs spread from the west to the east pursued by Mughals, in search of adventure and power, the warriors in the south remained a local community. The brahmins always obliged the ruling families with genealogy and *prasasti* (panegyric) and accepted their claim to be ksatriyas. The ksatriyization of Shivaji (1674) is a well-documented case. The south also had a flourishing business community.

Yet another widely prevalent assumption has been that brahminism is the dominant ideology which swept the whole country bringing within its fold all jatis and janas. That brahminism was a dominant ideology, which had a wide impact, is accepted. But there were peoples and territories which remained outside the range of the influence of brahminism or which were not subjected to its impact to the same extent as the areas under its direct influence were. Ghurye, as mentioned earlier, goes a little too far when he says that the idea of endogamy and other elements of caste were taken by the brahmin prospectors to other regions and that they devised their scheme of occupational segregation and endogamy of various groups according to their respective abilities.[12] Such a view underestimates the autonomy of various regions and of their social formations. Jati has been strictly a local institution like tribe. Both share many a characteristic, and have evolved norms and institutions in their habitat as they have settled down. Clan exogamy and tribe or jati endogamy are generally characteristics of settled, large and homogeneous communities. There is no evidence that these institutions were borrowed from the brahmins. Many tribes to this day practise rigid commensal norms and do not accept food and water from the brahmins. Behind this probably lay the belief about the sanctity and power of food to transmit certain qualities which are common to many primitive peoples, from whom the brahmins might have borrowed these ideas. Further, anthropological evidence shows that many castes and tribes, living far away from areas of brahminical influence, evolved a technology of their own which was suited to their eco-system and a set of beliefs and institutions generally independently of any outside influence.

The integration of jana with the cultural and economic system of jati is best studied in the regional setting. A *janapada* (region) is the unit of social history and of social formation. It seems that the people inhabiting a particular *janapada* broke up into functional jatis. The Abhiras split into both varna and jati categories; there were Abhira brahmins, Abhira ksatriyas, Abhira vaisyas, Abhira mahasudras, Abhira carpenters and goldsmiths.[13] The Gurjara people too had similar divisions along the varna and jati lines. There were pastoral Gurjaras also. In contemporary times a similar example is offered by the Mina tribe in Rajasthan who appears to have fissioned into various jatis defined by occupation. There are also indigenous jatis of brahmins and Rajputs, the Aranyaka brahmins of Orissa and the Lohtamiya Rajputs of Bihar, to mention only two of many examples. Aranyaka brahmins are said to have originated in an episode of the battles that raged between the Andhras and Oriyas in the course of which the Oriya ruler facing the threat of a defeat hastily collected a bunch of local tribals, conferred the sacred threads on them, paraded them as brahmins before the advancing Andhra army and thus stopped the war. The immigrant jatis who too are a feature of the local system were regarded as superior by indigenous jatis. Now both have started intermarrying.

The local setting is also important from another angle. Certain elements of kinship structure in many parts of India are territorial, cutting across both jatis and janas. Both practice clan exogamy and tribal or jati endogamy. Both observe a set of commensal norms. Both are local institutions, inhabiting relatively well-defined territories and thus sharing many characteristics of social and kinship structures—though jatis are relatively dispersed. There are also differences between the two. The jana is still moved by the strong sense of kinship which not only regulates social life but also controls resources including land which are shared. The tribal society is more egalitarian and less unequal.

There does not seem to be any anthropological support for the idea that a community on the move in the turbulent Vedic period which had not settled down could have developed a well-defined system of endogamy. The social system in the early phases of ancient society in India was in a state of flux and neither endogamy nor commensal norms acquired rigid forms for a long time and they did so probably only in the last phase of the ancient period or the early medieval period, or with the onset of mythical Kaliyuga as mentioned above.

Yet another assumption is about the mode of upward mobility for communities placed low in the jati or varna hierarchy. The authors of the smritis have spoken of *jatyutkarsa* or *jatyaprakash*.[14] (upclimbing or illumination in jati hierarchy). Others have spoken of *varnotkarsa* (upward mobility in varna hierarchy). These concepts underline the theoretical possibility of the rise in status of a varna placed low to a higher varna through appropriate marriages contracted over generations. This provision was supposed to lessen the rigour of the caste system. But as Kane rightly says, one does not know the extent to which the provision for mobility of this kind was acted upon. No example of *jatyutkarsa* occurs in the literature of dharmasastra or in inscriptions.[15] However, upward climbing was not so much a result of the marriages into higher varna described in the smritis, as a function of power and authority. There are umpteen examples of families and groups having risen from the ranks of sudras to be recognized as ksatriyas.

An analysis of the ancient texts shows that the integration of the outlying communities with the varna system was also an economic process. There were communities living on the periphery who came to perform specific economic functions in relation to the core community. Manu seems to make a distinction between what we call today a tribe and the untouchables. He speaks of the first in terms of the communities that dwelt around well-known trees and burial grounds, on mountains and in groves and were being functionally integrated into the local economy. Such communities were the Nisads who killed fish, Ayogava who did the carpenter's work, Andhras who slaughtered wild animals, Pukkasa who killed animals living in holes (like the present day Musahars in Bihar), Venas who played drums (like Doms and Ghasis in north India) and the Dhigvanas who worked in leather. There were also communities called the mlechchas whose speech was unintelligible, and those who ate the cow's flesh as some tribes do, and as some tribes did in middle India. Unlike these communities the Chandalas, who carried corpses for burial and executed criminals, appeared more closely integrated with village communities even though they lived outside the villages. Much the same system continues to this day.

While this kind of integration into the local economy was going on for the people on the periphery there were some among them who rose to found states and acquire political power. References to tribal chiefs or even Chandala chiefs are many, and Banabhatta rapturously describes in *Kadambari* a Chandala princess in a royal court. It was in the medieval period both early and later that we find the communities called tribes today emerging as custodians of political power. The Kharwars are first in the race followed by the Cheros and Gonds in medieval India. In the north-east the *Kiratas* set up their states. Even those who did not so directly participate in the endogenous processes of state-formation, were accepted as dominant communities. The *Ain-i-Akbari* mentions the Bhils, Gonds and Kolis as dominant communities in their region. Thus integration was a multiplex process that took place at economic, cultural and political levels.

II

During the colonial period many of the processes mentioned above gathered momentum. It is well known that the successive censuses triggered off the scramble for higher ranking within the varna hierarchy. Sanskritization was in full swing. It is not possible in this chapter to discuss the claims and counterclaims and the final gradation of jatis arrived at by census authorities after the examination of petitions filed by different communities. Suffice it to say that this upgradation business did achieve a measure of upward mobility for some sections of many communities. We also notice during this period the process of jatis emerging from their local matrices, swallowing up upjatis (subcastes) and seeking kinship with what are called their counterpart groups in other parts of the country and thus establishing their pan-Indian identity. Such communities laid down norms for the jatis as a whole including the right to wear the sacred thread. There was an economic dimension to the right to wear the sacred thread, as asserted by both backward castes (such as the Yadavas) and the Santal tribe in the 1920s and 1930s in Bihar, who sought a higher social status and also tried in the process to acquire an economic clout. The records of the caste mahasabhas should be examined for the purpose of delineating this kind of social mobilization.

The Rajput Mahasabha papers as also the proceedings of the Chamber of Princes might reveal the extent to which the model of Rajputization was carried to apply to the then ruling princes who were non-Rajputs.[16] Many such princes tried to acquire Rajput status through the mediation of the Rajput Mahasabha or through the Chamber of Princes or in spite of both. A Sikh prince from Patiala married into the Rajput family of Saraikela and vice-versa. A Wadiyar from Mysore married into the Rajput family of Morvi. Not all such marriages ended happily, but the trend was set. The Rajputs and Marathas intermarried first at the level of their princes (Baroda and Cooch Bihar) and then at middle levels. The recognition of Dogras as Rajputs was resisted for a while and then intermarriages began. Perhaps the best documented example, as briefly mentioned above, is that of the Raj Gond family of Khairagarh who at first failed to get recognition as Rajput through the Rajput Mahasabha probably in the 1920s, which held that they were Raj Gonds. Frustrated in their first attempt the Khairagarh family resorted to the time-honoured device of seeking a higher status; they got a new genealogy written to establish their claim to be Nagbansi because the status of the latter as ksatriyas was recognized in central India, and married into a Rajput family. An acrimonious debate followed in the course of which the well-recognized Rajput and the lower-ranked Rajput zamindars differed in their recognition of the Khairagarh chief as a Rajput. The genealogy was written by a scion of the Nagbansi family of Chotanagpur who was suitably rewarded by Khairagarh. Once recognized their status has not been questioned since.

Sociological studies have stressed primarily cultural integration of tribe with peasant. There are many variants of this model. The best known of the models centres on the sanskritization of the families which constitute the upper crust of the tribal society. The Cheros are a classical example. They not only changed to a new jati status by claiming to be Chyavanvansi Rajputs but also sought the varna status of the ksatriyas. However, while one segment of the Chero tribe became Rajputs in one region, another segment remained a tribal and backward community in another. On the other hand the Kharwars, Gonds and Nagbansis did not give up what we might call, for the purpose of convenience, their jati status—in fact they continued to take pride in their status as such, as the revenue and judicial proceedings of the 19th century show. They only claimed the varna ranking of the ksatriyas and got it recognized as such. Secondly, we have the example of a whole tribe being sanskritized. The Mahtos of Chotanagpur were recognized as a tribe in every census up to 1921. Then they went through a process of social mobility, discovered their kinship with the Kurmis of Bihar and the Kunbis of Maharashtra, found their culture heroes in Shivaji Maharaj and Sardar Vallabhbhai Patel and claimed the status of the ksatriyas. They were descheduled as a tribe in 1931. Now they are trying to reclaim the status of the tribe and the Kunbi-Mahto nexus has broken down, the Kunbis having disowned any historical or social links with the Bihar Kurmi- Mahto. Thirdly, there are segments of tribes which claim the status neither of a jati nor of a varna but are sanskritized. They have generally adopted the institutions of child-marriage and polygamy, acquired the notion of a Supreme Being, borrowed the rituals and life cycle ceremonies of the neighbouring Hindu communities. The recent trend, however, is to assert tribal identity and autonomy. In spite of the continuing acquisition of cultural traits the process of sanskritization has received a setback because no tribal today seeks a higher jati or a varna status, but "hinduization" is on.[17]

So ubiquitous has been the varna model that it was manipulated as an ideology in the course of a wide ranging debate on social reform in the modern period. Many reformers attacked the inequalities of jati and varna by invoking the philosophy of *advaita* (unqualified monism). Mohandas Karamchand Gandhi (the Mahatma) defended the varna but attacked the jati system. B. R. Ambedkar attacked the *chaturvarnya* system but described the sudras as degraded ksatriyas.[18] Thus he did not altogether reject the varna system. While, according to him, the concept of *chaturvarnya* preached the gospel of social inequality, he did not hesitate to embrace the Buddhist faith which too accepted the varna system, though in doing so it introduced 'positional' rather than structural changes within it by placing the ksatriyas above brahmins. Few scholars today are in agreement with Ambedkar's views that the ksatriyas were degraded as sudras just because they were denied *upanayana* (sacred thread) by brahmins.[19] The hero of the Battle of Ten Kings, Sudas, was not a sudra as claimed by Ambedkar but there was an Arya tribe called the sudras. While Ambedkar is right in holding Manu's concept of the *chaturvarnya* responsible for the degradation of the sudras, their degradation was not an accomplished fact with and after Manu. Recent researches have shown that sudras were liberated from the state of slavery that existed in the Mauryan period which he describes as the golden age and that they emerged as peasants enjoying rights as such and a measure of affluence, which was probably unthinkable in Manu's scheme of things. They could be teachers; they enjoyed the right to make gift in spite of Manu's injunction that they should not do so. Yajnavalkya reflected this trend by providing for a liberal dispensation for the sudras. Even though they did not become ksatriyas they were treated with a measure of tolerance as part of a far more broadbased system of production in the more expansive phase of the Gupta period.[20] Similarly, some of Ambedkar's views about the untouchables who stood outside the pale of the varna system do not hold good today. He is right in holding that the untouchables were on the periphery of the village society, that they were beef-eaters, that they had their own social system and world view, that some of them even looked down upon the brahmins, that they were 'broken men', i.e. remnants of conquered tribes living on the fringe of villages, and that there is no racial basis to untouchability as proved by the results of anthropometry. But his views that they were the Buddhists is not supported by studies.

Few scholars will be in agreement with the Mahatma's idealized views of Hinduism. According to him caste was a drag on Hinduism, and untouchability was not part of Hinduism, but an excrescence upon it. The varna system was natural, inherent in human nature, which specified the religious, social and economic needs of the community and a just division of labour. However, according to him varna had nothing to do with jati which was at the root of all evils. Therefore while jati and untouchability should go because they militated against the principles of social equality, varna should remain because it expressed natural divisions among men.[21] Such views went against the generally accepted opinion of the scholars that roots of jati and untouchability went back to the varna system. They found themselves more in sympathy with Ambedkar than with Gandhi on this point.

Two anthropologists pleaded in the 1930s that the varna status of ksatriya should be conferred on the tribals. Sarat Chandra Roy in one of his later writings noted with approval the concept of *varnotkarsa* which, according to him, showed considerable flexibility in the varna system, by permitting upward mobility of individuals, family or a whole clan.[22] The sudras could become saints. However, as far as tribals were concerned there was a certain ambivalence in applying the theory of *varnotkarsa* to them. They were treated as "nominally Hinduized", as the lowest of the low. Therefore Roy warned, if this attitude was not abjured and if the tribes were not given a respectful status either as ksatriyas or vaisyas with the prospect of rising still higher by merit, hinduization is calculated to rob them of their respect and to degrade them to the unenviable position of a deprived class. Roy did not, however, take note of the fact that powerful sections of the tribals had got themselves recognized as ksatriyas, too. As far as those tribes which had become peasants are concerned, they owed to the influence of Hindu peasant communities around them "the unobtrusive infiltration into the society of the concept of certain beneficent deities and certain ideas of ritual purity and cleanliness as an aid to inner purity which if properly appreciated might strengthen and illumine their inchoate ideas of taboo, holiness or the avoidance of spiritual uncleanliness". Under the impact of Hindu peasants such a process was already on with many tribes giving up eating beef and drinking liquor. While the tribals were moving towards this form of Hinduism, Roy argued, the Hindus on their part should give up their degrading notions about touch pollution and food pollution. Towards the end of his life Roy thus seems to have formed an idealistic view of varna, as he saw "inherent in the varna ideas of a natural social hierarchy an instinctive reverence for the pure in soul and the recognition of the supremacy of the spiritual motive in life".

Verrier Elwin carried his advocacy of the ksatriya status being conferred on the tribals a little too far.[23] In what was a polemical paper against the foreign missionary, he pleaded (with):

> ....all Hindu organizations interested in this problem to pass resolutions accepting the major aboriginal communities as ksatriyas, which is what they claim to be, to stop talking of them as 'backward' and 'depressed', to drop the horrible word 'uplift' from their vocabulary, and above all never to allow the slightest association in mind or organization between the Harijan movement and that for the establishment of the aboriginals in an honoured place within the Hindu fold....If they are to take their honoured place as kshatriyas in the Hindu social system, they must be trained in the arts of liberal thinking and educated to courage and the traditions of honour. It is particularly necessary that Government should forbid any proselytizing agency to function in any Tribal Area in the whole of India.
>
> I appeal therefore to the great Hindu community of India, you who have excited the wonder and admiration of men of intelligence in every part of the civilized world. to awake and rouse yourselves, there are five and twenty million souls, some of the most virile, the most delightful, the potentially most useful of all the inhabitants of your sub-continent in danger. They will be taken from you, they will be degraded in a score of subtle ways;

> they will become a thorn in your side for a hundered years unless you take immediate, urgent and drastic action. You must prepare for the day of freedom. Political liberty is the basis, but religious and spiritual freedom is the glorious and shining superstructure that you must erect above it. Men, money, brains, action, sacrifice, love, are needed. You must give as generously to this battle as you have given to the greater war of politics.

Neither Roy nor Elwin was cognizant of the fact that the Hindus had no centralized authority to confer such high status on any community, that upward mobility of the tribe they envisaged was strictly a local phenomenon, that it was a local raja who often conferred high status and that higher status was achieved by the effort and enterprise of the aspiring community.

The principal reason for the tribe acquiring the characteristic of a peasant jati was and is economic. The carrying capacity of swidden agriculture is low. Therefore as population multiplies, the pressure for adoption of the technology of settled agriculture grows. In the Indian context the transition from the tribe to peasant is facilitated in situations of culture contract between tribe and peasant jati. From ancient times and through the medieval period peasant jatis have been emigrating to tribal areas. This process was accelerated during the colonial period.

When the jana moves to the jati end of the pole, it acquires not only a new technology of production, but also a new set of relationships with peasants and artisans, traders and money-lenders, a new value system that enjoins thrift. The tribal way of life is not puritanical; consumption rather than accumulation is its credo. A tribal is a *homo ludens*.[24] Therefore as there is change to jati values among tribals successive social reform movements stress the importance of accumulation.

III

The peasant-jati model of integration repeatedly emphasized in cultural terms does not seem to go far as a model to explain fully the process of the integration of tribe not only with caste but with the larger system, which has been far too complex. Many segments of tribal community stand out of the cultural system of the jati and yet they are integrated into the agrarian and economic system of the region as small producers, landless labourers, artisans, producing for the market. The market is not an invisible factor but a part of the larger productive and distributive organization. Market also contributes to the growth of interdependence of tribes on the one hand and the non-tribal peasants and artisans on the other. There was no such interdependence in north-eastern India where the tribes and artisans belonged to the same community and the polarization between agriculture and crafts had not occurred along the caste-peasant axis as in middle India.

This process of economic integration has sometimes been called the Hindu mode of absorption. Bose describes how the Juangs of Orissa took to wet cultivation and to manufacturing bamboo articles.[25] This had less to do with their "being economically tagged on to the larger body of Hindu society" or their forming "only one cog in the wheel of advanced productive machinery of the Hindus" and more with the mode of production into which these primitive communities were being absorbed. The Juangs were responding to the pressure released by the colonial system that restricted their dependence on forest by adopting an alternative mode of subsistence.

Far more enduring is the process of integration of tribes into a new mode of production. This goes beyond the transfer of technology or acquiring the cultural attributes of jatis to a new state of production relationship.

Notes and References

This is the revised version of my paper "Varna, Jati and Jana, An Anthropo-historical Perspective" presented at the Indian History Congress, Burdwan, 1983, and published in the *Indian History Congress Proceedings of the Forty-Fourth Session*,Burdwan 1983.

1. D.D. Kosambi, *The Culture and Civilization of Ancient India in Historical Outline*, p. 81. See R.S. Sharma, *Sudras in Ancient India*, (2nd edn, pp. 331-44; also see *Indian Feudalism c. 300-1200 A.D.* pp. 232-3.

2. Romila Thapar, *Ancient Indian Social History*, pp. 353-4.

3. M.N. Srinivas, "Varna and Caste" in *Caste in Modern India and Other Essays*, pp. 63-9. Also see D.G. Mandelbaum, "Varna: Villagers' 'Theory and Theorists' Fallacy", in *Society in India : Change and Continuity*, pp. 21-7; "Varna as Referencə Category", pp. 448-53.

4. P.V. Kane, *History of Dharmasastra*, vol. II, Part I, pp. 42-55.

5. See Mandelbaum, op. cit., pp. 448-53.

6. L. Dumont, *Homo Hierarchicus*, 104-112; and Veena Das, *Structure and Cognition*, p. 85-6. K.N. Sharma highlights the intial difference between varna as *dharma* (style of life) and jati which is related to birth. He is right in pointing out the difference between the two levels of social reality today, even though they converge on birth as the determinant of status and occupation, that is *varna vyavastha* or varna as a principle of ordering or systematization and jati as a *pratha*, that is tradition or custom, "On the word "Varna", For a Sociology of India", *Contributions to Indian Sociology* (NS) Vol. 9, No 2.

7. G. Buhler, *The Laws of Manu*, pp. 401-17.

8. Kane op cit., p. 48.

9. S. Jaiswal, "Studies in Early Indian Social History: Trends and Possibilities", *The Indian Historical Review*, vol. VI, 1979-80 pp. 1-63.

10. Kane, op. cit., pp. 380-2.

11. Srinivas, op. cit., p. 66.

12. Ghurye, *Caste and Race in India*, p. 176.

13. See R.S. Sharma, *Social Changes in Early Medieval India*, p.24; also see Dasrath Sharma (ed.) *Rajasthan Through the Ages*, vol I, pp. 472-3.

14. Kane, op. cit., pp. 60-5.

15. Ibid., pp. 282-3.

16. Based on discussions with Maharaj Kumar Raghubir Sinh.

17. Furer-Haimendorf, "The Position of the Tribal Populations in Modern India", pp. 182-221; and *Tribes of India , The Struggle for Survival.*

18. Ambedkar, *Who were the Shudras: How They Came to be the Fourth Varna in the Indo-Aryan Society.*

19. See R.S. Sharma, *Sudras in Ancient India*, pp. 36-43.

20. Ambedkar, *The Untouchables : Who Were They and Why they Became Untouchables.*

21. M.K. Gandhi, *Hindu Dharma*, pp. 279, 324, 334-5.

22. S.C. Roy, "The Aborigines and the Depressed Classes in India", *The New Review*, August 1939, no. 56, vol X.

23. V. Elwin, *The Foreign Missionary Danger.*

24. See J. Huizinga, *Homo Ludens, A Study of Play-element in Culture.*

25. N.K. Bose, "The Hindu Method of Tribal Absorption", *Culture and Society*, 1967, pp. 204-15.

5

Tribalization

We have discussed the concept of brahminization in relation to tribal communities and its limitation as a model. In this chapter we turn to describe the countervailing process of tribalization. Some of the tribes, i.e. the communities who are idenitified as tribes in the Constitution of India, were also the dominant community in parts of India. As such they exercised political authority in the pre-colonial and colonial periods, laid down the law and set the example for emulation by immigrating communities. Even though this occurred on a small scale, it was an interesting process which continues in some respects to this day. We begin with the "traditional aspect" of tribalization[1], i.e. acceptance of tribal mores, rituals and beliefs by in-coming communities, which has been reported upon by ethnographers, among others, and then proceed to describe the relatively little-known aspects of it, namely tribals' participation in coronation ceremonies and their role as custodians and priests at Hindu shrines.

I

Historians have written about the Vratyas, the bands of Aryans who got mixed up with the non-Aryans and adopted their way of life. They neither performed *yajnya* nor practised Vedic rites . The early ethnographic accounts of what is the tribal belt of middle India today similarly speak of how the people who went in accepted the local deities and their priesthood, participated in tribal festivals and festivities, and borrowed many elements of tribal life-cycle ceremonies. The authors of the smritis allow for the acceptance of the customs of the locality (*lokachara*) and the country (*desachara*) if it is not contrary to the Vedic faith. In practice it seldom turned out as prescribed by the smritis. Varna system was lax and commensal norm far from rigid in such territories. The local raja could confer high status upon persons belonging to low jati by conferring the sacred thread upon them.

Social anthropologists have reported selectively on tribalization in terms of the acceptance by in-coming communities of the mores of the locally dominant tribal community. The brahmins and other high-caste people of Uttar Pradesh after they had emigrated to the hills, "ate meat, drank liquor and consorted with the hill women"[2] in deference to climate and social situation. In Bastar where the tribals are in a majority, many of the non-tribals have began to eat meat, drink alcohol, and participate in social and religious functions of tribals. In Barwani of Nimar, where the tribals again are in a majority, non-tribals speak the tribals' dialect (Barely), have adopted the tribal practice of tattooing, and participate in tribal dances while tribals provide music for festive occasions. This was antithetical to the sanskritic notions of purity and pollution. Such processes could also be described as "desanskritization" because the in-coming high caste groups gave up their sanskritic beliefs.[3]

Such a process is different from the tribalization of other categories of castes who with their background of "animistic' belief did not encounter any difficulty in being assimilated into the cultural world of the tribe. In fact, it seems that the acceptance of the tribal mores was easier for the middle and lower segments of the caste hierarchical order who moved in search of land or to offer their services and for artisans who served their tribal masters. In fact they got so mixed up with tribal communities that they were not considered "aliens" by tribes at any stage. They performed social and economic functions for tribes. A typical case is that of the Ghasi who play drums or the Lohara who unlike the non-tribal Lohar consider themselves tribals and are recognized as such in Chotanagpur. When tribal revolts occurred, these communities rose with tribals in Chotanagpur and elsewhere too, because the two had almost entered into a symbiotic relationship.[4] A paradoxical example of this is offered by the role of moneylenders both in Rajasthan and Chotanagpur. A moneylender in the tribal areas of Rajasthan exchanged gifts and participated in festivals; therefore a moneylender on horseback was the safest person in Bhil countryside. In Chotanagpur, some of the moneylenders in spite of their usurious practices got so mixed up with tribals on remote plateaus that two of them were among the leaders of the uprising of the the Kisans in 1921. This was of course an exception to the rule but shows the extent to which backward castes, artisans and even some moneylenders had become so tribalized that they participated in the tribals' spontaneous upsurge.

Fugitives went into the hills as individuals, families and communities. There is the example of Dudhnath Tiwari in the late 1850s, who escaped from the jail in Port Blair, sought shelter with the Andamanese who were quite numerous at that time married one of their girls, Lipaia, and begot a child, and then betrayed them by leaking out the secrets of their attack planned on Port Blair. Later, after many years Dhudhnath Tiwari returned to see his family which was not happy to see him back. Tiwari returned to the mainland. Such cases of betrayal were rare.

There were instances of the tribalization of the Rajputs who went into the Aravalli hills, a scene of turmoil and upheavals, as fugitives. Bhilalas were the progeny of Rajput fathers and Bhil women, but the Garasias are described as "tribalized Rajputs". According to Sherring, "the Garasias are said to be descended from Chauhan Rajputs who were in the country before the Sisodia conquered Chittor. They have lost most of their Rajput customs and are now a wild race, associating closely with the Bhils, whose daughters they take to wife, and now they live apart from more civilized people". This theory of the Garasias being tribalised Rajputs is now being questioned from the limited angle of the persistence of dissimilarities in the social customs of of Rajputs and Garasias, and with the role of the latter as forest dwelling antochthones overly emphasised.[5]

Another aspect of tribalization was respect for the tribal priest and medicine man and for tribal deities which was retained even after the tribals were driven out of a village. Their priests were maintained to propitiate the local gods who would otherwise become angry. We are told :

> Even where the landlord, and the majority of the tenants are Hindus it is still the custom to employ as the *pahan* or sacrificer one of the race of the original clearers of the village, or at least of an earlier dispossessed race. The idea underlying this is a belief in the existence of local spirits who must be proptiated by sacrifices, lest their anger vent itself on the fruits of the fields and cattle and the fertility of the women, or in the stirring up of disease for men and beasts. The jurisdiction of these spirits usually stops short at the village boundary; and it is therefore obvious that their peculiarities require the most intimate local experience. This is naturally found in the descendants of the original clearers: and so the Brahman or Babhan grantee or purchaser of a jungle village considers it a matter of mere common sense to retain by the attraction of rentfree land the Mundari or Bhogta *pahan* whose brethren have long since been expelled, that he may perform the customary sacrifices and placate the spirit when some unintended or even unknown injury has aroused their anger. The belief that a village can become unlucky is sometimes the cause of serious loss to the landlord. When this reputation has been gained the village is said to be *mahaant;* no one will live in it; and only with great reluctance, and at a great reduction of the usual rates of rent will neighbouring villagers take the lands for cultivation. The reputation need not be ancient; all that is required for its acquisition is unusual sickness or mortality.[6]

The patronage of such tribal deities was generally an article of state policy. In Orissa, for example:

> Up to the early 19th century the legitimacy of suzerainty of most of the Garhjat rajas over the tribal hinterland was mainly based on their position in the cult of the tribal 'thakuranis', who usually had become the rastradevatas of their states (e.g., Bhattarika in Baramba and Maninagesvari in Ranpur). Thakuranis were a direct link between the Garhjat rajas or chiefs and the tribes. The patronage of these powerful goddesses secured the kings the support of the tribes and thereby the safety of thier states: in their wars with each other they de-depended on the goodwill of 'their' tribes. In this period. i.e. 17th and 18th centuries, the Jagannath cult and its temples in the Garhjat capitals were of minor importance. In the tribal areas during the Moghal and Maratha period Jagannath temples were symbols of a political (semi-) independence rather than an

institution which influenced the legitimation and position of the within their tribal society.

But matters changed:

> after the immediate danger from hostile neighbour had been removed by the 'Pax Britannica' (after 1803) the cult of the tribal goddess increasingly lost its central function in the ideology of Garhjat rulers. No longer depending on the voluntary support of the tribes, feudal loyalties became a 'burden' for the rajahs and an obstacle in their efforts to be recognized by the British Government and by other feudatory rajas all over India as full Hindu Rajas. During the 19th century it was again the 'Puri model' which influenced the feudatory rajas of Orissa.[7]

II

There were any number of examples of a fugitive going into the hilly region alone, or with his pregnant wife, who delivered a child, and after having done so committed *sati* or died, leaving it to be brought up by a tribal family which tended it with care and affection, and helped it to found a state. Such legends, written down in brahminical accounts—the brahmins unfailingly described the mother as a brahmin girl—are to be found, sometimes exactly in the same form, all over the tribal middle India from Orissa and Chotanagpur to Gujarat and Rajasthan. The interesting point that emerges in such legends is the tribals' participation in the formation of state and their continued support for it. One aspect of the association of the tribals with the state formation is the high ritual status offered by the rulers to them. For example, the Nagbansi treat the Munda as their elder brother, and the latter would not visit Nagbansi households as such (*bhaisur/jeth*).[8] Commensal and connubial relations between Rajputs and Bhils were not infrequent. Sisodias and Bhils were on very good terms from the times of Bapa Rawal to Rana Pratap. In a grateful acknowledgement, the Bhils were at least in one case represented in the state emblem (Rana Pratap-Bhil raja on the Mewar emblem). The Mina, another old tribe, who unlike Bhils really ruled till 16th century, had a role in the coronation of the Kachchwaha chief of Jaipur. Every chief before his installation on the throne received the "tilak" on his forehead of blood obtained by incision of the toe of a Mina of Kalikoh. This practice fell into desuetude but the Minas continued to occupy important positions as custodians of archives and treasure at Amber, and earlier as the guard of the insignia of the state and the person of the prince and his seraglio.

This aspect of tribalization is however dramatically symbolized by tribals' participation in the coronation ceremony. The shastras provide for participation of many castes in coronation ceremonies but in the case of tribes it is symbolic of their partnership in the establishment and continuation of the state. Such examples are again strewn all over Garhjat (Orissa), Chotanagpur, Rajasthan and Gujarat. Putting a tilak on the forehead of the ruler was not only confined to Sisodia states. We are told,

> In many Rajputana, Malwa and Gujarat states, when a Rajput chiefs succeeds, his brow is marked by blood taken from the thumb or the toe of a Bhil. The Rajputs say that this blood mark is a sign of Bhil allegiance; but it seems to be a relic of Bhil power. The Bhils are always keen to keep the practice alive. The right of giving the blood is claimed by certain families and the belief that the man from whose veins it flows dies within a year fails to damp their zeal for the usage. The Rajputs, on the other hand, would gladly let the practice die. This they say is due to their shrinking from impure Bhil blood. But the true ground of this dislike is that the ceremony reminds them of the shortness of their rule and of the need of sanction by their lowest subjects.[9]

The dominant community of Bastar, the Halbas, exercises the right to invest each new chief of adjacent Kanker state with royal robes and to affix the tika or tilak i.e. the sign of office on his forehead. The chiefs of the Bhuiyas of Gangpur (Manjhi) exercised the right of conferring the tilak in token of the investiture of the Raja of Bonai, who later did not recognise it. The Khonds in Kalahandi (Orissa) not only participated in the coronation ceremony but also insisted on the marriage of a Khond girl with the Raja as a necessary ritual:

> The Khonds claim the right of placing the Chief on his *gadi* and until this has been done the Chief is not formally recognised by them: this custom is similar to that in vogue amongst the Bhuiyas of Keonjhar and Bonai states. Lieutenant Elliot in his report thus describes the ceremony:
>
> 'The ceremony observed on the installation of a new Raja is curious and appears worthy of mention. There is a place called Jugsaipatna about 24 miles east of Junagarh, where it is said a large village formerly stood (probably at one time the principal town of the dependency) but now covered with jungle. Near this, lives a Khond family the eldest members of which is called the *patmanjhi;* when the Raja dies, his funeral rites are performed and his corpse disposed of by the orders of his succesor who does not take part in the ceremony: after the due completion of these office, the zamindars and principal persons in the dependency assemble at Jugsaipatna for the purpose of installing the young Raja, which ceremony is conducted in the following manner. The *patmanjhi* or Khond above mentioned having seated himself on a large rock at Jugsaipatna, dressed in rich cloth given him for the occasion, a rich cloth is thrown over his lap on which the young Raja sits while his turban is tied by the *Baghe* or *Diwan*, all the zamindars and principal persons and others then present their *nazars* (gifts) in token of obedience to their ruler. The origin of the custom of celebrating the ceremony in the lap of a Khond is attributed to a convenant said to have been entered into between some former Raja and the Khonds of the country. but unfortunately the legend has been lost; it does not appear that his particular Khond exercises any authority over his tribe.'
>
> The description given above represents traditional custom, but omits to notice an important feature, namely, that the Chief must marry a Khond girl. This marriage ceremony is performed by presenting a girl to the Chief who immediately returns her to her parents and the tribe by the Khond system of divorce, whereby a fine is paid by the husband to the tribe for divorcing his wife.[10]

The tribals' participation in the coronation ceremony was thus not limited to putting only a tilak on the forehead of the ruler, it went beyond it. The Bhuiyas of Keonjhar took a direct hand in selecting the chief, who founded the dynasty, provided him with concubines from their own clan (from such unions sprang the Rajkuli Bhuiya) and selected the site for his fort:

> The installation of a Chief is the occasion for a mustering of the Bhuiya clans in their strength, headed by the hereditary master of the ceremonies. The Bhuiyas march into the courtyard of the residence of the Chief to the crash of drums and wild fantastic airs, their leader carrying a pumpkin, as a token of submission or allegiance. After the company is seated the Chief enters the apartment prepared for the ceremony and distributing *pan*, confections, spices and garlands to the company, retires. Then to the clash of the musical instrument of the wild Bhuiyas, the Chief re-enters mounted on the back of a Bhuiya leader, who plunging, snorting and neighing. embodies the war-steed of the Chief. Dismounting from his human steed the Chief is seated on the lap of a Bhuiya leader. The attendant Bhuiyas then receive from the servants of the Chief imitations of the insignia of royalty—banners, *pankhas*, *chamars*, *chhatras* and canopies, and the hereditary office bearers range themselves round the the Chief. The principal Bhuiya leader then goes through a religious ceremony by binding round the turban of the Chief a light flexible forest creeper as the *siropa* or honorary head dress conferred by the Bhuiyas : the bands strike up, bards chant odes of praise and the Brahmans recite the Sama Veda and finally the principal leader of the Bhuiya marks the forehead of the young Chief with sandal wood, thereby conveying the *tika* or emblem of investiture. The Brahmans and the *Bawaria* or prime minister, then in their turn mark the seal of the *tika* with sandal wood. A sword is then placed in the hands of the Chief and one of the Bhuiya leaders coming forward kneels before the Chief, who touches him on the neck with the sword: this ceremony is symbolical of actual human sacrifice in earlier days: the Bhuiya leader who has thus been touched with the sword at once disappears and does not return for three days when he presents himself to the Chief as miraculously cured. The Bhuiyas then make offerings to the Chief of rice, pulse, *ghi* (clarified butter), milk and honey and their leaders then solemnly address the new Chief, impressing on him that in accordance with the authority exercised by them from time immemorial they have invested him as Chief to rule the State with justice and mercy. The Chief then withdraws mounted on his human steed. Soon afterwards or on a subsequent date the Bhuiyas return, and prostrating themselves before the Chief ask for forgiveness of

> former misdeeds. Their leader then addressing the Chief inquires after his health, his establishment, horses and elephants. In turn the State *Karan* (writer) reads from a palm-leaf document prescribed inquiries touching the health of the Bhuiyas, their families, cattle, hill streams and fields. The leaders thereupon prostrating themselves raise the left-foot of the Chief and place it alternatively first on one shoulder and then on the other, then touching the Chief's foot with their forehead retire. This ceremony is annually repeated in the month of May, but the installation portion of the ceremony is omitted. The Bhuiyas desire in their Chief a leader to whom they can appeal and obtain advice and have no desire for independence: they claim, however, a prescriptive right to approve of or resent the administrative acts of the Chief whom they have themselves created; the periodical rebellions which have taken place have been due to dislike of the individual ruler by the Bhuiya clans. This attitude was manifest in the rebellion of 1890-1893 when the Chief fled to Cuttack leaving his family in the *garh* whieh could easily have been taken by the Bhuiyas. The Bhuiyas, however, made no attack on the *garh* as they had no animosity against the family The Bhuiya pirs (tracts) have always been the property of the Rani of the State, and the Bhuiyas hold her in high veneration, styling her "the mother". In one of their rebellions the Bhuiyas entered the *garh* seeking for the *Bawaria* (prime minister), they found him in the Rani's apartments, where he had fled for sanctuary; horrified at the sacrilege that he should have seen the face of their revered mother they put him to death.[11]

The question that again arises at this stage is whether tribals' participation in coronation ceremonies, which were a complex affair, in spite of all that has been said above, could still be considered a dimension of tribalization. That it represented more than putting a tilak on the ruler's forehead is evident from the manner in which the tribals lent their support to the raja—whether it was in Mewar or in Keonjhar-where the Bhuiyas rebelled in the latter half of the 19th century whenever they found their raj in danger. This is also evident from the manner in which many chiefs of these states tried to "detribalize" themselves later by playing down the element of tribals' participation.

III

Another dimension of tribalization has been the tribes' association with some of the Hindu shrines. The Todas serve as the palanquin-bearers of Shiva at Bhavaneeshwar temple at Ooty. One of the reasons why no pollution attaches to such tribes could be that they are the autochthones who do not perform any "polluting" function. A distinguished anthropologist expressed surprise at the attachment of the Chenchus, a primitive community of food gatherers, to the major Hindu shrine of Sri Sailam, described it as an "unusual phenomenon" and stated, "it is remarkable that despite a long symbiotic relationship the basic economy of the group has not significantly changed".[12] This could not have changed because the Chenchus served in the temple, as he says, as palanquin bearers and sweepers and acted as watchmen and have hereditary rights to only a share of the offerings given by pilgrims. This was not unusual when seen in the historical perspective. Shiva was a "tribal deity" to begin with and forest-dwelling communities, including those who have ceased to be tribals and those who are tribals today, were the custodians of such shrines located in remote areas all over Chotanagpur, central India and in the Western ghats. Some of them still have tribals (and non-brahmins too) as custodians and priests. The striking fact about such association is that, as mentioned earlier, no "pollution" attaches to tribals, and that their role as priests and custodians is accepted by the larger community. Brahminical versions of the association of tribes with the shrines assign a central role to them. Here is an example of the "Bhil" (there are no Bhils in Bihar) deity apotheosized into Shiva at Deogarh in Santal Pargana, Bihar:

> According to the Padma Purana the Brahman to whom Ravana entrusted the lingam deposited it in due form, consecrated it with water from a neighbouring tank, repeated his prayers and then departed. A Bhil who was present when this was done received instructions from the Brahman as to how the worship of the emblem should be conducted, but having no vessel at hand, brought the water required for libations in his mouth.

When Ravana at last returned, the Bhil related all that had happened, and pointed out that the Brahman was no other than Vishnu himself. Ravana then exacavated a well with an arrow and brought into it the waters of all sacred pools on earth for the fitting worship of the god. According to other traditions, not noticed in any Purana, the lingam lay neglected after the death of Ravana until it was noticed by a rude hunter, Baiju by name, who accepted it as his god and worshipped it daily, proclaiming it to the world as the lord of Baiju (Baidyanath). [There was also] a band of Brahmans settled on the banks of the beautiful highland lake beside which the holy city stands. Around them there was nothing but the forest and mountains, in which dwelt the black taces. The Brahman placed the symbol of their god Siva near the lake and did sacrifice to it; but the black tribes would not sacrifice to it, but came as before to the three stones which their fathers had worshipped, and which are to be seen at the western entrance of the holy city to this day. The Brahmans, moreover, ploughed the land and brought water from the lake to nourish the soil; but the hillmen hunted and fished as of old, or tended their herds, while the women tilled little patches of Indian corn. But in process of time the Brahmans finding the land good, became slothful, giving themselves up to lust and seldom calling on their god Siva. This the black tribes, who came to worship the great stones, saw and wondered at more and more, till at last one of them, by name Baiju, a man of a mighty arm and rich in all sorts of cattle, became wroth at the lies and wantonness of the Brahmans, and vowed he would beat the symbol of their god Siva with his club every day before touching food. This he did: but one morning his cattle strayed into the forest, and after seeking them all day he came home hungry and weary, and, having hastily bathed in the lake, sat down to his supper. Just as he stretched out his hand to take the food he called to mind his vow; and worn out as he was, he got up, limped painfully to the Brahmans' idol on the margin of the lake, and beat it with his club. Then suddenly a splendid form, sparkling with jewels, rose from the waters, and said:—'Behold the man who forgets his hunger and his weariness to beat me, while my priests sleep with their concubines at home, and neither give me to eat nor to drink. Let him ask of me what he will, and it shall be given.' Baiju answered: 'I am strong of arm and rich of cattle. I am a leader of my people: what want I more? Thou art called Nath (Lord). Let me too be called lord, and thy temple go by my name.

> 'Amen,' replied the deity: 'henceforth thou art not Baiju, but Baijnath, and my temple shall be called by thy name'.[13]

This may be bad history but it is a good myth. The tomb in which the mortal remains of Baiju are said to be deposited could not be more than 200 years old, but to this day on a certain day in the year the tribals crowd into the large courtyard to dance and perform worship in their own way.

There were other instances too. The shrine of Shiva on the Panchmarhi hills was under the hereditary guardianship of the Korku chiefs. The Jagannath temple of Orissa is associated with the Savaras; the deity sculpted in wood is described by some tribals as a uniquely tribal innovation (according to them the Hindu deities in contrast are in clay or in stone). Similarly, Sri Venkateswar temple of Tirupati, one of the foremost shrines in India, has been associated with Kurumbas, who have now moved away to the Nilgiris, and with Lambadies. Among the other tribes who worship at this shrine are Yenadi, Yerukula and Chenchu. The Yerukulas have been related to Sri Subramanyam temple of Palani and Tiruttani. The interesting point here is that most of these temples in central and north India belong, among Hindu gods, to Shiva and the mother goddess who are associated with *tantra*, magic and witchcraft which is widespread in tribal areas. In Chotanagpur, there are plenty of temples[14] of which the local tribe priest, *baiga* or *pahan*, is the priest. Tanginath, a temple on the border of Madhya Pradesh in Ranchi, is one example and the temple of mother goddess at Diuri another.[15]

It would be interesting to describe the tribalization of the rituals at this temple. Diuri is a tribal village situated at a distance of sixty kilometres from Ranchi on the national highway connecting the steel city of Jamshedpur. Predominantly inhabited by the Munda tribe, it was founded by its Kamal lineage, whose members form a landowning and privileged category (*khuntkattidar*) by themselves. As the nomenclature of the lineage suggests sanskritization has been at work among the Mundas for a long time. The Panchpargana region of which Tamar, the block headquarters, is a part—the village is about three kilometres from Diuri—has also been the scene of intensive interaction between the tribals and peasants at the cultural and economic levels. However, as the first wave of sanskritization represented by the construction of this temple receded, the tribals firmly took over the management of the temple services and sought to establish their identity with the temple. The raja of Tamar issued a land grant to a brahmin of Disipara to perform worship, but a good working arrangement seems to have been established between the brahmin and the *pahan* (tribal priest) about ritual services to be performed in the temple in which the *pahan* plays a major role. The brahmin turns up every Thursday, a day of special *puja* for the mother deity, and on the *mahaasthmi* to conduct the *pujas* as laid down in the scriptures. On other days and on the occasions of major festivals the *pahan* holds sway. There are thus sanskritic aspects too, of the worship at the temple.

The Mundas insist that the village name was originally derived from the combination of the two words, *diuri* and *diri*, where lay the slab (*diri*) which is worshipped to this day, belonging to the priest (*diuri*) who still retains this nomenclature among the Ho tribe living across the hills. This was even before the temple was constructed. After the temple was constructed and the tribals took over the management, the mother goddess inside it was identified with the *bonga*, the benevolent spirit, particularly with that of *jah-era*, the female presiding deity of the sacred grove, the *sarna* of the village which is close by. Thus, as the *pahan* explains, the mother goddess as a *bonga* has been worshipped from time immemorial by the Mundas who flock to this temple to offer prayers.

While the brahminical rituals are complex, expensive and time-consuming, the ritual services performed by the *pahan* are simple, the prayers are short, the offerings consist simply of *laddus* (sweets) and red flowers dear to the goddess. The *pahan's* conduct of the *puja* is reminiscent of his conduct of the worship in the *sarna* with this difference that liquor and fowl are not offered in the temple. The prayers are the Mundari translation of the Bengali and Sanskrit prayers of the *Durga Saptshati*, or adaptation of traditional Mundari prayers to the Singbonga, such as:

O Mother *devi*
You are mother and father
You rise like milk
You set like curd
This earth is yours, this creation is yours
We stand under your protective umbrella
This person has come to you
You know what he is suffering from
Point out the way to end suffering
Take away his sorrow and suffering.

The temple is also linked with many other aspects of tribal religion. The slab kept on the platform is worshipped when the tribals offer homage to the ancestral spirits every year. The village deity (*gram deota*) is worshipped in the precincts of the temple. among other places. Other tribal religious ceremonies are performed in houses and in the *sarna*. The temple is not associated with the underworld of black magic, with the practice of *sabar mantras*, or the witches' dance (*najom susun*), we were assured.

In fact, the most remarkable aspect of the village is that it look like an *agrahara*, a cluster of houses with thatched roofs, tucked away in groves. According to tradition, no house in this temple village can be built of baked bricks; houses are made of either stone slabs or of earth. Non-Munda outsiders wanted to construct houses of bricks but they discovered to their horror that the brick kilns were severely damaged by a hailstorm, as villagers recall. The mother goddess in the temple does not "like" baked bricks and has a preference for thatched roofs. This, a sanskritic relic, is probably the most impressive testimony to a living tradition in what undoubtedly was a seat of shakti worship and an ashram organized around it.

This discussion raises an important question whether the Munda religion has accepted the concept of a female deity or that of a mother goddess. The Singbonga is a male god, an *avatar*, who came down to destroy the Asurs. He is the Supreme Spirit, invisible and distant, known only through symbols and signs. He is without a female companion. However, there are female spirits in the Munda pantheon. Apart from the *jah-era* there are the *chandi bongas* presiding over various activities. There is also the concept of the mother earth (*dharti enga*). The Munda epic *Sosobonga* contains a beautiful invocation to a virgin goddess (*devi kumari*):

> O Singbonga, O Virgin Goddess
> This is your land, this is your country
> This land which is spread in all directions
> East, west, north, south
> Is your creation
> The tanks filled with lotus,
> the reservoirs filled with flowers of various kinds
> Trees and plants, cows, birds and all grazing animals
> All are your creation, your handiwork.

In other prayers the Singbonga is mentioned as the lord of heaven and the *devi* as the goddess of earth. If the partial tribalization of a sanskritic heritage is a pointer, the Singbonga is now likely to acquire a female companion, a wife!

A question may be asked whether these instances of the association of tribals with temples, as functionaries, custodians and priests and of the tribalization of temple services could be described as a process of tribalization. It should be noted that such shrines are located in what once upon a time were and what continue to be today the regions where tribals lived and were a dominant community. The tribal belt was dotted with the shrines dedicated to Shakti, Shiva and Vishnu, with the centres of *tantra* worship, which is closely associated with the underworld of magic and witchcraft. We could therefore look upon this phenomenon as a continuation of the tribals' role in the management of these temples, which seems to have been accepted by Hindus. As the tribals remain associated with them and perform the services in their own way, the concept of tribalization appears to be relevant.

It is debatable if the recent trends regarding some of the former tribes such as the Kurmi-Mahtos of Chotanagpur, who were descheduled as a tribe in 1931, and of other communities, seeking tribal status to avail themselves of the privileges of being a "tribe" granted under the Constitution of India could be considered a dimension of tribalization. The Mahtos of Chotanagpur do claim that they share many social characteristics with tribes, but these are not spelt out. Similarly, the Bhumij who once claimed to be kṣatriyas have now discovered fresh merit in "re-tribalisation". The Bhotiyas of U.P., who acted as traders across the Himalayas before the Indo-China conflct, once claimed the status of Rajputs. Later as border trade came to a standstill and their economic condition deteriorated, they laid claim to be members of a scheduled tribe. Claiming tribal status is one thing, accepting tribal mores is another. Evidence on the part of such claimants regarding their newly discovered affinities with tribes, participation in tribal festivals, and worship at tribal shrines is still weak. However, with the increasing politicization of such of these communities as live on the border line of a tribe and a backward community, this trend deserves to be noted.

We have discussed the three dimensions of tribalization, adoption of the tribal ways of life by different categories of non-tribal immigrants, their role in state formation as symbolized by their involvement in coronation ceremonies and their management of and ritual control at temples. All aspects flow from the tribes' position as the dominant community in some regions and therefore are parts of the over-all processes of tribalization. There was, as mentioned above, also an attempt at whittling down of the first two elements as the non-tribals involved in them tended later to look sideways and elsewhere for legitimacy. However the trends remained broadly undisturbed. The third component remained generally unaffected. Put together these three processses also represented, as they do even now in some respects, the recognition by non-tribals of the relevance of tribalization for them.

Notes and References

My interest in the study of "tribalization" was aroused by the first visit to Diuri on foot from Tamar in 1961 to see the temple When I came back to Ranchi in 1978, I visited Diuri a number of times to oversee the implementation of a couple of development projects we had taken up. The first visit to Diuri and similar places resulted in a study which formed the subject of a paper, "Temples in Ranchi District".

1. B.R. Chauhan describes tribalization in terms of the withdrawal of a tribe "from the mainstream of the larger culture, into a secluded life in an inaceessible area thereby redefining its own world view". See B.R., Chauhan, "Tribalisation" in *Rajasthan Bhils.* This "tribalization" of tribes is very different from the tribalization as it has been described by others and myself.
2. M.N. Srinivas, "Sanskritization", in *Social Change in Modern India*, pp. 18-19.
3. See S.L. Kalia, "Sanskritization and Tribalization".
4. Ranjit Guha, *Elementary Aspects of Peasant Insurgency in Colonial India*, pp. 180-88.
5. Rev. M.A. Shering, *Hindu Tribes and Castes* p. 81; for the counter view see B.L. Meharda, *History and Culture of the Girasias* pp. 12-13.
6. E. Lister, *District Gazetteer, Hazaribagh*, pp. 76-77.
7. Hermann Kulke, "Kshatriyaization and Social Change, a study in Orissa Seetting", in S. Devadas Pillai (ed)., *Aspects of Changing India, Studies in Honour of Professor G.S. Ghurye.*
8. K.S. Singh, "Chotanagpur Raj: Ramification, Structure and Mythology", presented at the seminar on State Formation in Eastern India, Calcutta, July 1982.
9. J.M. Campbell, *Gazetteer of the Bombay Presidency: Khandesh*, pp. 79, 86.
10. LEB. Cobden-Ramsay, *Feudatory States of Orissa*, pp. 202-3.
11. Ibid., pp. 43-6.
12. Furer-Haimendorf, *Tribes of India, Struggle for Survival* pp. 167-8.
13. L.S.S. O'Malley, *District Gazetteer, Santal Pargana*, pp. 253-55.
14. K.S. Singh, "Temples in Ranchi District". op. cit
15. K.S. Singh, "A Temple in a Tribal Village", presented at the seminar on village, Festival of India, London, April 1982.

6

Colonialism and Anthropologists

Anthropology gradually emerged as a major influence to sensitize the colonial administration to the issues concerning primitive communities.[1] While anthropologists generated information about the tribes, some of them and the administrators-turned-anthropologists, played a significant role in shaping public policy on tribal people. We take up a crucial phase of constitutional reforms in India (1928-47) to study the interaction of the colonial officials' and anthropological viewpoints as revealed by the primary sources including the constitutional records for the period 1928-35 and Transfer of Power papers for the 1945-7 period. Not so well-known are the political proclivities of the anthropologists, who were otherwise known for their competent studies.

I

One is struck at the dichotomy between the colonial ethnographer's and the administrator's perception of the primitive society in early literature.[2] The ethnographers took a placid, even a synchronic view of the tribal society. The conceptual framework developed by the British administrators-turned-ethnographers and by anthropologists was inspired by the then prevailing model in anthropology. Tribal communities were treated as isolates, tribals as Noble Savages, and the primitive condition was described as a state of Arcadian simplicity. The deterioration of tribal communities was attributed to the sanskritization of the semi-tribal chiefs and to the vulnerability of tribal character, as mentioned earlier. There was little understanding of the nature and function of the tribal mode of production and of the role of colonial system in its subversion, and of the economic factor underlying the process of change in the tribal area in most of the ethnographic literature. Through their writings the anthropologists rationalized the colonial system and projected it as the benefactor of tribes. In striking contrast to the anthropologists the administrators took a diachronic view of the tribal society and described the pattern of change and development affecting the tribal people. Their accounts set out changes in the agrarian system, exploitation by aliens, progress of "material culture", and what is more the rash of riots, and depredations, outbreaks of violence, etc., which suggested that the primitive people were not so immune to the impact of colonialism. While some of the colonial officers formed an unfavourable, even unflattering view of tribal character in the early stages, others chastened by their experiences of tribal revolts were prone to take a romanticized view of the tribal people. The tribal country, its undulating terrain and forests brought back nostalgic memory of their homeland to colonial officers; the tribals' love of freedom, their free life, their simplicity and straight forwardness aroused their admiration. The authors of census reports collected and interpreted data in terms of transformation of tribe into caste. The controversy whether the tribals were to be registered as Hindus or animists did not appear to have been satisfactorily resolved. The anthropologists displayed a one-sided view of the process of interaction between the Hindu and the tribal communities in terms of brahmanization, hinduization or sanskritization of the latter. The interaction was, however, a two-way process. The historians unlike the anthropologists were aware of the survival of autochthonous forms and structures in the larger society.

Some of the earlier studies by anthropologists, however dealt with change in tribal society in time. *The Mundas and their country* (1912). the first work of Rai Bahadur Sarat Chandra Roy, the father of Indian ethnography, is more a work of history than ethnography in its content. A later work of his on the Kharias is, in a way, a model of local history. The Rai Bahadur was, however, too obsessed with his loyalties as a British subject—and his early writings are paeans to the "beneficent" British rule—and too influenced by his close association with the missionaries to make a critical assessment of the impact of colonalism and missionary activities. It was only towards the end of his life that he confided in Verrier Elwin his misgivings about the latter. Roy's monographs on the Oraons (1915 and 1928), Kharias (1937) and Birhors (1925) provided a model for similar studies. Little attempt was made to study the cohesive nature of rural communities, the role of non-tribal artisans who contributed to the self-sufficiency of the village system, settlement of tribals as peasant communities and their development as such. The composite character of the society in the exposed tribal regions, in general, was overlooked in such studies. The influence of the "functionalists" was hostile to history. However, these studies helped shape tribal consciousness and define tribal identity *vis a vis* non-tribals in the 1930s.

II

Chotanagpur had a tradition of militant struggles waged by tribals in defence of their rights in land through the different phases of the colonial rule. Around the turn of the century there was a great upsurge led by Birsa Munda, which apart from other consequences resulted in a sharpening of the awareness of the tribal unity and solidarity. In 1916, the Chotanagpur Improvement Society was formed to work for the educational, cultural and economic advancement of the Chotanagpur tribals. In 1918 it stressed the need for the preservation of tribal identity in the changing political context and for continued administration by sympathetic European officers. Behind it lay the influence of a tribal middle class coming up in urban areas. Roy knew many of its members intimately, and he was particularly close to the members of the Roman Catholic Church and its political wing, the Catholic Mahasabha. Roy was thus no closet anthropologist; but he related his study of tribes to action-programmes oriented to their welfare. He was a member of the Legislative Council of Bihar and Orissa for many terms by reason of his expertise in aboriginal affairs. He was elected a member of the provincial committee that sat with the Indian Statutory Commission (popularly known as the Simon Commission), and also of the Indian Franchise Commission (the Lothian Committee). It was as a member of these two bodies that Roy was able to give shape to and articulate his political ideas. One also gets the impression that although Roy tried to disown any direct link with Bengal, he did champion the interests of the Bengalis who occupied a dominant position in education and services and as landlords in Chotanagpur. They were not happy over the separation of Bihar from Bengal and nursed the hope that they would be recapturing their status and power if Chotanagpur was separated from Bihar. Roy was also the spokesman of a certain section of the missionaries who demanded a separate political dispensation for tribals so that they could work more freely among them.

As a member of the Provincial Committee, Roy pleaded for the creation of a separate political system for Chotanagpur because the aboriginal tribes had their requirements and needs which people of a different race and different mentality and different social system failed to appreciate. With the introduction of the Reforms of 1919 the authorities were hardly in a position to give the tribals much help. The representation in the Council of the aborigines by one or two out of a total of 76 elected members was farcical. Owing to the cultural and racial divergencies between Bihar and the aboriginal tracts, the administrative union of these two areas could not create anything like a "common nationalism". The artificial union of Chotanagpur and the Santal Pargana with Bihar was rather an obstacle than a help to their political, social, economic and educational progress. Therefore, he suggested three alternative schemes :

(1) The separation of the aboriginal tracts from Bihar and their formation into a separate province under a sympathetic and well-informed administrator directly subordinate to the Governor-General.

(2) The formation of a separate province composed of the aboriginal tracts and the Oriya-speaking tracts, with certain safeguards for aboriginal interests.

(3) Constituting the aboriginal tracts into a sub-province under a major province.[3]

Roy's own preference was for the first scheme because Chotanagpur had little affinity with the rest of Bihar. Chotanagpur would not be a deficit state because the untapped mineral resources could generate sufficient revenue and the central government could provide special funds for the development of the backward population. It would not be a small province either because the "Greater Chota Nagpur" in which the feudatory states of Orissa would join would have an area of 66,600 square miles, being thus much more than that of England and Wales put together. The new province would have a population of 12,383,376, being slightly less than that of the province of Burma. While the aboriginal population formed 58% of the population of Chotanagpur, the remaining 42% of its population were also 'mostly all aborigines in origin" whose interests were not in any way "adverse to the interests of the aboriginals". Again, of this there were only about 10 percent, "mostly alien Hindus", whose interests were "frequently in opposition to the interests of the aborigines". If the first scheme was not accepted he would prefer the union of Chotanagpur with Orissa, which would be more equal than that with Bihar, because Orissa districts had a large aboriginal population, and the feudatory states of Orissa were inhabited largely by the tribes of the same stocks and similar culture and speech as the Mundas, the Oraons and the Santals of Chotanagpur. In Chotanagpur districts of Ranchi and Singhbhum there was also a certain proportion of Oriya-speaking population. Geographically and economically as much as ethnologically and sociologically Chotanagpur had a close connection with Orissa.

Nevertheless, Roy was in agreement with the nationalist opinion on the point that the aboriginal tracts should not be excluded from the operation of the constitutional reforms and placed under the direct rule of the Govenor of Bihar and Orissa through the Commissioner of the Division. He felt that it would be an administrative anachronism. The tribals had enjoyed the right of directly electing their representatives to the Legislative Council since 1920. Democratic institutions were not "new things to the aboriginal", but were indigenous to them and suited to their genius. The results of the three general elections for the reformed councils since 1920 showed that the aboriginal voters evinced greater enthusiasm for the Council elections than the more advanced people of the Province. The proportion of the votes polled in the aboriginal districts of the Province were higher than in most of the advanced districts of Bihar proper. The proportion of aboriginal voters who attended the polling stations was greater than that of the Hindu and Muhammadan voters in Chotanagpur. Aboriginal voters, at least in the principal districts, also exercised their rights of voting with proper discrimination. He gave yet another reason, which was critical of the colonial rule. He stated:

> Beyond a partial protective policy, Government has so far hardly formulated, much less systematically pursued, any constructive policy of social and political uplift for the aborigines. Thanks to the Christian missiondries and other non-Government agencies and the education imparted through Government and mission schools, the aborigines of the Province have now outgrown the state of spoonfeeding at the hands of a paternal Government.

A separate administration for Chotnagpur was the only answer. If this was not created, disaster would follow. Roy sounded a note of warning:

> The last European war, travel in and outside India, foreign Christian missions and political and politico-religious movements, education and a taste of local self-government in the District Boards and Muncipalities and in the Reformed Councils, have unleashed many forces and created many aspirations and if they can find neither satisfaction nor even self expression in the Council and in a constitutional manner they may perhaps seek it elsewhere and in other ways. And there may not improbably grow up subterranean and extra-parliamentary organisations of sufficient power which may seek to force the hands of the authorities and wrest from them more drastic constitutional changes.[4]

This, however, did not cut any ice with the majority of the members of the Provincial Committee who rejected Roy's suggestion because "the implications of his scheme" were "so great and the practical difficulties so varied" that the very idea of a sub-province or separation must be "ruled out altogether as beyond any practical politics." There were also the administative reasons: paucity of funds as the size and revenue of Chotanagpur were not sufficient to constitute it into a separate province, and they were not enough men to be found to run it. However, they accepted Roy's suggestion that the electoral franchise should be widened so as to include headmen, and that a large number of representatives from the tribal tracts should form part of the future legislative council. Roy saw in the extension of franchise an opportunity for improving the position and status of the tribal people who appreciated the value of the vote as much as their more civilized and well-to-do neighbours did.[5] Roy's own thoughts graduated to a higher level. He sought later for them in a posthumously published paper[6] the status of a minority community.

Thus, though Roy's ideas of political separatism were rejected out of hand, the debate for and against the formation of a state for Chotanagpur is still being carried on, 50 years later, along the lines laid down by him.

III

A little later and at the higher level, two administrator-anthropologists, J.P. Mills and G.H. Hutton sought to influence the political opinion in London in favour of their proposal regarding complete exclusion of tribal areas from the operation of constitutional reforms so as to keep the tribals under the direct control of British administration. The Report of the Statutory Commission, which took into account the views expressed by officials and representatives of the aborigines, contained various recommendations about the backward tracts. The Commission introduced new terms, excluded and partially excluded areas to replace the old term 'backward tracts' which offended some people and sounded derogatory. The Government of India accepted some of the recommendations and restricted the number of excluded areas to four and that of partially excluded areas to eleven tracts.

It was at this stage that some backbenchers of the Conservative Party led by Cadogan and James (their full names were not given) revolted and pressed, probably instigated by the anthropologists waiting in the wings, for an enlargement of the list of excluded and partially excluded areas and for a larger measure of protection for the tribals. Winston Churchill quipped that the whole of India deserved to put into an excluded category; which outraged the nationalists. Later he claimed that he was an anthropologist in his own way and had opposed exclusion because when major tasks were being assigned to the new Indian bodies, tribal affairs being only a comparatively minor administrative duty it should not be withheld from them.

Both Mills and Hutton were at that time in London. Mills was on leave, examining for the anthropological tripos at Cambridge, but he found time to keep in touch with the constitutional developments. He also helped the authorities by preparing a report on Chittagong Hill tracts.[7] Hutton played an open-handed role and submitted an amended memorandum of evidence on the excluded areas before the Joint Committee in September, in which he pleaded for the total exclusion of tribal areas, for self-determination and for creation of petty states. This was based on Hutton's assumptions that the aboriginals were an absolutely distinct element in India which was not amenable to the political treatment which was being adopted in the non-aboriginal tract, and that the administration was accustomed to make too many mistakes in dealing with the aboriginal areas by too blindly applying principles and precedents applicable elsewhere. According to him the only effective remedy was to greatly extend the area of total exclusion in any distinctly aboriginal areas.[8] Partial exclusion would not help. Hutton's ideas were found to be too radical and liable to cause misapprehension. However, even though Hutton revised his draft amending the portions likely to offend, he did make an impression at the lower echelons. Meanwhile the Tory backbenchers were active. They pointed out that large pockets of tribal habitation had been left out of the list of partially excluded areas and that the members of the Indian Civil Service would not be able to attend to the wants of the primitive people. Out of these informal discussions emerged suggestions to extend the aboriginal areas and identify the Governor's special responsibilities to cover cases of such tribes as were left out.[9] Both the excluded and partially excluded areas were extended by 300 to 400 percent. The backbenchers and their anthropologist advisers had won in the end.

The nationalist opinion saw in the new constitutional provision for partially and fully excluded areas the shades of a by then familiar imperialist design to separate the tribals from other communities and thus weaken national unity and undermine the freedom struggle. The Indian National Congress at its session held at Faizpur in December expressed its opinion as follows:

> The creation of excluded and partially excluded areas and Chief Commissioner's Provinces including British Baluchistan from January 1937 and covering an area of 207,900 square miles and inhabited by 13 million people is yet another attempt to divide the people of India into different groups, with unjustifiable and discriminatory treatment, to obstruct the growth of uniform democratic institutions in the country....This Congress is further of opinion that the separation of these excluded and partially excluded areas is intended to leave out of popular control, the dispositions and exploitation of the mineral and forest wealth in those areas and to keep the inhabitants of these areas apart from India for their easier exploitation and suppersssion. This Congress holds that the same level of democratic and self-governing institutions should be applicable to all parts of India without any distinction.[10]

The nationalists reacted sharply to the attempts to isolate the tribals from the mainstream. The isolationist school of policy-makers comprised anthropologists and British members of the I.C.S. of whom G.H. Hutton was the arch exponent. However, it was Verrier Elwin who got more closely identified with the isolationist stance in the pamphlet *The Loss of Nerve* published in 1941 in which he recommended a policy of isolation of the tribals and suggested that their administration should be so adjusted as to allow them to lead their life without interference from outside agencies. In conclusion he said:

> I am not one of those who advocate a policy of absolute isolation, but I do urge a policy of isolation from debasing and impoverishing contact. The aboriginal cannot remain as he is—but is it necessary for him to pass through a long period of degradation before he emerges as the civilised man of the future? Could we not keep him in his innocence and happiness for a while till 'civilisation' is more worthy to instruct him and until a scientific age has learnt how to bring development and change without causing despair?[11]

Much the same thought was expressed a little later in another pamphlet, *The Aboriginals:*

> I advocate, therefore, for the aboriginals a policy of temporary isolation and protection, and for their civilized neighbours a policy of immediate reform....The essential thing is not to 'uplift' them into a social and economic sphere to which they cannot adapt themselves, but to restore to them the liberties of their own countryside...But whatever is done, and I would be the last to lay down a general programme, it must be done with caution and above all with love and reverence. The aboriginals are the real swadeshi products of India, in whose presence everyone is foreign. These are the ancient people with moral claims and rights thousands of years old. They were here first; they should come first in our regard.[12]

Elwin spiritedly denied having been an isolationist; he affirmed that he had condemned the policy of isolation. But the confusion arose out of the inept phrase, "the National Park", that he coined in the late thirties to underline the need for the protection of the tribes against exploitation. He admitted later that when he spoke in terms of preserving tribal culture, he thought a little statically. Later he thought in a less static way and spoke about the unity of the hills and plains as essential to the general national interest. Elwin edged closer to the nationalist school in this respect[13], which will be discussed later.

IV

As negotiations for transfer of power got underway in the mid-1940s, the bureaucratic and anthropologist lobby became active to ensure the protection of tribals' interests. Administrators like Sir John Hubback floated many ideas. Sir John had worked as Commissioner of the Chotanagpur Division in 1932 and later as Governor of Orissa and thus had considerable experience of handling tribal affairs. He prepared a note on the "Backward Tribes" (1944)[14] at the instance of the Viceroy. Sir John was of the opinion that the British interest in tribal affairs should continue to operate even after the transfer of power because they had a moral responsibility for the protection of tribals. He suggested that the treaty with the Government of India should mention that in return for a substantial subsidy similar to that already made to the Crown Colonies of Basutoland and Swaziland in South Africa the Indian Government should agree to allow the employment of officers whose function would be the uplift of backward tribes. These officers would work under a British High Commissioner and keep their eyes and ears open to actions adverse to the interest of of the backward tribes. The High Commissioner would be assisted by an officer posted in each agency for the express purpose of watching the interests of backward tribes. The Crown Representative might also discharge the function of the High Commissioner. Declaration of minority rights for the tribal communities on the lines of Articles 73 and 74 of the San Francisco Charter could also be considered. Elwin suggested appointment by the Central Government of a fulltime adviser on aboriginal problems, one who would study the problem and prepare a twenty-five year plan of gradual regulated development. Hubback also suggested the formation of a triumvirate of an anthropologist, an administrator and a missionary, which according to him would do considerably more for the hill tribes than an anthropological dictator suggested by Elwin.

There was another set of proposals put forward by Messrs Mills, Mitchell and McGrie on the future of the Hill tracts of Burma, Assam and Bengal. They were of the opinion that the

Mongolian inhabitants of these hill tracts could not be classified as Indian or Burman. Their self-governing institutions had survived. So they suggested the establishment of the union of the Hill tracts of Burma, Assam and Bengal under one agency, with the Governor of Burma and Governor of Assam and Bengal being responsible to the Secretary of State for their welfare.

Both Sir John and Sir Kenneth Fitze who had served in western and central India and acquired considerable experience with the Bhils shared great admiration for the missionaries whose role, they were sorry to see, was going to be circumscribed in free India. Both were critical of Verrier Elwin's openly professed aim of the hinduization of the tribes. According to them Elwin believed with astonishing optimism that the Hindus could be pursuaded to admit the aboriginals into the higher grade of the society, even though the Hinuds had no such self-executing social mechanism for ensuring conversion on a large scale. The Secretary of State was also critical of the gospel preached by Verrier Elwin, which was that the backward tribes should be isolated in reservations, and shut off by ring fences from the rest of India. This was impracticable and could even prove dangerous, to say nothing of the political morality of maintaining these people as 'museum pieces'. Development of communications, largely as a result of the war, and the exploitation of the mineral resources in the eastern states whose inhabitants had so far been protected from exploitation and opperssion by their very remoteness from civilization had opened up new vistas. While the British government had a moral obligation to see that the backward areas received special consideration in the constitutional settlement, it was under no solemnly recorded obligation to do so. England was going to be a poorer country after the war and "it would be difficult to pursuade the British taxpayer to agree to financial and administrative commitments being under-taken in an independent India, for a class so numerous and so remote from their normal range of concern".[15]

The Provincial Governors' reactions were even more adverse except to the part of the proposal regarding the creation of a special department for the affairs of the backward tribes.

Governor T.G. Rutherford of Bihar was against any form of intervention in tribal affairs by the Government of India. He handed down, at the close of the British raj, probably the most damning indictment of its policy toward the tribals:

> While we (the British) have been in power we have not done much for them beyond a certain amount of protective legislation which functions effectively when the officers responsible are really sympathetic, and—largely with the aid of missionaries—we have done a little to educate them. The tendency on the whole has been to treat them as delightful primitives whose simplicity and customs are a welcome relief from the sordid details of administration among the ordinary Hindus and Muslims.[16]

Thus the realities of the situation could not be wished away. The then Government of India concluded that the proposal regarding the removal of the tribes from the jurisdiction of the provincial governments and their transfer to the control of an outside authority—a British High Commissioner, the Crown Representative, or an international body—was impracticable. The nationalist opinion was already disturbed over the existence of exluded and partially excluded areas which was to a "Congressman like a red rag to a bull." "If India was fit to govern herself, she must *a fortiori* be able to look after her aboriginals." The British Government also strangely thought that the backward tribes were probably better off in the princely states than in the British Indian provinces as the more primitive conditions of the states were congenial to them. In other words, prevalence or continuation of primitive conditions was better for a tribal than change and development. The Secretary of State was therefore advised to drop the matter as tribal affairs was a small subject compared to the major political issues that awaited action.[17]

In all these goings on about tribal affairs, tribals were nowhere in the picture. The Adivasi Mahasabha hardly attracted any notice; its leader Jaipal Singh did not canvass the case for political autonomy for tribals. Hubback was of the opinion that while the scheduled castes threw up a leader like Ambedkar, the backward tribes had none of his stature and Jaipal Singh's influence did not extend beyond the Mundas. "His prowess on the hockey field was not necessarily combined with sound political judgement".[18] Hubback apparently had his difficulties with Jaipal Singh.

V

To sum up, the anthropologists have generally been accused of exaggerating the segmentary and pluralistic foci of the colonial societies to serve the colonial masters' interests of divide and rule.[19] This was no doubt partly true. The facts narrated above show how the administrator-anthropologists were keen to maintain the colonial hold on tribal society through various devices, not only in 1935, but even later during 1946-7 and after the transfer of power. The educated sections among the upcoming tribal middle class demanded a separate political dispensation for which an Indian anthropologist presented the first cogently argued case. The British anthropologists felt a sense of moral responsibility shared by their Government in the matter of the continued protection of the tribals to the point of their exclusion from the fast-moving political processes. They had no perception of the larger issues of social change and economic development, and they even thought that continuance of primitive conditions was good for tribals. Exclusion was equated with the *status quo*. This was a grave fallacy. While they had a point in stressing protection—the principle of partial and full exclusion was later embodied in the Indian Constitution—constitutional guarantees of protection had to be combined with programmes of rapid development, which did not find any place in the colonial frame.

Notes and References

This is a modified version of the paper "Colonialism, Anthropology and Primitive Society: the Indian Scenario (1928-47)", presented at the Second Indo-GDR History Seminar on Imperialism and Nationalism, Department of History, University of Delhi, 8-10 December 1981, which was subsequently published in *Man in India*, December 1984.

1. Talal Asad, (ed.) *Anthropology and the Colonial Encounter*.

2. K.S. Singh, "Colonial transformation of the tribal society in middle India", *Occasional Papers on Tribal Development*, 22, Ministry of Home Affairs, New Delhi, 1978. Later published in the *Economic and Political Weekly* 29 July, 1978.

3. *Indian Statutory Commission*, vol. 3, *Reports of the Provincial Committees appointed to confer with the Indian Statutory Commission*, pp. 554-556.

4. Ibid.

5. Ibid.

6. S.C. Roy, "The Aborigines of Chotanagpur: their proper status in reformed constitution" (written in 1936), *Man in India*, Administration Number, June 1946, vol. XXVI, No. 2, pp. 120-136.

7. India Office Library, (I.O.R.) File No. L/P& J 3712 & 343, London.

8. I.O.R.: L/P & J, 9/51, ibid.

9. I.O.R.: L/P & J, 4077 C., ibid.

10. I.O.R.: L/P & J, 9/343. Also see L P & J (C) 8712.

11. Verrier Elwin, *Loss of Nerve*. A comparative study of the result of the contact of peoples in the aboriginal areas of Bastar State and the Central Provinces of India, Essay submitted for the Wellcombe Medal 1972.

12. Verrier Elwin, *The Aboriginals*.

13. K.S. Singh, "Mahatma Gandhi and the Adivasis", *Man in India*, vol. 50, No. 1, January-March, 1970.

14. I.O.R.: L/P & J/6787, Backward Tribes.

15. Mr Amery to Field Marshal Viscount Wavell, India Office, 28 September 1944, L/P & J/7/6787: ff 171-6, ibid.

17. Field Marshal Viscount Wavell to Mr. Amery, New Delhi, 3 Deceber, 1944, L/P & J/7/6787: fiff 101-2. ibid.

18. I.O.R.: L/P & J/7/6787, Backward Tribes, op. cit.

19. J. Pathy, "Imperialism, Anthropology and the Third World", *Economic and Political Weekly*, April 4, 1981.

7

Tribal Movements

In this chapter we propose to deal at length with the tribal movements in the two phases of 1765-1857 and 1857-1920, briefly outlined in the first chapter, in terms of ideology, structure and leadership. There has been generally a tendency to link up all tribal movements, no matter how distanced they are in time and to lump peasants and tribes together[1]. Such an approach tends to gloss over the diversities of tribal social formations of which tribal movements are a part, both being structurally related. Our efforts in this chapter will be to underline the variety of tribal movements in keeping with the transformation of tribal society brought about by colonialism. In official reports on such movements written by colonial officials an attempt was made to emphasise the element of protest against the local functionaries of the raj and ignore the thrust against the British and other European personnel. In April 1858 Colonel E.T. Dalton, a distinguished administrator-ethnographer, expressed the view that the tribals were "not impelled by feeling hostile to the British Government but they cannot resist the temptation of following any chief who will lead them on plundering expeditions".[2] Of course, the rebellions of the latter half of the nineteenth century were still far away, but those of the first half did not support such optimism. Recent studies have, however, shown that these movements were basically anti-colonial, directed against the policy, system and personnel of the colonial administration. Similarly, such movements have been described as defensive[3] because the tribals rose in revolt only when they were driven to the wall. This is no doubt partly true but such characterisation does not help us to understand the totality of the movement in which all the elements that held tribal society together were brought into play in situations of rebellions in which the tribals also went on the offensive.

Even before the East India Company set about the task of extending its influence and conquering territories the tribes such as Gonds, Bhils and Kolis were in a disturbed state. The Mughals had suppressed the uprising by the Kolis in north-west Poona; in the process they hunted down Kolis and either made them prisoners or slaughtered them, destroyed their leader (*naik*) and his clan and took the prisoners to Junnar and had their heads cut off and piled into a pyramid; a platform was built over them which is still known as the black platform (*kala chabutra*).[4] Owing to their shrinking subsistence base, the tribals would take to plunder. Matters would become worse in a famine when they would descend from hills to loot villages, which invited heavy reprisals. One of the famines turned the Bhils who had acted as village watchmen into robbers. The Marathas retaliated by the most cruel massacres and other forms of savage punishments.[5] Divested of their political power by the Marathas the Gonds also turned into robbers and marauders of "a daring type, who would make a dash into the rich country of the Narmada valley, and after looting and killing all night returned straight across country to their jungle fortresses guided by the light of a bonfire on some commandng peak",[6] of which they built quite a few on the most inaccessible hills in the jungle. The Marathas continued to harass the hill Gonds, who were said to have lost "every vestige of humanisation" and become "the cruel, treacherous savages"[7] that the colonial officers found them to be and described them as such in an effort to present their treatment of the Gonds in a favourable light.

After the East India Company took over, the tribals ravaged by a famine coninued to plunder. We may distinguish raids from resistance during this phase as two sub-phases, though sometimes they are mixed up. The Paharias in the 1770s would come down the hills to loot. The weakening of the authority of Indian states made matters worse. The story of the Chuars of the Jungle Mahals who spread destruction is relatively well documented.[8] The introduction of the colonial system in tribal areas resulted in the displacement of the zamindars following the sale of zamindaris for failure to pay rent and depriving their men of service-land (*paikans*). So the contumacious landlords and their *paiks* combined with the "wild, untamed, ferocious, spirited and uninformed" tribes—many of them their kinsmen—to start what has been called the Chuar rebellion. The "Chuar" is a derogatory term, meaning a barbarian or a robber, who would go down to loot, commit dacoities and kill. The Chuars appear to have been a mixed lot consistng of the people belonging to the" low caste Hindu" such as the Kurmi, Rajwar, and Santals who were later compelled by the disturbances to move into Birbhum, but the Bhumij preponderated with their kinsmen, the Munda coming in at a later stage. Their popular base widened as *raiyats* joined them. The Chuar rebels were supported with food and shelter by the people. Although Chuar sardars started offering resistance to the colonial system from before, the Chuar rebellion was at its peak from 1795 to 1800; the Chuar "dacoities" however continued to be reported till 1816. The Chuars sought only restoration of their land, and not political independence. They killed the agents of the East India Company, plundered the "alien" zamindars, robbed the "Bengali and Hindu" (the Hindi-speaking people) who had come to the Jungle Mahals as purchasers of land. However the Chuar rebellions were put down with a heavy land.

The Santals were disturbed too. From this phase emerges a character, larger than life, Tilka Manjhi, who is now being made into a cult figure, *a la* Birsa Munda. A definitive history is sought to be reconstructed out of the mass of myths that surrounds him. He is said to have been born on 11 February 1750, which is too exact to be true, and is given a life-span of 1750-1784. He was devout, endowed with spiritual powers, treated all communities equally and sought to secure justice for all. After the Paharias were pacified by Augustus Cleveland, Tilka started the revolt against the Britsh in 1781. He was like Robin Hood, who would loot the British treasury to share the spoils with the poor. He organised a guerrilla warfare in which Santal women partcipated, attacked Bhagalpur in 1784, shot an arrow through the chest of Augustus Cleveland, which killed him (?). The revolt was crushed with Tilka having been captured and hanged, while his wife and brothers were killed. The place where he was buried became a shrine (*majaar*), where his statue stands today, visited by all seeking relief from the *baba* he has now been apotheosized into[9].

The rajas, zamindars and *muttadars* led the uprisings in this phase of what has been described as "baronial resistance" in which the tribals also played a role. The Kuricciyar of the Wynad in Kerala were probably the first after the Chuars to have joined the Palassi rebellion led by their raja (1802—4), one of the most serious outbreaks against the British supremacy in south India.[10] Another instance of resistance to the British fiscal system by the zamindars' soldiery was offered by the Khonds in 1817-18.[11] They also misconstrued the measures taken to suppress human sacrifice and female infanticide as an attempt on the part of the British government to appropriate their land and tax them. They revolted in 1846 against the attempt to eradicate Mer ah sacrifice. The Gond and Binjhal zamindars revolved twice, in 1827 and 1839, when they found their privileges threatened and their land enchroached upon by Hindus.[12] The Savaras in 1853 made inroads into parts of Parlakimedi and were put down by the troops who burnt their crops and drove off their cattle as the most efficient means of punishing them for their outrages. The Savaras resorted to plunder again in 1856, inviting heavy reprisals.[13] In western India when the fortunes of Mewar declined in 1818 the Bhils, Minas and Mers indulged in ravaging activities. The Kolis of the Sahyadris and Ramoshis were so integrated with the Maratha political system that when it was dismantled, they rose in revolt. The Koli revolted in 1828, 1839 and 1844-45 because they had been rendered unemployed or with an avowedly political objective of the restoration of the Peshwa rule in collaboration with others. Occasionally, as in 1824, they would just indulge in depredations, loot and burn down villages in Gujarat up to Baroda. In 1857 the Kolis and other hill tribes also attacked their moneylenders, who exploited them. The pacification of the Bhils both in Khandesh and princely India, who were found raiding and plundering at all times and all around was reported extensively by colonial administrators.[14]

The episodes we have discussed above representing resistance to one or another sub-phase of colonialism belong to the genre of primary resistance movements among tribes. It was in Chotanagpur and the Jungle Mahals, which bore the brunt of colonialism in its first phase, that we could see the development of the first series of tribal insurrections under traditional tribal leadership, a pattern which repeated itself elsewhere in parts of tribal middle India much later. In Chotanagpur we are in a position to identify the early phase of tribal resistance. The Panchpargana was part of the territory ravaged by the Chuars, Mundas' kinsmen, as mentioned earlier. Apart from the climate of lawlessness that prevailed, there were also agrarian issues mixed up with the factors of tribal discontent. As early as June 1789, the Mundas of Tamar rose in arms against their landlords. Within next ten years Bishnu Manki led the Mundas who committed several outrages before they could be put down. Ten years afterwards the rebels mustering five hundred strong under Dukhan Sae, still commemorated in folklores for his chivalry, attacked and burnt down a number of villages until he was captured on 14 March 1808. Earlier the adjoining parganas witnessed commotion and lawlessness in the wake of the aggression on the rights of the Mundas, who burnt down twelve villages of the raja of Rahe, and plundered his fort between 1796 and 1798. The culmination of this series of uprising was reached in the Tamar insurrection of 1819-20. The Munda uprisings from 1789 to 1820 marked the resistance of the tribe against the break-up of their agrarian system in the region. Driven out of the plains of Panchpargana the Mundas retreated into the hills of southern Khunti and eastern Tamar leaving behind the seeds of discontent which blossomed into the insurrection of 1831-32.

The Kol and Bhumij insurrections[15] (1831-2) represent a high point of this process. These uprisings were in the nature of a regional (even class) upsurge in which the tribals played a dominant role; they were led by the scions of the tribal aristocracy which had suffered in the hands of the colonial authorities. The historians and anthropologists have mistakenlyi attributed the Kol uprisng to the hinduisation of the Nagbans chiefs. In fact the hinduisation of the chief and his kinsmen was but one aspect of the process of state formation in the tribal society which had introduced a new set of production relations not only in Chotanagpur but elsewhere too. Even so, while the medieval state system in tribal regions sought to preserve tribal autonomy, the colonial system in the first flush subverted it. None of the colonial officers showed any understanding of the peculiarities of the political system of Chotanagpur, the rights and privileges of the chiefs recognised by the Mughals as autonomous chiefs. The British identified the Chotanagpur chief with the Bengal zamindar and the tribals with raiyats, subject to the same pattern of duties and obligations. As pressures built up on the meagre resources of the Chotanagpur chief and his subordinate tenure holders to pay more taxes and spend more, they were compelled to invite *thicadars* (farmers) from outside who could generate more income for them. The new class of *thicadars* not only grabbed as much of the tribals' land as they could, once foisted on the traditional tribal chiefs such as the Mankis and Mundas, they also missed no opportunity to harass and humiliate them. The immediate provocation for the Kol insurrection came from one of many such situations which could best be described in the words which remain probably the most eloquent ever uttered during this phase of tribal rebellions by a tribal chief, Bindrai Manki, a leader of the uprising :

> I borrowed a pair of old buffaloes from Burju Bania of the Sonepur pargana. This man came to my house accompanied by 60 men and took from me six cows, and calves, and four buffaloes, seized both my brother, Singhrai and myself, and took us to his house. We succeeded in effecting our escape, but my cattle were not released. I complained to Moomkera Singh, Raja of Bandgaon, of the Banias' treatment of us. He listened to me and gave me 35 men for my protection with whom I went to Surgaon, where not finding the Bania, we seized two men and a pair of bullocks which we took to the Raja. For this an inhabitant of Surgaon, named Singh, preferred a complaint against me at Sherghati. My brother Singhrai and self and Bahadur were seized by the Chakradharpur Munshi and Jamadar who came to Bandgaon for the purpose. I requested them to send us to Sherghati, if our seizure were in consequence of the orders from there. They

> replied that they would give us answer on paying them 100 rupees. After remaining confined on the stocks for fifteen days and suffering great pain, we escaped. When our flight was discovered, the Munshi and Jamadar carried off my two wives. They released the older, who was pregnant, but the other, who was young, was detained and ravished by the Munshi and two of his Musalman peons; the Singh of Surgaon has besides taken away two of my sisters by force, who are still in his house. At the Dasahara of the present year, Singhrai, Bahadur and I waited on Raja Achet Singh of Porahat; Soie Munda also accompanied us. We complained to the Raja of his Munshi's having aided with his father-in-law and deprived my wife of her chastify and of the Singh having forcibly taken away and kept my sisters. When we had told the Raja our grievances, we returned home. We four were subsequently sent for by Krishna Dewan, who told us that, as we were Kols, we might do as we pleased, but be careful, not to involve Raja Achet Singh in any difficulties by our conduct. We returned home, invited all the Kols our brethren and caste to assemble at the village Lankhan in Tamar, where we had a consultation. The Pathans had taken our honour and the Singh our sisters, and the Kuar Haranath Sahi, had forcibly deprived of our estate of twelve villages which he had given to the Singh. Our lives we considered of no value and being of one caste and bretheren it was agreed upon that we should commence to cut, plunder, murder and eat. We said, if any were hanged it would be us four; if any put in irons, we should be the four. We four should be answerable and if the gentlemen sent for any it would be us, who were ready to attend and submit to whatever might be the sentence. It is with this resolution that we have been murdering and plundering those who have deprived us of both honour and homes, conceiving that committing such outrage our grievances would come to light, and that, if we had any master, notice would be taken of them and justice rendered.[16]

This was however only the immediate cause. The roots lay deeper. As mentioned earlier, the colonial system introduced a new system of administration, an array of new taxes, and an army of petty officials. The tribals accustomed to pay quit rent now had to pay fines for crimes; excise duty on spirits including their favourite drink, rice beer; the various *salamis*, postal taxes, etc. They had also to render forced labur. The new taxes were realised ruthlessly by the zealous agents of the local authority. Then the traditional system of land control broke down. Not only were the hereditary tribal chiefs deprived of their estates, the tribal cultivators, too, lost their land to the newcomers. The Kol insurrection (December 1831 to May 1832) was thus like the bursting forth of a prairie fire. It spread over most of the regions of modern Chotanagpur, Singhbhum, Manbhum and Palamau. It was unique in that it saw for the first and probably the last time in Chotanagpur in the nineteenth century a confederacy of many tribes. Not only did the militant Ho tribes (Laraka Kol) and Munda lead and join the uprising *en masse*, the passive Oraons (Dhangar Kols) also joined hands. The Cheros and Kharwars of adjoining Palamau also rose in rebellion, though the links between them and the Kols could not be clearly established. The uprising started in the heart of the Munda land, Sonepur, situated on the periphery of the Munda and Ho homeland. It was a spontaneous upsurge against all outsiders (the *suds*, and not *dikus*)—the *thicadars*, moneylenders, traders and petty officials. The tribals attacked and killed them, plundered their property and set fire to their houses. It was an orgy of slaughter, an outburst of primordial savagery. The official returns put the number of persons murdered at 304, houses burnt at 4086, of the number of cattle seized at 17,038 and of the quantity of grains burnt at 822,922 maunds. The non-official estimates of the loss were bigger, However, it is interesting to observe that the tribals spared the non-tribal artisans who performed useful services for the village community such as the chowkidars who belonged to the Ghasi community, the milkmen, the ironsmith (lohar) etc. The Nagbansi chief and tenureholders were also not touched. This gave rise to the suspicion that the Nagbansi and Rautias, their militia men, having lost their authority, had incited the rebels, but on inquiry this was found to be untrue. The colonial authorities moved in troops to quell the disturbances which took three months. The rebels lost ground rapidly and their leaders were arrested. About 350 Mundas were put on trial for cases involving killing of persons. Eight tribals were executed for such crimes: many others received life sentences. A general amnesty was proclaimed later as a gesture of conciliation. The Kol insurrection was followed by the Bhumij rebellion in 1832-33 in Dalbhum and Manbhum (Barabhum, Patkum, etc.) under Ganga Narain, who was joined by Bindrai Manki, a leader of the Kol Insurrec-ion. The uprising was put down only towards the end of the year 1833, Ganga Narain having been killed on 7 February 1833. The insurrections, though short-lived, made the authorities aware of the depth of tribal disaffection. The understanding of the tribal problems led to a modification of the pattern of regulation administration and the formulation of a number of administrative measures to redress the local grievances. The most important of these was the formation of the South West Frontier Agency, which embodied the concept of a non-regulation administrative system under a benign, paternalistic agent. The Agency was also the precursor of the administrative division of Chotanagpur. After the insurrections a large number of tribals left their homeland, and when they returned years later, they found that they had lost whatever had been left of their lands. They demanded the restoration of their land, which when resisted led to the Sardar movement, the *mulkui larai*, the struggle for land. The Kol insurrection thus contained the seeds of the peasant movement led by the Sardars, which lasted forty years, and culminated in the *ulgulan*, the Munda uprising led by Birsa Munda.

In the north-east the sub-phases of tribal rebellions could be similarly demarcated. The Garos and Hajongs who submitted to the British rule to escape the tyranny of their zamindars, came under the influence of the Pagal Panthi. Their chief, Tipu who became the leader of the oppressed peasantry, founded a kingdom and was arrested. The Khasis were engaged in acts of deprediations in the plains they raided from 1787 to 1825. The Singphos, Mishmis, Lushais, Khamptis and Daflas raided plains and killed people. The Khasis opposed the construction of the road, and the confederation of Khasi chiefs resisted the British attempt at the occupation of their country, led by Tirot Singh. The British sent out expeditions to punish the Lusahis,

Mishmis etc. As in middle India, this phase ended with the revolt of Maniram Dewan and Saranga Raja of Assam in 1857.

This phase of tribal uprisings reached its finale in the first war of independence of 1857. The Chero and Gond zamindars participated in this, the most celebrated of the latter being Narain Singh, the zamindar of Sonakhon. In Hazaribagh while the Santals became excited and resorted to a certain amount of plundering, some of the dispossessed Bhuiya chiefs saw in the Mutiny an opportunity to recover their land from the purchasers then occupying them, an objective which was supported by their tenantry. The Bhils raised the banner of revolt. The Bhils at Manpur, the headquarters of the Deputy Bhil Agency, in contrast, guarded the Europeans, and the names of these faithfuls were included in the tablets so that "their gallantry and faithfulness may not pass out of remembrance". In Gujarat, the Bhils, Kolis, Thakardas and Naikdas rose in revolt against the established authority. One can see the continuation of this phase in the endeavour of Wasudeo Balwant Phadke (1845-1883) to free the country from the British rule by violent methods. He raised an army of Ramoshis and Dhangars and enlisted the support of Kolis, but with no great success.

II

In the second phase (1857-1920) we take up, tribe-wise, the rise of peasant-cum-revivalistic movements. Various episodes including raids, armed uprisings and movements for social reform were part of the procession of a tribal movement. A crucial factor in the formation of such movements was the mobilisation of the tribe as a whole under the leadership of one of its own members,who was not necessarily a chief. This helped articulate issues regarding alienation of land, erosion of right in forest, levy of taxes and illegal casses which affected the community as a whole. In this phase we could trace the beginning of the rise of a peasant culture among the tribes, based on the concept of individual proprietorship, and led by peasant leaders particularly in eastern India. There were four factors that brought about this change. First, the breakdown of the tribal agrarian system continued unabated. As the foundations of the raj were firmly established, the economic consequences of it operated with a far more disastrous effect. Introduction of cash rent, commutation of praedial conditions and services into money rent, advent of money economy and moneylending communities, alienation of tribals' land were the facets of the rapidly changing situation. Secondly, the autonomy of tribal systems was gradually whittled down as alien land laws and rent laws were introduced. Together with the new economy that came to tribal areas, they helped to create individual proprietorship of land. The village community was not recognised. Land became saleable, inheritable, transferable, and a commodity. The third factor in the formation of such movements was the culture contact with peasants,which has been described elsewhere in this book. The peasants spread the rudimentry notions of Hinduism among tribes such as Mundas, Santals, and Bhils who have been long in symbiosis with them. The millennial ideas such as the "divine-inspiration" for movements derived mainly from Hinduism, though later these were reinforced by the influence of Christianity. Fourthly, Christianity in Chotanagpur stimulated the concept of peasant proprietorship in tribal areas where communal systems once prevailed. Christian priests emphasised the peaceful and constitutional means of change, as against the violent means adopted by the tribals, and they acted as the watchdog of colonial interests, and would cry wolf and see sedition in the most innocuous of tribal movements.

The Santals as the largest and most resilient tribe in eastern India, were the first to wage what could be described as the peasant war in tribal India. It foreshadowed peasant-cum-revivalistie movements among the Mundas, Bhils, and minor tribes of Orissa and Maharashtra. The Santal uprising, called *hul*[17] (1855-56) began paradoxically in a relatively happy economic situation. The Santals had settled down as peasants in their new homeland, the Damin-i-koh, where they were more prosperous than their kinsmen elsewhere. Employment at indigo factories and in the construction of railways brought in ready cash which filled the Santal's girdles with coins and their women were bedecked with silver jewellery. What turned this happy homeland into a storm centre was the sense of humiliation that the Santals, who had innovated the unique institution of *bitlaha*, that instrument of collective Santal action against non-tribal offenders suffered when they saw themselves exploited economically by moneylenders and also socially. This was the time of stress for all including the four Santal brothers, Sidhu, Kanhu, Chandu and Bhairab, inhabitants of the village Bhagnadihi, a short distance south of Burhait, which had suffered much from the usurers. All four were landless men. The more sensitive among them, Sidhu and Kanhu had long been brooding over the wrongs when :

> Thakur or god appeared to them in the form of a white man, dressed like a native, with ten fingers on each hand. He wrote in a book which he gave the brothers, together with 20 pieces of paper in five batches. He then ascended upwards and disappeared, after which two men appeared, each with six fingers on each hand, and having told them the purport of the Thakur's order, likewise vanished. For some time the god appeared to the two brothers every day; at one time as a flame of fire, with a book, some white paper and a knife; at another in the form of a solid cart wheel. A shrine was erected consisting of a mound of mud crowned by a cart wheel, at which the villagers were instructed to present offerings of grain and milk, and to sacrifice kids and buffaloes. Here the worshipers were shown the slips of paper and the book (which proved to be none other than the Gospel according to St. John), and were told that in them were written the orders of the god. The news of the miracle spread far and wide, and messengers were sent to all the *manjhis* of the Damin-i-koh, bearing a branch of the *sal* tree, which, like the fiery cross of the Highlands, was a signal to the people to gather.[18]

The Thakur also called upon the *dikus* (aliens) and *sahebs* to clear out of the Santal land and go back to the other side of the Ganges or "the Mother Ganges (*Ganga mai*) will come to His assistance and fire will rain from heaven". The *hul* of 1855 thus directed its fury against the *dikus* such as *mahajans* (moneylender and traders) who exorted, the *amla* (petty officials) who were corrupt, and the *saheb*, who not only neglected them as pointed out by colonial officials but also exploited them. Even before the *hul* occurred a number of *mahajans*' houses were attacked. The Damin-i-koh was the centre of the *hul* but it spread over the Santal belt, comprisng Bhagalpur, Birbhum and Girdih. At Parasnath a Santal chief tried to organise the Santals of the south into an independent kingdom. The *hul* was marked by "scenes of inhuman cruelty, e.g., slow roasting of men, torture of children, the ripping up of women, the drinking of blood, etc". Villages were burnt and property pillaged. The "most brutal outrages" were committed on the moneylenders. "When a *mahajan* fell into their hands, they first cut off his feet with their *pharsas* or battle axes with the taunt that that was 4 annas in the rupee, then cut off his legs at the thigh to make up 8 annas, then cut him into two at his waist to make up 12 annas, and finally took off his head to complete the 16 annas, shouting '*pharkati*' i.e. full a quittance". A "savage sense of humour" was displayed in chopping up the body of a zamindar into 22 pieces, one for each of his ancestors. Though the rebels are said to have declared that they warred against the Bengalis and not against the English, they did murder Europeans as well and burnt down their bungalows and destroyed railway works. In one case two European ladies were cut down and in another an old planter and his three sons were murdered.[19]

A feature of the *hul*, often highlighted, is that not only the Santals but also Mal Paharia tribe with whom they were not on the best of the terms joined them. All artisan and service-performing communities belonging to the so-called semi-Hinduised "low castes" such as barbers who performed ritual services, carpenters, blacksmiths (who manufactured arms for them))and Doms (who acted as messengers and drum beaters) also jointed the *hul*. The participation of so many communities under the leadership of the Santals gave the *hul* a broad based character. This is supported by the punishment meted out to the rebels of different castes : Out of 251 prisoners, 191 were Santals, 34 Nais (barbers), 5 Doms, 6 Dhangars, 7 Kols, 1 Gwala (cowherd), 6 Bhuiya and 1 Rajwar. They belonged to 54 different villages[20]. When the Europeans were killed the

Calcutta press screamed for Santal blood. Martial law was proclaimed in November 1855. The army moved in. Repressive measures followed. The *hul* was quelled but its lessons were not lost. The Santal Pargana was consistuted into a separate non-regulation district and kept out of the application of general laws.

In 1866 the Santals revolted in the Bamanghati pargana of Mayurbhanj which was one of the best governed native states, over its officials' attempt to introduce a survey and settlement of land which was made distasteful by the manipulations of petty officials (*amlas*) who falsified measurements and did not grant receipt for the tax paid and demanded *rasad* (provision for raja's local agents). Four chiefs (sardars) of Santal *pirs* (divisions) were arrested for refusing to provide *rasad* and carried off to Baripada. The rising began. The Santals started committing a series of dacoities for a month and called a conference of Santal sardars. When negotiations with the state authorities broke down, the Santals openly plundered the outsiders (*hattooaha*) while sparing the autochthones (*deslog*) such as the Kol and Bhumij. They were called upon to worship the broad arrow as the common symbol of the uprising and set up a bamboo pole with a bundle of straw tied at the top, as a mark seeking protection. The outsiders included the cultivators (Chasas) and Mahantees (Oriyas). The result of the uprising was that the raja's authority in Bamanghati was suspended and the Singhbhum model of administration introduced. The Santal sardars were permitted to exercise police powers, and restored to their old position. They could collect rent, and settlement for all villages was made under written agreements with them. The old system of plough tax was also restored though at a higher rate.

The reverberations of the Santal *hul* died away, albeit slowly. Its benefits appeared to have been washed away a few years later by the application of all laws to Santal Pargana; extension of the Civil Procedure Code brought back lawyers and the extortionate rate of interest; Santal headmen were evicted from their office, and Santals from their land. This caused general unrest. The Santals of Dumka and Godda held meetings, complained bitterly about their condition to the British Officers, which created a panicky situation. A Santal drum sounded and the memories of the *hul* revived. An inquiry resulted in the promulgation of the law which restored the benefits of the *hul*, and reaffirmed the exemption of the Santal parganas from the general laws; it restored dispossessed headmen, settled rents and reduced interest on debts.

It was in these unsettled conditions that the Kharwar movement took shape.[21] Bhagirath Manjhi, a resident of Tardiha (Godda) preached thus : "No human being created the earth or sends rain and sunshine, no human being cleared or ploughs our land, but ourselves; *ergo*, no human being but ourselves has a right to a share in the produce". This gave expression to the idea of freedom embedded in the Santal psyche when the Santals were free, did not worship spirits but only one God, and when they as the original reclaimers of land were its master, a position that had been irretrievably lost to the *dikus* and the other aliens. This ideology was interpreted as fuelling a "rabid socialistic political agitation, a statement of absolute anarchic independence, which even the most advanced English liberal would hardly be prepared to advocate". The famine of 1874 gave Bhagirath an opportunity to declare himself as the person "who was commissioned by God" to redress the grievancesas of the Santals, to fight for them and to be their king. On 24 July 1874, he was appointed the king of the new Santal raj at Baunsi. Bhagirath's first act as the king was to abolish all demand for rent and to order the slaughter of pigs and fowls, being unclean, and to prohibit drinking and dancing. The new Kharwar religion was couched in Hindu idioms. The presiding deity of the Kharwar was the *singbahini* (mother goddess) of the *diku*, followed by the Santal sun god, (Chando). His adviser was one Hindu, Matadin; a shrine was set up at Tardiha on Hindu principles with a Santal *panda* to conduct services. The missionaries were scared of the Hindu influence on the movement, saw sedition in it and a disaster for native christians. Bhagirath was arrested and sentenced to two year's imprisonment, and his shrine was dismantled. However, the Kharwar cult and its votaries, the "clean Santals" (Sapha Hor) survived Bhagirath's death in March 1879, and the Kharwar movement continued spawning *babas* (the holy men), some of whom were described as having been 'pervert christians' earlier. Their influence was far and wide, and it could be seen at work among the Mundas.

The *meli* (Santal disturbance) of 1917 in Mayurbhanj had its origin in the officials' attempt to raise a labour corps for the war in France. While, as it was rightly said, the ideas of serving across the seas in a semi-military capacity was strange to tribals, they were by no means averse to recruitment as coolies for tea gardens in Assam. The Santals had of course their grievances, against the forest department which prevented them from collecting jungle fruits and forced restrictions on sale of forest produce and extracted *begar*; against the excise department regarding prohibition of illicit distillation of liquor and brewing of rice beer (*handia*) for sale etc. But the real reason appeared to be political :

> The records of the trials show that the series of disturbances were only indirectly connected with the recruitment campaign. Before they arose it was well known that no man would be taken against his will and that recruitment had in fact been stopped. But once the unrest in the Sadar subdivision had taken the form of open revolt, the idea which loomed large in the aboriginal mind was that the time had come to make a bid for independence. The yearning for a return to the golden age when they had no over-lords is one that periodically returns to the Santals and other aboriginal tribes. It seemed to the Mayurbhanj Santals that the present time was opportune. The Sahibs had nearly been killed by the German god and they were forced to ask the Santals for help in men and money. The events of the earlier rising in the Sadar subdivisions were misrepresented, partly in the natural spread of rumour, partly of set purpose. The would be rebels were told of the great success of their fellows at Betnoti and elsewhere successes against which the State had been able to do nothing striking in the way of reprisals. All the restrictions of rent payment, excise rules and forest laws to which they had hitherto submitted with patient resignation, became suddenly galling and intolerable, and the desire for emancipation from them became a passion which could not be extinguished without a trial of strength.[22]

The uprising had two well-marked phases. In the first it occurred in the Sadar subdivision and culminated in the cutting of the railway and the sack of a bazar in May 1917. In the second phase, in June, the disturbances spread over the Bamanghati and Panchpir subdivision, a bazar was looted, and acts of robbery and murder were committed after a meeting of the Santals was held. Order was restored by the armed police and regular troops. Out of 1118 persons tried 977 were convicted. Four were sentenced to death and 33 to transportation for life. This was the biggest trial of its kind involving the largest number of tribals.

With the spread of Christianity in Chotanagpur from 1850 onwards among the Mundas the agrarian question took a new turn. Tortured beyond all endurance for nearly fifty years, they believed that at last the day of their deliverance was drawing near. During the Mutiny of 1857, the zamindars attacked the German mission at Ranchi and persecuted the Christians in the villages. With the suppression of the Mutiny, the tide turned in favour of the Christian raiyats. The Sardar agitation led by Christian raiyats put them on the offensive against their masters. The forty years of Sardar agitaion or *mulkui larai* (the struggle for the land) from 1858 aimed at expelling the zamindars, protested against the incidence of forced labour and praedial conditions and reminded the people of the deeds of the heroes of the tribal insurrections. Its leaders adopted the means of prayer, protest and petition to win back their kingdom. They distrusted the *dikus*, the non-white judges and the administrators who were alleged to be the relations of zamindars. They would sometimes not pay rent, turn out rent-collectors and sought forcibly to dispossess their landlords of the lands they claimed to be theirs or their ancestors. They raised funds for fighting the legal battle necessary for the restoration of their lost rights and lands. The widespread disturbances during 1858-59 marked the beginnning of the movement. In October 1858, the Christians of the villages near Jhagra resisted their zamindar who oppressed them; in November 1858 at Bala there was a clash between a Jagirdar and his ryots. The *bhuinhari* area was in ferment. During 1862-88 there were clashes between zamindars and their raiyats. In September 1867, 4,000 Christians filed a petition against local officers and the raja of Chotanagpur. The agitation, however, continued and passed into a revivalistic phase during the eighties. In a petition dated 25 March 1879, the Mundas claimed that Chotanagpur belonged to them. In 1881 a party of Sardars calling themselves the 'Children of Mael' under one "John the Baptist" set up a kingdom at Doesa, a former seat of the raja of Chotanagpur; the leaders were prosecuted. From 1890 the Sardar movement turned against all Europeans, both missionaries and officials, who were suspected of acting hand in glove with the zamindars. The Mundas thought that all had turned against them, and that there was no alternative to fighting unaided their own battle for the recovery of their land. The constitutional methods had not yielded any results. The situation was ripe for the rise of a new leader of the Munda movement.

The movement led by Birsa Munda (1874-1901) is easily the best known of the socio-political movements of this phase because it is very well documented and has a vibrant folklore. The movement sought to establish Munda raj and independence. In its socio-religious aspects, it was like any other bhagat movement, with this difference that it was also influenced by Christianity, and it used both Hindu and Christian idioms to create the Munda ideology and world view. The rebels attacked police stations and officials, churches and missionaries, and though there was an undercurrent of hostility against the *dikus*, there was no overt attack on them except in a couple of controversial cases. The uprising was quelled, and its lessons were acknowledged in the passing of an agrarian law that protected the Munda land system[23].

The pacification of the Bhils in Khandesh and Mewar accomplished, their reclamation to settled agriculture, aided by various measures such as induction of peasants (Kunbis) taken by the government and the operation of market forces, was a slow process. This could be observed at work more among the Bhils in the plains than among their kinsmen on the hills. However, their social organization remained cohesive. Their villages under the headman (*gameti*, *rawat* and *mukhi*) were grouped into *pals*, a larger organization under the chiefs, who were recognised by princely states. This structure of organization which remained largely undisturbed made for effective mobilisation during Bhil uprisings in the latter half of the century. It is important to emphasise this because the colonial records speak more of Bhil raids and less of Bhil movement or of the latter in terms of raids. Not that these did not exist—in fact the Bhils have probably more of "social bandits" than any other tribe—but it is pertinent to go into their social roots. Many colonial administrators have commented upon the predatory habits of a tribe—and in the first phase of colonial encounter there are umpteen examples of this, the Chuar rebellion being one of them, as described above. Even if a rebellion was quelled, the *chuari* (predatory) habits survived, and they revived particularly in every famine and period of scarcity. This did not take the form of any large-scale violence or an organized opposition to constituted authority, but it expressed itself in recurring outbreaks of dacoity, of loot of grains. This formulation applied more to the Bhils than to any other tribe. Even after their pacification, with their dwindling resource base and subjected to all kinds of pressures exerted by traders and moneylenders and revenue authorities from outside, the Bhils did turn into "social banditti". A number of them are mentioned : Kajar Singh (1833-60), Tulia Naik (1867-1876), Tantiya Bhil, etc. Tantiya Bhil graduated from petty theft to dacoity; he kidnapped people to obtain a ransom. His depredations lasted from 1878 to 1889. He was a friend of the poor, and so great was his influence on the Korkus and other backward communities who fondly called him Tantiya *mama* that when he was captured, crowds of people flocked to see him and the Nagpur bar submitted an appeal on his behalf. He was hanged in 1889. Tulia Naik was about six feet tall and of powerful frame. For years, he lived quietly with his family. He was known as bold and manly, a brave hunter, and a leader among his people. According to his own story, it was his love for hunting that proved the beginning of his troubles. His story reads like this :

> After following a big panther for many days, I killed him, took the skin to the Government treasury at Pimpalner, and was paid £1 4s. (Rs. 12). No sooner had I drawn the money than I was beset by the treasury servants asking for a share. I paid 6s. (Rs. 3) to messengers and others, and then said I would give no more. One of the men I refused, who was a constable, threatened to bring me to trouble; but I was not one who cared for threats, and I paid him nothing. Taking what was left of the reward I called some of my friends and feasted them. We had a goat and plenty of liquor, and afterwards music, and dancing. Towards midnight a message came from the police that the music must stop and the party break up. I had drunk freely and would not listen, and when the police tried to break up our party, I resisted and was taken into custody. Next morning I was started to some villages where the chief constable was. Two constables were in charge of men, one of them the man whom I had refused a share of my reward. All the way he kept gibing me, saying, 'ah, you would not give me a rupee, very good, wait a little, you will have to go across the sea'. I feared that I might, and watching my chance, I ran away.[24]

He was sentenced to seven years' imprisonment. On completing his term, he got himself a job as a watchman and worked as such till a complaint of rape was brought against him. He fled, and then when, all attempts to catch him had failed:

> One day, as Major Probyn was driving along the Selbari road, Tulia walked out of a *Babul* tree into the middle of the road, and said he had come to give himself up. He got into Major Probyn's pony cart, was driven to the Magistrate's camp, convicted of rape, and transported for life.[25]

The Bhils' passage from "raids" to the movement was well underway in the 1870s. The Bhils rose against moneylenders, in times of scarcities, a little before the Kunbis struck at Marwari moneylenders in the Deccan riots. The money relations between the Bhils and Gujar landlords had always been uneasy in Khandesh. However, the Bhils were worse off economically in the princely states. The Bhil rebellion of 1881 is probably the first well-documented story of their movement. It started in Mewar. The establishment of a customs post along the border made the Bhils suspicious that they were going to be deprived of their traditional right to levy "protection money" (*bulwa*). The census of 1881 was also misconstrued as a prelude to additional taxation, a device to recruit the able-bodied Bhils for the Afghan war, which would result not only in their women being taken away by non-Bhils but also in a mal-exchange of women, the fat women being given to stout men and the lanky to the lean ones. To rumours such as these were added the oppressive demand by Mewar *durbar*. In March 1881 the Bhils revolted at Padona, and after a few skirmishes, forced the Mewar *durbar* to sign a 21-point agreement. This was a notable victory for them, because among their gains was the continued recognition of the Bhils as protectors of roads and withdrawal of the customs outpost, stoppage of census, reduction of taxes and general amnesty for all. As the Agent to Governor-general said, "The Bhils have succeded in extorting by force and murder unreasonble concessions and this is sure to have the most mischievous effect, although it may ensure a temporary truce".[26]

This sounded prophetic. The Bhils of Mahikantha, encouraged by the success of their kinsmen across the border, rebelled. A violent mob of the Bhils forced the chief of Pol to sign an agreement to which the political Agent, Col. Goodfellow was forced to put his signature, making wide-ranging concessions such as reduction of land tax, not only for Bhils but also for other castes. Later the Government of Bombay did not approve of this agreement because it was concluded under duress. The Bhil uprising spread to Alirajpur in central India, and to other parts of the princely states in Gujarat of the Bombay Presidency. Behind this sweep lay a similar set of grievances, namely, the extortions of the *durbars* through high assessment, the harsh conduct of their functionaries and maltreatment of Bhil chiefs. An interesting feature of this movement was that the Bhils were only the "front" behind whom rallied many communities such as moneylenders (*banias*), carpenters, potters and menials, as in the Kol and Santal insurrections. But the Government of India saw the hand of *banias* behind it because by instigating their debtors they would reduce the claim of the state and improve their own position in consequence. That the Bhil disturbances were taken seriously will be evident from the fact that a Bhil Enquiry Commission was set up. In its report the Commission exonerated the state chiefs from any responsibility for the grievances of the Bhils who were squarely blamed for their own ills.

However the process towards mobilisation of the Bhils for redressal of their agrarian grievances had started. The famine of 1899-1900 saw the Bhils revert to social banditry. No uprising followed immediately but one did 14 years later. It was led by Govind Giri, a Banjara by caste, who started as a *hali* (forced labourer) in the Sunth state, and after having lost his wife and children in the famine, he settled down at Vedesa in Dungarpur, as a preacher. The Bhils, who had already been acculturated through bhagat movements listened to Govind Giri, as he too preached on similar lines in favour of monotheism and against witchcraft; he also enjoined personal cleanliness, abstention from killing animals and giving up drinking liquor. But there was a typical twist to his teachings. The Bhils were asked to set up fire-pits (*dhunis*), flags (*nishans*), wear yellow turbans (*safas*) and beads (*rudraksha*). They were not to carry arms but only iron tongs. They were exhorted to behave like *savkars* (higher castes) and become *sagras* (civilised) as against the *nugras* (uncivilized) that they then were. The Bhils were the owners of land, and therefore the establishment of a Bhil raj where it existed at one time in the Bhil tracts of Sunth and Banswara states was inevitable. Evidently Govind Giri's teachings caused a tremor. Sale of liquor fell. The French missionaries warned the authorities that the movement was "seditious". The Bhils attacked a police outpost, carried off two constables, and went on to attack the fort of the raja of Sunth towards the close of 1913. Govind Giri explained that his followers were only trying to retrieve the goods captured by the *durbar*. Govind Giri and his followers assembled on the Mangarh hill on the border of the Sunth and Banswara state and demanded, in the course of negotiations, apart from the freedom to preach his religion, non-increase of land revenue (*vero*), exemption of the holdings of the poor people from payment of tax (*vighoti*) and non-levy of interest on loan (*taccavi*). In an address, couched in religious idioms, and not without political overtones, he said:

> Here (on the hill) we have facilities of water and firewood and so my disciples come here to pay their respect on the fair days such as the new moon and full moon..on the one side (our side) is the word (divine word), on the other (your side) is order (i.e. power or authority). One party is *vedi* (i.e. knower of truth), the other party (your) is *bhedi* (practiser of all worldly activities)..Females of banias, brahmins and rajputs become child widow and then practise immorality. Can they be called *satis* (chaste) or *papis* (sinner)? These (Bhils) are poor people—worms of earth—they till land and throw a handful of grain in it..The thanedars of Idar, Lunawada and the uncle of the durbar asked for bribe from me, and as I did not give it to them, they said they would ease themselves on my *dhunis* and kill fowls and goats in them and would molest my flags.. I have completed six years of my worship and six more are remaining..because none of the States would allow me to live below (in the plains) and because they would molest me and my worship, therefore I have taken myself to this hill..I am innocent. I am the disciple of Rajugarji who was a disciple of Solaganji who again was the disciplle of Ghotagarji of the great Akhanda (institution) of Bundi. I am a *sansari*, i.e., worldly man and I have children. *Bhekh* (begging) is the attribute or symbol of God Shankar. Have fear of the lord. All have to die, (so) have some mercy and religious spirit. Do not attack me through anger. If my intentions be fraudulent towards the raja or raiyats, then let the very *bhekh*, the religion swallow me. And if you practise any fraud against me, then let your religion swallow you..He who digs a pit will fall into it. As one sows, so he reaps..You should decide all this and render us justice and then go your way: otherwise your field will be spoiled (i.e. perhaps the whole affair will be spoiled). I am guru of these people; these are the things for a guru (priest) to raise these people from their wild habits [through] Guru-Mantra.[27]

On 14 November 1913 the hill was attacked by the troops. Govind Giri was arrested along with patels and other Bhils, around 900 of them. He was sentenced to ten year's rigorous imprisonment. The Dungarpur *durbar* issued orders restricting *begar*. No major reforms were considered expedient for the Indian states as long as they were in position to quell the uprisings of the Bhil, as they had done. Bhil depredations continued. In 1907 the Bhils gathered at Alwa (Dangs) to kill officers and loot the treasury. In the 1920s the Bhil uprising against the states of Sunth and Lunawada was nipped in the bud by the combined forces of Alirajpur, Baria, and the two states.

The millenarian movements were not confined to major tribes alone. The Konda Dora of Salur (Vizagapatnam), particularly one of its two divisions situated in the plains (China Kondalu), was acculturated enough to generate a movement of sorts. A Konda Dora, Korra Mallayya, declared himself to be the incarnation of one of the five Pandava brothers and his infant son as the god Krishna. He also announced that the English would be driven out and the country would be ruled by himself. Therefore, his followers should be armed with bamboos which would be "turned into guns", while he would change the weapons of the authorities into water. His followers killed two constables. Eleven of his followers were killed in turn when the police went in. The Swami died in jail and his infant son died too, ending the movement. This movement stood out of "most of its predecessors" in its "desire for loot and political aspiration",[28] as also for religious fervour.

There was another millenarian movement among the Naikdas, a small forest-dwelling tribe who lived in a remote situation and were notorious for their savage cruelty. They were earlier not in a culture contact situation : they showed no respect to brahmins and cared little for brahminic rites, fasts or feasts. Yet in 1868 they were led by one of their "holy" men (bhagat) to a rebellion, their second in ten years, Joria of Jamughode who gave out that he was the supreme lord (*parameshwar*), gifted with the power of working miracles. He preached the purest morality, made converts and showed a surprising knowledge of Hindu mythology and ritual. There was nothing to show that a brahmin was behind it and that Joria had not himself worked out all the details. Then he joined hands with Rupa Singh, "a pardoned rebel and outlaw", gave up his scheme of moral reform and decided to set up a kingdom of which he would be the spiritual head with Rupa Singh as its temporal chief. Rupa Singh sacked Rajgad:

> During these days the Naikdas at Vadek were full of the wisest trust and zeal. Almost every soul, for about twenty miles round, believed that the British Government was at an end, and that under Rupsingh and Joria a *dharamraj* or religious rule had begun. In their former fights with trained troops the Naikdas carefully avoiding the open, by sudden night attacks, had wearied their opponents. But now, as they seemed to have given up their old tactics, every effort was made to lose no time in letting them try the chance of an open fight.[29]

The Naikdas clashed with the British troops on February 16. They plied their arrows with such effect that the *risaldar* of the Poona Horse was killed and the captain narrowly escaped twice. Emboldened by this success the Naikdas kept advancing until a shot from each of the three district officers laid low the leader in red and yellow and two of his chief supporters. With the loss of nine of their men the Naikdas fled, and the rising was at an end. Joria and Rupa Singh were captured and hanged later.

We may now discuss the tribal agrarian movements which were without any millenarian content. In Orissa,[30] the Khonds of Kalahandi in 1882 rose against the Kultas (the Oriya), whom they killed in hundreds and whose villages they plundered. Excited over the overassessment of tax and extinction of their rights in land and forest, the Khonds were particularly irked by the lease of their villages to the outsider Kultas. They invited other Kondhs to join by circulating the head, fingers, hair etc. of an early victim. Nothing came of it. The Savaras attacked the Pans, who stole cattle, charged high interest on loan, and acted as the intermediaries between the Savaras and the outside world. In 1899 the Savara headmen (*naiks*) of sixteen villages in Jeypore organised attacks on the Pans' houses which were razed to the ground. Next year, the Savaras sent around the jack branch, a well recognised form of the fiery cross "to invite all except Pans" to assemble, but it was intercepted[31]. In 1891 the

Juangs and Bhuiyas of Keonjhar took to arms to protest against the oppression and exaction of the raja.[32] They committed dacoities, looted villages, and finally when they were quelled they came in to do the homage in the most solemn manner to their raja. In December 1893 the Kondhs with their penchant for palace intrigues, rose in a full-blown *meli* in Nayagarh, instigated by a dismissed diwan, which resulted in political murders. In 1894 the people in Rangpur rebelled against the oppression of the chief and his officials and their interference in the forest and other rights of tenants. The village headmen (*gaontias*) and leaders (*naiks*) in Gangpur committed a series of docoities in defiance of the state. In 1912 the Savaras resisted reservation of forest and resulting encroachment on their rights. But it was in Daspalla that the Kondhs, once again incited by a claimant to the throne, committed serious murders. Out of a population of 12000 Kondhs 1500 of them and about 170 villages were involved in them. Ninety-seven persons were convicted including seven to death. In western India, a Koli leader, Honya, began a series of attacks in the north-west of Poona in 1873 on the moneylenders who cheated and oppressed hill tribes and at intervals drove them into crime, until he was caught in 1876. Many of the moneylenders were killed and some of them had their nose cut off. This was both the precursor and spill over of Deccan riots when the Kunbis attacked Marwaris money-lenders. Gang robberies erupted in 1879, led by Kolis and Ramoshis, jointly.

Yet another type of rebellion during this period resulted from the disturbance of the ritual relationship between tribes and their non-tribal chiefs, the nature of which has been highlighted earlier in this book. The Bhuiyas of Keonjhar who had the right to enthrone the ruler, disturbed over the issue of succession, rebelled under Ratna Naik (1861-68). Both Bhuiyas and Juangs supported the *rani* and her protege. The Bhuiyas refused to recognise one Dhanunjay as the ruler and boycotted the coronation ceremony, but Juangs attended it. The Bhuiyas held out for sometime, and then on being released from the oath of allegiance to the *rani*, whom they regarded as their mother, they along with

Juangs performed the investiture ceremony. But their leader Ratna Naik remained unreconcired. In April 1868 the Bhuiyas led by him looted the Keonjhar bazar, carried off the raja's *diwan* who had antagonised them and killed him, besieged the raja for a while and plundered villages. By August, Ratna Naik was captured and the rebellion crushed. But during the trial that followed, barring six persons involved in the murder of the *diwan*, others were let off lightly because the Bhuiyas had "only acted according to their immemorial custom".[33] In a similar fashion the Marias and Bhattras of Bastar protested when their ruler Bhairondeo who was the head priest of Danteshwari, the apex goddess of the tribal belt, planned to visit Bombay in 1876 to see the Prince of Wales. In spite of the fact that some of the *diwan's* attendants shot dead a few Murias, about 10,000 of them along with the Bhattras sat out most peacefully around Jagdalpur. The ministers were banished.[34] But there was more to the rising of 1876. The tribals were giving expression in their own way to their fear of misgovernment; and they had their reasons. Bastar in the latter half of the nineteenth century resembled the Chotanagpur of the first half. There was the same syndrome : influx of aliens, enchroachment on tribals' land and other rights, as the tribal areas were opened up under the colonial rule:

> An alien police from 'civilized' India was soon followed along the gradually expanding lines of communication by Bania and Rohilla tradesmen, and by low-paid esurient subordinate officials 'lent' to the State, who regarded service in a native state only as a means to the rapid acquisition of wealth. Cultivation was to be expanded by the formation of new villages by alien immigrants; instead, the aliens were given long established Bhattra, Muria, Parja or Maria villages nominally as lessees, over the heads of the traditional village headmen; and the lessees at once proceeded as fast as possible to get the best land into their own hands, to make the headmen's lives a burden by their repeated demands for forced labour and supplies to ignore the use and wont of village life, especially the *sari-bori* or co-operation in supplies and labour for village bread-winning and village festivals, to introduce Hindu and

> Mussalman settlers, and to turn the natives of Bastar into bondservants little better than slaves by advancing them money, on terms which made repayment practically impossible, in return for their labour or that of their sons. Every immigrant trader even considered it his right to demand the labour of half a dozen 'Murias' to carry his wares for him.[35]

This process did not substantially change afterwards, in spite of the good administration provided by a couple of officials. In the first decade of the century, the same factors, multiplied manifold and their equation relatively changed, were at work. Behind the tribal uprising of 1910, locally called *bhumakal*, emerged the forest question as the key factor. With the reservation of forest, restrictions were imposed on the tribals' immemorial practice of shifting cultivation. They also had to offer *begar* or forced labour and were forced to sell grain at a much lower rate to local government officials. They objected to the spread of education, because they had to build school buildings and maintain school teachers. Village lessees and petty officials oppressed them.

The tribals' strategy, as in 1876, was to sit around Jagdalpur, its capital, and to starve it out. They converged on Jagdalpur, but this time their plan did not work. The *bhumakal* developed like the Kol insurrection into an allround attack on the aliens, the *pardeshi*, who were mostly "low-caste" people from Chattisgarh settled in the state, and the officials. The Murias, Bhattras, Parjas and Bison-horn Marias joined hands, while the primitive Marias of Abhujhmar and the Murias of the zamindaris abstained, in committing arson, robbery and violence against the *pardeshis*, who were savagely beaten, and in some cases murdered, their womenfolk stripped and turned out naked. It was a movement to keep Bastar for the Bastaris i.e. Bastar forest dwellers. Aliens had no place in it. The *bhumakal* was brutally suppressed. The rebels were disarmed, the ring leaders hanged and several hundred men flogged, because "flogging was considered more humane for such primitives than imprisonment". By way of reform the state was once again brought under the the government management.[36]

Between land and forest, the latter thus emerges much later than land as the focal point of tribal unrest, with the increasing restriction placed on shifting cultivtion. The latter was an aspect of the commercial exploitation of forest resources from the 1870s. Probably the first uprising, resulting from this process, occurred in 1879-80, known as the Rampa (and Rekapally) rebellion, after the place of its occurrence, Rampa, a village in the Chodavaram division of Godavari district, rather than the tribe who led it, the Koyas. The Rampa part of the rebellion was over new toddy rules, a new *abkari* regulation, preventng the drawing of toddy for domestic purposes and leasing the toddy revenue to renters who demanded that tribals' masters, *muttadars*, should pay fees (*chigurupannu*) for the right to tap toddy. The *muttadars*' chief, *mansabdar* threatened to levy an additional tax (*modalupannu*) at the rate of one-half to two-thirds of the *chigurupannu*. This was the proverbial last straw. The old grievances were revived: the constables extorted fowls; the traders, taking advantage of the civil law grabbed their land. In Rekapally, restrictions had been imposed on shifting cultivation (*podu*), and the customary tax of four *annas* an axe had been trebled by the Madras government, which also imposed a tax on the felling of certain species of reserved trees. This was part of the policy of the reservation of forest. The colonial records attribute the rebellion to the "oppressive acts of the *mansabdar*" and the "absence of proper supervision and control on the part of European officers". In fact the two could not be separated. The rebellion started in March 1879. Two constables were sacrificed before the chief shrine by the insurgents. In its sweep the Rampa-Rekapally insurrections could be compared with the Kol and Santal insurrections. The area affected comprised about 5000 square miles of wooded hilly country in which the rebels resorted to guerrilla warfare, avoiding confrontation with troops. They attacked isolated police-stations and looted the villages of those who collaborated with the government. The gravity of the rebellion for the authorities could be assessed by the strength of the forces they deployed to quell it. Harassed by guerrillas, and struck down by malaria, the state forces, aided by Hyderabad, succeded in capturing or killing its leaders and suppressing the rebellion.[37] The Rampa-Rekapally rebellion resulted in the abolition of the *mansabdari* of Rampa, establishment of direct administration by government and reduction of toddy taxes.

In the north-east the Kuki uprising[38] in the state of Manipur had its origin, like the Santal *meli*, in the British need to raise a labour corps to serve in the battle-fields of France. Raising of the first labour corps presented no problem, but as demand for more labourers came in, the people expressed their reluctance, and the local officers retaliated by burning down the offending villages. The Kukis raided some Nepali and Manipur villages, and the rebellion lasted two years. The Kuki killed 289 men and women and burnt 34 villages. The British destroyed 80 villages and lost nearly 192 men of the Assam rifles through death or killing. The Kukis could mobilise 40,000 men, women and children over 6,000 square miles of rugged hills. The Kukis' grievances were building up over issues such as the British ban on formation of new villages, administrative indifference to the famine and forced labour (*pothang*). As the movement developed the Kukis established rapport with Meiteis, the settled agricultural community. The traditional structure of tribal chiefship came into full pay, as also the time-honoured mode of communication by circulating burnt wood, a chilli, a bullet, gunpowder or a kuki earlead, each conveying a specific meaning. Intra-tribal conflicts also surfaced.

III

Let us pull together the strands of our discussion. There was a diversity of tribal movements in the two phases, the first one of primary resistance, both baronial and "plebian" sub-types, and the second one when they centred around agrarian and forest questions, the political issue of the formation of raj and achieving independence and, finally, social reform. While periodisation helps us to understand the changing profile of tribal movements, there are certain processes that tend to overlap.

For example, the drive against the outsiders which marked the Kol and Santal insurrections stirred the Kondhs, Savaras and the Bastar tribals much later. The reason for this is that the penetration of the colonial system in their area was slow, and in princely states all efforts were made to maintain the *status quo*, though market forces operated there without let or hindrance.

The all-out operations against the outsiders who went in as agents of the colonial system need to be seen in the tribals' perspective. The tribe made a distinction between "we" and "they". The latter was, to begin with a territorial and geographical concept, which acquired an economic connotation in the colonial context. The Kol insurrection was directed against the *sud* or *sadan* (not *dikus*) who were the communities settled on the periphery of forest. The *diku* was a Kolarian concept, evolved by the Korku (*de-ko*, the others), picked up by the Santals to identify and chastise the non-ethnic moneylenders, traders and *amlas*, and later applied by the Mundas to the same class of people during the *mulkui larai*. The word *diku* is a generic term for various functional groups belonging to the category of the outsiders as perceived by tribals. Similar terms are in vogue in the north-east. Elsewhere the tribals identify as outsiders either one community such as Pan or Kulta or describe a bunch of communities as *pardeshis*. As market forces penetrated deeper, the *dikus*' position in tribal economy became unassailable, and there was no alternative to putting up with them. Thus the thrust of Birsa's rebellion was not so much against the *dikus* as against the raj that made their exploitation possible. The participation of the communities subordinate to the tribes and the collaboration of various tribes in a rebellion is again an aspect that deserves to be highlighted, because it tended to get attenuated with the tribal movements projecting an ethnic dimension later. By the time we reach the end of our period, tribal movements have become an affair of a tribe or a group of tribes.

Out of a large number of the communities now listed as tribes, only over a dozen participated in tribal movements, the Santal, Munda, Ho and Bhumij of the Chotanagpur—Santal Pargana region, the Kondh, Koya and Savara of Orissa-Andhra, the Bhattra, Parja, and Muria of Bastar, the Bhil, Koli, and Ramoshi, with a few minor tribes such as Juang, Bhuiya, Konda Dora, and Naikda. The tribal aristocracy of the Chero and Gonds was active in the first phase. The Kondh and Savara appear to be more involved in palace intrigues. The Bhils conducted raids and then went on to stage a large-scale movement. As every movement shows, the tribals' dream of primeval freedom embedded in their psyche stirs in some "holy" man (*baba*)'s head in situations of stress, and the vision of the tribal raj returns, and religious movements slide into uprisings, almost effortlessly. It was left to the Chotanagpur tribes to articulate their demands in social, agrarian and even political forms. The dream of a raj haunted the Bhils also, but it was only the Santals and Mundas who tried to give it a shape. Similarly, the movement for social reform influenced only a few tribes who were in touch with Hinduism and later with Christianity. It is wrong to say that by acceping Hindu idioms the Santals tried to subvert Hinduism.[39] There is nothing to indicate that they seriously did so. The Kharwar movement went on, steeped in Santal traditions and influenced deeply by Hinduism.

The movements described above appear to have been confined to the three regions: (i) Chotanagpur-Santal pargana and the adjoining areas of West Bengal and Orissa, peopled by Chotanagpur tribes, (ii) Bhil-Koli-Ramoshi belt of south Rajasthan, north Gujarat, west Madhya Pradesh and north Maharashtra and (iii) South Orissa-Andhra-Bastar region—in that order. The first region accounted for the largest number of rebellions and movements, unless some of the Bhil "raids" are counted, followed by the Bhil-Koli belt, with Orissa-Andhra-Bastar coming last. In the three regions the larger tribes were capable of effective mobilization through their traditional institutions of chiefs and clan or village assembly. Tribal assembly held the key. All elements of the tribals' corporate life were carried into their movements. Dacoities, loot,and murder were the modes of the rebels' strategy, ruthlessly enforced. Spontaneity and speed of the tribal movements have often been commented upon, but the elements of planning and organization behind them also deserve to be highlighted.

The results of the uprising were also not uniform. While in British India they achieved a non-regulation administrative system for tribes and special agrarian laws to protect tribal land, little was done or allowed to be done for them in princely states, in spite of the fact that the political agent did intervene to uphold status quo rather than promote change. This ambivalence was typical of the colonial system. While the leadership of the first phase emerged from the upper crust of tribal society, that of the second rose from the lowest rung of it. The Santal brothers were landless, Birsa Munda was a raiyat or a *parja* (crop-sharer) and Govind Giri was a *hali*. The goals of the movement ranged from the restoration of service tenure (Chuar) and land (Sardar) to expulsion of outsiders, social reform, political independence and establishment of the tribal raj. The composition of the movements varied from a confederacy of tribes and the castes sub-ordinate to the tribes to a tribe.

Yet one more aspect of the tribal movements is the correlation between tribal and non-tribal movements. The phase of baronial resistance saw non-tribal zamindars and their rank and file such as *paiks*, *bissoyis*, *muttadars*, *mansabdars* and *naiks*. revolt as the system to which they were linked broke up. There were also many points of similarities between the peasant and tribal-peasant movements later. Like peasant movements, tribal movements were local, confined to a particular tribe or a group of tribes. Few tribal and peasant movements cut across local and community barriers and developed into a regional and nationwide movement. However, the tribal movements were far more numerous than peasant movements during this period. While the peasant movements tended to remain purely agrarian as peasants lived off land, the tribal movements were both agrarian and forest-based, because the tribals' dependence on forests was as crucial as was their dependence on land. A tribal was both a peasant and a non-peasant. There was also the ethnic factor. The tribal revolts were directed against zamindars, moneylenders and petty government officials not only because they exploited them but also because they were non-ethnics, aliens. The social horizon of the tribal movements was wider than that of the peasant. The tribals sought a higher social status and a better political dispensation through their movements. The peasants integrated within the politico-social framework of the larger society sought the solution only of agrarian problems. The socio-cultural factor was well articulated in tribal movements. The peasant and tribal movements did not generally merge or form a common front because ethnic differences between the two were sharp and certain sections of the peasants exploited the tribals. There were some cases of involvement of the tribals in peasant-led movements organised by the political parties later, but it was only marginal at that stage of development, and the tribe-peasant equation is still in the process of being established in ongoing movements.[40]

Note and References

1. See, for example, Ranjit Guha, *Elementary Aspects of Peasant Insurgency in Colonial India*. In this excellent study Guha tried not only to link up horizontally the Kol Insurrection, *hul* and Birsa's movement to trace the broad traits, overlooking the crucial differences between them, but also tribal and peasant movements. The leaders of peasant movements have described the tribals as aboriginal *kisans* and contented themselves with observations like this: "The Santhal rebellion of the last century and the Koya revolt of the thirties of this century and the recent agitation among the Bhils of Dahenu, the tribes of Mymensingh, and Mayurbhanj have shown that these aboriginal tribes too have in them the irrepressible spirit of revolt that can shake up modern capitalist hegemony to its very roots."See N. G. Ranga and Swami Sahajanand Saraswati, *Agrarian Revolts*, p. 75. Even in perceptive writings little attempt has been made to identify the similarities and differences between tribe and peasant and the structures of their movements beyond the bland observation that some of the "most successful communist-led peasant actions" such as those of Tebhaga in 1946, Telengana in 1946-48, Naxalbari in 1967, and Andhra Pradesh in 1969-71 involved "a large component of tribal people",Kathleen Gough, "Indian Peasant Uprisings", A. R. Desai (ed.) *Peasants Struggles in India*.
2. Quoted in *District Gazetteer*, *Manbhum* (1911) pp. 65-7.
3. Christoph von Furer-Haimendorf, "Aboriginal Rebellions in the Deccan" *Man in India, Rebellion Number*, Dec. 1945; also see his Forword

to K. S. Singh, *Birsa Munda and his movement* 1874-1901.

4. *Gazetteer of the Bombay Presidency, Poona District* Vol. XVIII, Part II, 1885, pp. 227-8.

5. James M. Campbell (ed.), *Gazetteer of the Bombay Presidency, Khandesh*, Vol. XII, p. 254.

6. R. V. Russell (ed.) *Central Provinces Distt. Gazetteer, Betul District* 1907, pp. 37-8.

7. Charles Grant, *The Gazetteer of the Central Provinces of India* 1870, pp. IXXXV-CV.

8. S. B. Choudhary, *Civil Disturbances in India* 1757-1857, pp. 67-72.

9. Samar Ku. and B. Hansda, "Amar Shahid Baba Tilka Manjhi," *Adivasi* 9/16 August, 1984, Ranchi.

10. A. P. Ibrahim Kunju, "The Kuricciyar and the Palassi Rebellion" (unpublished).

11. See for details, S. B. Choudhary, *Civil Disturbances in India.*

12. L.S.S. O'Malley, *District Gazetteer, Sambalpur* 1909, pp. 26-27.

13. T. J. Maltby, *The Ganjam District Manual,* pp. 193 & 196.

14. M. Campbell, James, op. cit. pp. 256-61.

15. See J. C. Jha, The *Kol Insurrection in Chotanagpur*, The *Bhumij Revolt* 1832-33,

16. J. Reid, *Final Report on the Survey and Settlement Operation in the District of Ranchi* 1902-1912, p. 22.

17. For the *hul*, See, W. W. Hunter, *The Annals of Rural Bengal*; K. K. Datta, *Anti-British Plots and Movements before* 1857; N. B. Roy, "New Aspects of the Santal Insurrection of 1855-6," *Indian Historical Records Commission Proceedings*, Vol. XXXV, Part II, Feb. 1960,

18. LSS O'Malley, *District Gazetteer, Santal Pargana,* pp. 48-52, 1910.

19. Ibid., pp. 52-54.

20. K. K. Datta, op. cit. p. 106.

21. For the Kharwar movement, See Rev. P. O. Bodding, "The Kharwar Movement Among the Santals", *Man in India*, vol. I, September, 1921; A. P. Jha, "Nature of the Santhal Unrest of 1871-75 and origin of the Sapha Hor Movement", *India Historical Records Commission Proceedings*, Vol. XXXV, Part II File 1960; and Narahari Kaviraj, "The Santhal Agitation over the Rent Question", *Problems of National Liberation* vol. I, no. I, November 1974.

22. India Office Library, L/P & J/6/1488

23. K. S. Singh, *Birsa Munda and his movement.*

24. See James M. Campbell, *Gazetteer of the Bombay Presidency, Khandesh*, pp. 309-14.

25. Ibid.

26. Quoted in C.S.K. Singh, Tribal Movement in Rajasthan 1920-47 (Unpublished thesis).

27. Ibid.

28. W. Francis, *District Gazetteer of Vizagapatnam*, 1907 pp. 304-5.

29. W. J. Culshaw and W. G. Archer, The Santal Rebellion, *Man in India, Rebellion Number* Dec. 1945; Kalipada Mitra, "Santal Insurrection in Chotanagpur," *Bengal Past and Present*, vol. VIII, Jan-June, 1940.

30. *Bombay District Gazetteer*, *Panch Mahals*, *Gujarat*, pp. 254-8.

31. Foreign Political Department 1932 No. 643 (I) National Archives of India.

32. Verrier Elwin, "Saora Fituris" *Man in India*, *Rebellion Number* op. cit. The Savaras' bloody attacks on Pans who had become Christian, came in January, 1941.

33. Foreign Political Department 1932, op. cit.

34. L.E.B. Cobden-Ramsay *Feudatory States of Orissa*, pp. 215-22.

This relationship of the Bastar ruler with his tribe was dramatically confirmed when he was killed with some tribals on 25 and 28 March, 1966. See Justice Kanhaiya Lal Pande, *Report on the Disturbances which took place at Jagdalpur on the 25th and 26th March 1966.*

35. W. V. Grigson, *The Maria Gonds of Bastar*, p. 14.

36. E. Clementi Smith, "The Bastar Rebellion," *Man in India*, *Rebellion Number*, pp. 252-3; also pp. 16-17.

37. F. R. Hemingway, *District Gazetteer of Godavari* (Madras District), 1907, pp. 36-37, 270-76.

38. Gautam Bhadra, "The Kuki (?) uprising (1917-1919): Its Causes and Nature," *Man in India* January-March, 1975.

39. Ranjit Guha, op. cit. p. 73.

40. K. S. Singh, "Agrarian Dimensions Of Tribal Movements," A. R. Desai (ed.) Agrarian Struggls in Post-Independence India (forthcoming).

8

The Freedom Movement and Tribal Sub-movements

The tribal people, by and large, remained isolated and backward, and their participation in national politics, unlike that of the harijans, was inconsiderable. They were almost the last of the Indian communities to be politicized. But research into the freedom movement in different parts of the country, which has been recently undertaken in terms of the social composition of regional movements, has revealed a rich pattern of the involvement of local communities in regional politics. Evidence suggests that like other communities, tribal groups participated intensely in local politics, but with a difference. There was an attempt on the part of the tribal community to seek integration into the regional and national systems and also to preserve its identity.

Jawaharlal Nehru, speaking retrospectively of the nature and range of tribal prarticipation in India's freedom movement, observed:

> For half a century or more, we have struggled for freedom and ultimately achieved it. That struggle, apart from anything else, was a fresh liberating force. . .We must remember that this experience of hundreds of millions did influence the tribes in Central India to some extent but, in the frontier areas of Assam for instance, they remained almost unaffected by it. This was partly due to the inadequacy of the means of communication available to us in the old days. Of course, there were other reasons too.
>
> One of the reasons was that the city people were a little afraid to leave their familiar haunts and go into the mountains. . . . Apart from our own lack of initiative, we were not allowed to go there by the British authorities then in power. That is why our freedom movement reached these people only in the shape of occasional rumours. Sometimes they reacted rightly and sometimes wrongly, but that is beside the point.[1]

Jawaharlal Nehru's views were typical of the nationalist appreciation of the tribal question, which was concerned with larger issues and which tended to play down the role of parochial (caste and communal) politics in the formation of movements.

In contrast to the nationalist approach, which reacted understandably sharply to the separatist movements and assumed too much unity and uniformity in an essentially pluralistic situation, there was another line of thinking. The latter assumed that separatist movements in tribal India were typical of Indian conditions, and were the precursor of the Indian states' "inevitable" process of disintegration. Here is a specimen of this line of thinking in what is otherwise a good piece of writing on the Jharkhand movement:

> Harrison, a perspicacious American commentator reminded us, as late as 1960, that the *unity* if India was based on tenuous foundations, foundations perpetually inclined to disintegrate and thus make room for a possible emergence of Communist take-over....It is pointless to harp on cultural similarities between the victim and the victor....nothing can be deduced about *inergroup relations, particularly power relations, if* we *begin* analysis via the concept of culture. The crucial questions to be asked in this context are: who can compel whom, when, in which respect, and how?
>
> Let us remember the facts: creation of Pakistan, separatism *par excellence;* carving out of Andhra; consolidation of Maharashtra; earlier, separation of Bihar and Orissa from Bengal in 1912, the birth of Orissa in 1936; now, the Punjabi Suba agitation and the birth of Haryana as a separate state; the DMK movement, muted for the time being; the demand for Jharkhand. If analysis succeeds in rising above the cloud of *cultural* confusion, the answer to the question, 'who compels whom', will emerge vividly.[2]

Within four years of the publication of this piece of prognostication, the Jharkhand party had merged with the Congress and the Jharkhand movement had become moribund.

This approach overlooks the fact that nation-building is a continuing process and that the search for identity by small, backward, and sensitive communities should not always be considered antinational.

In the present chapter an attempt has been made to analyse the historical processes of integration during the pre-independence phase, their assimilation with regional movements, and their search for identity. It should be noted that the social milieu of tribal middle India is entirely different from that of the north-east. In the first region, tribal people do not constitute the majority except in about eight districts and forty *taluqas*; they live with other communities. The society and economy are composite in nature; interaction, and not exclusiveness, has been the important element in social formation. Therefore, in this region separatism has never developed into secessionism, the tribal demand for autonomy as will be described later, has been expressed in constitutional terms.

Documentation of the processes of tribal politics (1920-47) has not been easy. The story of the tribal movement from the 1920s onwards exists piecemeal, often under misleading labels, and such accounts as are available are not without a slant. It is not easy to piece together the fragments of the story from private papers and archival sources and field study, stay clear of the existing stereotypes that have conditioned our thinking on this subject, and seek an understanding in terms of the tribals' own perception of the issues at stake.

Tribal politics in the pre-1920 phase could be described in terms of a series of revolts, sporadic, isolated and spontaneous. Led by tribes who were settling down as agrarian communities, they resisted erosion of agrarian and forest rights. Inspired by the primeval dream of freedom, these movements aimed at the total restructuring of the primitive system which was breaking down under the impact of the colonial economy. They were violent, and were ruthlessly crushed. Certain tribes, such as the Bhil and Mina who had been uprooted and lived in conditions of turmoil, had adopted banditry as a form of social protest. Their leaders, officially described as 'pests', were in fact peasant rebels.

The phase of tribal politics which began after 1920 was relatively free from such episodes and was marked by movements which could be sustained only by organization and through external stimuli. The latter were provided by the nationalist struggle which came to the tribal world in the 1920s through the message and personality of Mahatma Gandhi, to be described later.

Among the tribes which responded to the movement and the Mahatma[3] were the Santals, Oraons, Bhils and Gonds, all major tribes. Among them, the sections which responded particularly were those who had already been sanskritized or sensitized to Vaishnavism. The leaders of these sects were the bhagats steeped in the bhakti tradition, like Hindu peasants elsewhere, and they understood the idioms in which Gandhi's message was couched. The Bhil bhagats, the Tanabhagats among Oraons, and the Sapha Hors among Santals, the Haribaba movement among the Hos (1930) and the Rajmohini movement among the Gonds, saw in the freedom movement led by Gandhi an opportunity for the recovery of the tribal raj and the rights as agrarian communities which they had lost, for continuing social reforms such as temperance, purification and education, and for seeking social uplift and establishing an equation with peasant castes. Most of these bhagat sects in their origin antedated the freedom movement. They received a fresh lease of life through Gandhi's reconstruction programme. Many bhagats became faithful followers of the Indian National Congress and clung tenaciously to its programme in the most adverse circumstances. They became standard-bearers of the freedom movement among tribes in the backward regions. Interestingly, most of the leadres of the movement among the Hos and the Bhils called themselves the *chelas* of Gandhi. The significance of the "nationalization" of the bhagat movements was considerable, even though the bhagats were only a minority among their people.

The best known of bhagat movements was the Tanabhagat movement[4] which started in the manner of a nativistic movement. On April 21, 1914, an Oraon youth of 20 to 25 years of age, Jatra Oraon, proclaimed that he had received the divine message from the Dharmesh, the Supreme God, in a dream, together with the divine power and supernatural gifts necessary for the restoration of the Oraon raj. He would be a raja and his followers would share his kingdom and be rajas too. He had also been entrusted with the mission to teach incantations (*mantras*) to pull out (*tana*) ghosts and spirits whose worship degraded the people and to purify and reform their lives so that they could be equal to the Christian and Hindus in social status. Monotheism, 'vegetarianism' and 'teetotalism' were the elements of the new religion. Jatra was the new god, and none was to be obeyed except him and his disciples. As the movement progressed, the agrarian issues came to the fore. The ghost-haunting drive gave way to a no-rent payment campaign. Jatra was arrested on 21 April 1914 on the charge of carrying on a mischievous propaganda which endangered peace. On his release on 2 June 1915, he was heartily welcomed back by his followers, but he would not burn his fingers again and faded out. A succession of 'gurus' followed. A woman, Litho Oraon, declared herself a goddess and preached along the same lines as Jatra did. The Tanabhagat movement spread among the Oraon population of Ranchi, Palamau and Hazaribagh. She too was charged like Jatra to stand a trial. On her release, she too faded into oblivion. In November, 1915, Mangra Oraon proclaimed himself a god and suffered the same fate. The movement slumbered until March 1919 when it showed renewed activity under the leadership of Sibu Oraon and Maya Oraon. Sibu Oraon, a boy of 20 years, solemnly declared in March 1919 that he was destined to become the leader of the world, that the raj would shortly return to the Oraon and that a great change in the order of things would take place after the Holi festival. In his new order, zamindars, traders and Government and Christians would have no place. Collecting about 700 to 800 followers Sibu proceeded to Satpahari (Chandwa) where his followers expected the advent of a deity, a saviour. Sibu and Maya were arrested at Murma on 17 March. The movement led by Sibu fizzled out by the end of the year.

The Tanabhagats had however been able to create a state of excitement and unrest among the entire population, both tribal and non-tribal, and bring the agrarian issue to the fore. Another factor which made for instability was the removal through deportation of the German missionaries who had exercised restraining influence on the Oraons at the beginning of the First World War. This was the background to the uprising, a short-lived affair, on the plateau of the Jamira Pat which lay across the border of Surguja state (Madhya Pradesh) and Palamau (Bihar). The Oraons and Kisans (Nagesia) preponderated in this sparsely populated region. The Tanabhagat movement came to this region in 1915. Meetings were held in villages. People gave up drinking alcohol; domestic birds and animals were turned out of houses and killed in large numbers because they harboured evil. The tribals also gave up tilling lands. When the authorities took action, the movement went underground. By March 1918, the message of the revolution, scribed on *sal* leaves, began to circulate from village to village. On 16 April, the clarion-call went out. The rebels under their leaders two of whom were *banias* (moneylenders) set up their camp on the Panchpahari (the five hills). On 21 April, they started looting villages, murdering the aliens; the first victims belonged to the Ahir and Kahar castes. The rebels' ranks swelled as they achieved success on April 25. A large number of rebels making horrible war cries, displaying their weapons and dancing widly raided the camp of the state's magistrate at Jalgali, who was killed. Villages were deserted. The "aliens" and *sahebs* fled. Those who remained in villages were savagely killed with characteristic tribal vengeance. Between 21 April and 4 May 1918, the rebels looted fourteen villages and killed fifty one non-tribals. Gopahatu became their capital. The State forces advanced setting fire to tribals' houses. The backbone of the rebels was broken after engaging them in a few skirmishes. The rebels' headquarters at Gopahatu was dismantled; a rebel leader who claimed possession of the mysterious weapon was killed. The two *bania* leaders were arrested and sentenced to death. Those who did not take any leading part were let off; those who did were sentenced to corporal punishment. All was over by 27 May.

The uprising over, the Tanabhagat movement in the heartland of the Oraon country, sought a new outlet and merged with the Congress-led non-cooperation movement when it arrived in the tribal region in 1921. The Congress worked upon the corpus of agrarian ideas then prevailing and reminded tribal people that they were the original rajas of the country, who had become coolies. If they gave up drinking liquor and using foreign cloth they would become raja again. The Gandhi raj would usher in the tribal millennium. Gandhi was a god or a demi-god, who was going to drive out the English without the help of guns and soldiers and establish a *dharam* raj (the kingdom of righteousness). The Tana movement subsequently integrated with the political mainstream and the Congress ideology. Under the impact of the new forces the agrarian issues were first radicalised. The Tanabhagats declared that they would not pay rent and hold their lands rent-free, which resulted in the sale of their land in many cases. The Tanas' agrarian movement tapered off as they got involved in the freedom struggle. They became the strong bastion of the Congress movement in Chotanagpur,

While the tribes accepted the nationalist programme and joined the mainstream of the national movement they were also not unmindful of the demands of their situation. Swaraj meant not only freedom from British rule, but also freedom from the oppression of the *dikus*, money-lenders, zamindars and feudal-overlords. *Ràm rajya* was interpreted as a restoration of the tribal world of primitive freedom, of the golden age of the race, the memory of which had survived. Freedom to them meant restoration of agrarian and forest rights.

The impact of Mahatma Gandhi and the mechanics of the reconstruction programme as it was conceived and implemented in the tribal areas needs a little more elaboration. Recent research has revealed a much more extensive impact by the Mahatma on the tribes of the remote regions than has been assumed. Gandhi *Baba* found his way into the tribal rituals and pantheon, but more suggestive appears to be his impact on tribal folklore in an isolated region like Bastar—leaving aside, of course, the more exposed Halbas and Mariass.[5]

An excellent case-study of the reconstruction programme (1922-47) among the adivasis of Vedachi (Surat)[6] shows how, with the Vedachi movement, the trend for social reform had already been initiated among the tribes. Even before the Gandhi movement began:

> ....a sort of religious movement had begun among the Kaliparaj (Adivasis). A goddess was moving about and was preaching to the people to not drink liquor toddy. In some districts of Gujarat the movement broke down. But the Chaudhries stuck to the orders of the goddess.[7]

The Gandhian workers built upon the movement of social and economic reform started by the tribal people themselves, which enjoined abstinence from liquor, toddy and meat, after the norms of the high caste Hindus. The Gandhians added a political dimension, and brought tribal and non-tribal communities together on the same platform:

> The Adivasis who distrusted the non-Adivasis could see that the programme of political movement and their own had a good deal in common. The new movement was therefore acceptable to them. This movement helped in blunting the edge of the Adivasis' distrust of the non-Adivasis and served the Adivasis and non-Adivasis to a common good, programme and ideology enunciated by the non-Adivasis.[8]

The Vedachi movement popularized khadi spinning, introduced education, promoted thrift and debt relief and tenancy reform. It brought economic benefits and "strengthened the property-owning strata" among them. In fact a "small committed and dedicated stratum of educated and education-oriented adivasis with new outlook and aspirations",[9] had emerged, ready to act as agents of change in their own society.

Much the same pattern of developments resulted from the operation of the reconstruction programme elsewhere in India and from the rise of autonomous movements for social reform among the tribes. In 1938, Gula Maharaj, a Bhil reformer, who worked as an ordinary labourer, urged his followers to give up drink, in Tolada taluka of Bombay.[10] His influence spread far and wide in the Bhil country.

The political aspect of the tribals' urge for reform was brought out through their participation in the Prajamandal movements. The tribes who responded particularly to these movements were the Bhils, Gonds, Kharwars, Mundas and Khonds. Most of them had a notion of property, private or communal, in land, which had been threatened by the colonial system and feudal exploitation. The agrarian issues which excited them were the demands for *begar* or *veth* (compulsory labour without payment) *rasad* or *magan* (free supply of provisions for visiting officers), and exactions other than rent (*abwabs*). Rent by itself was not a burning issue, because its incidence was very low in unsettled tribal areas (the exception being the Gangpur agitation against the enhanced rate of rent which lasted from 1939 to 1942). By the 1920s the process of the reclamation of tribes to 'civilization' had been almost completely implemented everywhere, and aided by economic factors, tribes in many parts of the country had settled down as agricultural communities which resented feudal exactions. The Kisan movement in Bihar (Palamau) and the Prajamandal agitation in Orissa, although led by non-tribal people belonging to the castes which were traditionally antipathetic towards the tribes, evoked support from the latter. The Khonds participated in the Prajamandal agitation in 1939 which sought to secure their agrarian and forest rights. The Kisan movement on the periphery of Chotanagpur agitated against feudal imposts.

The tribals' participation in peasant movements deserves to be discussed in some depth at this stage. The impact of Kisan sabha, the best organised peasant movement in Bihar, on tribals in Chotanagpur and Santal Pargana was minimal, in spite of the efforts made by its leader, Swami Sahajanand to establish its bases in Chotanagpur. One reason for this could be that the Chotanagpur's tribal peasants enjoyed the rights and privileges which had yet to be recognised elsewhere in Bihar. The other reason could be that the tribals were getting involved in the political movement seeking a new identity for themselves. They kept out of the Kisan movement as much as this movement kept out of the tribal areas. This is strikingly shown by the experience of the Santal movement which swept parts of Monghyr and Bhagalpur during the period 1932-35. This agrarian movement was directed against the *thicadars* who took away Santals' land, the zamindars who arbitrarily imposed high rent and collected illegal cesses, the zamindars' agents who restricted tribals' traditional rights in forest and against the moneylenders who charged exhorbitant interest. Yet the Kisan sabha did not take up any of tribals' demands, nor did the Swami make any reference to them in his speeches and writings. Besides, neither the Sabha nor the Congress had any strong foothold in the tribal areas, and their cadre with a few exceptions largely consisted of the elements that exploited the tribals. The Santals however managed to win recognition of their rights without the support of the Kisan Sabha, and the authorities amended the Bihar Tenancy Act to protect tribals' land against alienation. In Chotanagpur a Kisan sabha of sorts was set up in 1931 by the Oraon tribals led by Theble Oraon but nothing came of it. In Gujarat the tribals (*kaliparaj*) did not likewise gain from the "non-tribal" Patidars' agrarian movement. However, the movement among the Bhils and Garasias led by a non-Bhil political activitst Motilal Tejawat, turned out to be a good example of tribal mobilisation. Like peasant movements, the Bhil movement was directed against high incidence of rent, *begar*, *rasad* (free supply of provisions for visiting officers) and other "feudal" exactions. Motilal combined agrarian issues with social reform, popularised by bhagat movements, such as abstention from drinking liquor and eating meat, and discontinuance of bride price, and sought to articulate them through his organization "Eka". Although Motilal was described as an "emissary of Gandhi" and the Mahatma did intervene once to praise the "good effect of his work", the movement did not remain non-violent, with the "armed Bhils" swelling its ranks to harvest crops forcibly. The Garasias clashed with the Sirohi authorities on 12 April, 1922, and lost three of their men before being driven off into hills. On 4 May eleven Bhils were killed at Rohera by the state forces which also burnt down their houses and destroyed their grains. The rebellion became widespread. At its root lay the Bhils' distant dream of founding the "Bhil raj" and their immediate anger over over-assemssent of rent, payment of cesses and revenue in kind and rendering of *begar*. The Eka was broken. Motilal was arrested on 3 June 1929, but was released later. The agrarian issues affecting the Bhils were later taken up by the Prajamandal and Congress movements and continued to be pressed under their auspices by Motilal till 1947.

The CPI-led Kisan Parishad organised the Warlis in Thane to launch a movement (it was called and dealt with as a revolt) seeking the abolition of forced labour (*vethi*) which they, no better than serfs, performed for their masters. This went on for two years from 1945 to 1947, and resulted in the Warlis gaining freedom from serfdom and adequate remuneration for work. The Warlis were also sufficiently politicised, in the process, to take part later in the movement for Samyukta Maharashtra in the mid-1950s.[11]

The leaders of the freedom movement in the tribal regions of the Central Provinces and the Bombay Presidency oriented their strategy to involve forest communities. Manufacturing salt was not as easy as violating the forest regulations. The no-rent payment campaign affected settled peasant communities, but the forest satyagraha in the 1930s involved the tribes, viz., the Korkus (Betul), Gonds (Mandla) and Kolis (Bombay). The forest satyagraha stemmed from the discontent caused by the restrictions on grazing rights, erosion of the traditional rights to take fuel and fodder from forests, and the oppression of forest officials. The leadership of this movement came from outside, but the tribal response was most enthusiastic. The incidents always turned violent despite the exhortations to remain non-violent, in characteristic tribal fashion. A Congress report said: "The Gonds went in a mass to break forest laws. Here unfortunately the illiterate Gonds could not maintain the spirit of non-violence, and were successfully provoked by the police to some act of violence". The Bhils acted similarly in 1922 and the Kolis in 1931 in Bombay.

Both within the ambit of the Congress-led movement and without the forest question revolved around the frictions between forest officials, particularly the subordinate ones, intent on demaracting the boundaries of forest and the tribals seeking to resist it by asserting their traditional right to reclaim land and cultivate it. The Gonds' clash with the forest and police officials, called *fituri* in 1940, dramatised the conflict between these two notions. The Gonds led by a charismatic leader Kumra Bhimu, cultivated the land, which the Forest department claimed to be its own, at Babejheri for past five years. For Bhimu Babejheri was the end of a long journey in search of land, and all that he and his people wanted was a *patta* (title deed) which "outsiders" could manage to get so easily. The forest department tried to evict Bhimu and his people from the land they had occupied and shift them elsewhere. At this stage:

> It seems, however, that Bhimu and the Gonds of Jodeghat decided to resist evacuation by force and collected several hundred malcontent Gonds to support them. There are some indications that Bhimu claimed magical powers and the faculty of hearing the voices of gods, but in this there is nothing extraordinary, for in almost every Gond village there is a *bhaktal* who is capable of trance-experiences and at certain ceremonies is possessed by 'gods' and prophecies under their inspiration. Bhimu was apparently of the same mental disposition, but possessed in addition great intelligence and power of leadership. Hence he was able to voice the latent dissatisfaction and exasperation of the Gonds and to arouse several hundred men to active resistance against the forest subordinates, and this involved them ultimately also with the police....far too much has been made of his reputation as a religious leader; the idea that he intended to found a "Gond Raj" or had any such-reaching plans seems entirely erroneous; his and his co-villagers' aims were always strictly limited, namely their undisturbed cultivation of land in Jhoreghat. The fact that hundreds of other Gonds rallied to his cause is a symptom of their bitterness against the forest subordinates, and in this way they hoped they might rid themselves of their burdens.[12]

The inevitable followed:

> ....The Taluqdar decided to march to Jodeghat with a force of 100 police, accompanied by the DSP [Deputy Superintendent

of Police], the Civil Surgeon, and the Asst. Taluqdar and Tahsildar. They left on the 4th *Aban* and camped at Vaudham from which they sent messengers to Bhimu in an endeavour to bring him to his senses. Bhimu continued to send defiant messages, and a reconnaissance of the hill showed that drums were beating and hundreds of men were shouting defiance. Early on the 6th before dawn the force made its way 800 feet up to the plateau on which the Jodhighat is perched. They may lay through thick jungle. On reaching the village before 7 a.m. it was found that some 500 Gonds collected from various places were massed outside the village, fully armed with guns, swords, spears, hatchets, and lathis,. For four hours the Taluqdar and and his other officers endeavoured by persuation to induce the mob to lay down its arms. They were allowed by the hand of Mahdeo to reduce their grievances to writing, and the Taluqdar went to the extent of giving them in writing an order to the DFO [Division Forest Officer] that no dues should be collected until the court case was completed. This did not satisfy the crowd. Eventually Deoji and about six others, who formed a deputation, gave the Taluqdar an ultimatum that he must leave with the police, otherwise they would be killed to a man. Cries of 'come back' were heard in Gondi, and it was understood that on their return the attack would begin. The deputation was therefore passed between the lines and detained. At once the mob began to approach at a fast walk from its position 80, yards away. The Asstt. Taluqdar says he saw a number of bullets fly past. The Taluqdar decided in consulation with the DSP that the moment had come for use force. The Gonds had ample warning, and had been shown the force at his disposal. Several began to sway to and fro, as if possessed. . . . a sign that bloodshed would follow. Orders were given to use buckshot, but when this proved of no avail to stop the mob, ball and 'quick fire' was ordered. A fusillade began. Bhimu fell ten yards in front of the line of police, and near him his nephew. The crowd broke and fled into the jungle, leaving, eight others dead and 13 wounded. Several Gonds were arrested inside houses, with loaded guns.[13]

This was a typically "official" version of the incident which was sought to be corrected at other levels. However, this incident, among others, demonstrated the extent of the influence of the forest factor, alongside land, in the mobilisation of tribals.

While the tribals showed a penchant for protest movements

they had no interest in the sedate constitutional politics of the local and district boards in the 1920s and the 1930s. The Bhils and Gonds remained indifferent to the elections to these bodies, and had to be nominated to them. Even so, they were not interested in their deliberations and activities. In fact, this indifference born of ignorance was considered sufficient reason for perpetuating their backwardness through their exclusion from the operation of the Government of India Act of 1935 and for delaying their recognition as a *minority* in India politics.

By the 1940s tribal involvement in the freedom movement had become widespread, even though there was less manifestation of unrest than in 1930-2. Several regions of tribal middle India, which had not been affected by the Civil Disobedience movement, felt the impact of the Quit India movement. A typical example was found in Koraput. Lakshman Naik, a Bhumia, who had given up hunting and become a vegetarian under the influence of Gandhian ideology, offered satyagraha in 1939-40. He organized resistance to payment of taxes and led a march of the Bondo highlanders on 31 August 1942. They picketed liquor shops, and there was a scuffle in the course of which a forest guard was was killed. Lakshman Naik was implicated in this case and hanged on 29 March 1943, even though he was universally believed to be innocent.[14]

It was not always the politics of the non-violent movement and social reform that interested the tribal people. The Koyas and Jatapus of the Agency area (Rampa) of the Madras Presidency participated in a rebellion or *fituri*[15] (1922-3) and guerilla warfare waged by Alluri Sitaram Raju (1898-1923) who sought to overthrow the British raj and set himself up as the raja. A ksatriya, he had acquired the reputation of a sanyasin, astrologer and magician which attracted the rural folk. Influenced by the Non-Cooperation Movement, he preached temperance and the wearing of khadi which did not go down well with hill people. While there were factors of agrarian discontent arising from the restrictions on *podu* or shifting cultivation, extraction of forced labour and illtreatment of coolies, the movement was essentially political, designed to achieve independence. Raju, with the support of the *doras* the upper crust of tribal society, was able to establish a mass base for his movement. He took "scrupulous care not to antagonise the people" and in turn enjoyed their support. He denounced the British officers and the police establishment but there were no "incidents" involving the "Indians". The agrarian issue, which was relegated to the background, did not manifest itself in any attack on the moneylenders or the traders. The movement was suppressed, but Raju's martyrdom helped to strengthen the freedom movement in the Telugu region.

The north-eastern tribal region remained relatively free from the political influences of the kind that bore upon the tribal situation in middle India. However, there were two exceptions. The movement launched by Jadunang,[16] (1929-32) and the Riang movement led by Ratanmani, were structurally closer to the tribal movements in middle India. Jadunang, like the leaders of tribal social movements elsewhere, started as a reformer and religious leader. He acquired a reputation as a mystic, healer, soothsayer and prophet. He preached monotheism, which alone could provide a base for unity among the tribes worshipping a multitude of spirits and deities. Gradually, his movement, which had turned revivalistic, developed political overtones. Jadunang had seen Gandhi when the latter visited Cachar in 1927 and even composed a song in his honour. This was the only apparent link with the national movement, but its impact appeared to be deeper. Jadunang called upon the people to disobey unjust laws, stop payment of taxes and refuse to render forced labour. The British raj, it was rumoured, was coming to an end, and a Naga raj under Jadunang would be established. (This has been the refrain of all tribal movements in middle India, too.) Jadunang was captured and hanged on 29 August 1931. Rani Gaidinliu, who took over the leadership, established an even stronger link with the national movement. She was arrested and Jawaharlal Nehru sought to secure her release. He described her as the "brave child of her hills, with the free spirit of the mountains in her, whose story India ought to know and to cherish".[17]

Like Jadunang, Ratanmani[18] started as a reformer and a

guru among his people. "The Riangs",[19] he would say, "are simple and foolish. They do not know God and religion. Seeing this I decided to propagate the name of God among may people. Now many are reciting the name of God. They are thirsty for the message".

He preached a form of Shaivism which brought him into conflict with the religion of the establishment, Vaishnavism. It did did not take long for this religious movement to turn political (1942-3). Though it professed loyalty to the Maharaja of Tripura, the distant feudal lord, it demanded that the intermediate feudal structure consisting of the *rais* or the headmen be reformed, that they should be elected rather than nominated by the Maharaja, and that they cease to impose fines and collect taxes. Ratanmani set up an alternative government. He declared that he was a friend of the poor and it was therefore right to protect them against injusticc. His followers disobeyed and defied the traditional *rais* and *choudhuris*, who exercised judicial powers and oppressed the people. Meanwhile, a famine had ravaged the land. Ratanmani's disciples set up a few grain depots in their villages to distribute grain. There were two instances in which the property of the *choudhuris* was looted. The authorities apprehended resistance to the recruitment of the Riang youth for the army.

Over-zealous intelligence officers, alarmed at the possibilities of Japanese invasion, reported that Ratanmani and his followers had organized "a revolutionary party consisting of 10 to 12 thousand workers....had committed treason and equipped with arms and ammunition, were robbing the rich of their valuaable property". They were also charged with forming a heinous conspiracy to dethrone the Maharaja, and place Ratanamani on the throne. Later reports, however, denied the existence of any fifth columnist conspiracy and dispelled the impression that Ratanamani was pro-Japanese. There was nothing to indicate the existence of any link with the freedom movement or with the I.N.A. With the Japenese knocking at the gate, the government felt that it could not afford to allow the movement to continue. It was put down by the army. Ratanmani was arrested; he was stated to have died of cholera in December 1943. A large number of his followers were hauled up and complelled to wear the sacred thread and to shave their heads in token of their reconversion to Vaishnavism.

We have briefly discussed the impact of the freedom movement on the tribal region and the attempts by small tribal movements to seek to identify themselves with it. There was also the countervailing process of the tribes moving away from the mainstream of national politics to seek a political identity of their own. The process of political separatism started as the era of constitutional reforms after the First World War dawned. Like some other communities, the tribes demanded special privileges. In the east, a Naga club was set up to formulate demands to be placed before the Simon Commission. Its political aspirations, as reflected in the memoranda, did not go beyond the demand for the withdrawal of Nagaland from the framework of proposed constitutional reforms and for continuation of direct British rule for the Nagas. This was not accepted, despite intensive lobbying by the British administrators in London. However, the officials did not give up. In the early 1940s they formulated a plan for the establishment of a Crown Colony[20] This too did not make any headway.

The unfolding of these two developments—viz., tribal identification with the nationalist movement and the quest for a separate identity suggests that political separatism was not a force to be reckoned with until the beginning of the Second World War. Elsewhere in tribal India, a group of Bhils at the beginning of the Second World War demanded regional autonomy, but this was never followed up and no organization was set up to achieve it.[21] A movement for political separatism really developed in Chotanagpur and will be discribed later.

To conlcude, tribal involvement in regional politics was deeper than is generally known: it was also more diverse, as it centred around specific issues concerning land and forest; its manifestation was often violent, despite the valiant attempts by the bhagats to remain non-violent. Further, there was the process of sanskritization. All this made for integration into the regional system.

The process of integration, however, did not extend to the national level: tribal problems never figured in the resolutions passed at the Congress sessions; and few Indian leaders, with the exception of Mahatma Gandhi and Rajendra Prasad, showed any keen awareness of the tribal issue until the early 1940s. Tribal isolationism was the backlash of a sense of neglect and fear of losing identity: it was the charcteristic response of backward communities at a certain stage of their development.

Notes and References

Revised version of the article, "The Freedom Movement and Tribal Sub-movements 1920-47", in *Essays in Modern History*, Oxford University Press, 1980. It was, originally presented under the title 'From Movement to Party: A Study of the Tribal Politics in Middle India, 1920-63', at the Nehru Memorial Museum and Library on 29 March 1973 , and was later substantially revised with a new title. The latter part of the original paper dealing with tribal separatism has been developed into another article, "From Ethnicity to Regionalism: A Study in Tribal Politics and Movements in Chotonagpur from 1900 to 1975", S.S. Malik (ed.), *Dissent, Protest and Reform in Indian Civilization*.

1. J. Nehru, "The Tribal Folk", in *The Tribal People of India*, p.3.
2. P.C. Ganguly, "Separatism in the Indian Polity: A Case Study', in M.C. Pradhan, R.D. Singh, P.K. Misra and D.B. Sastry (eds), *Anthropology and Archaeology: Essays in Commemoration of Verrier Elwin*, 1902-64 pp. 104-5.
3. See the author's two papers on Gandhi's impact on the tribes, "Haribaba Movement in Chotanagpur, 1931-32", in *Journal of the Bihar Research Society*, vol. xiix, Jan-Dec. 1963, and "Mahatma Gandhi and Adivasis", *Man in India*, Jan-March 1963.
4. The material for this paper, except where otherwise indicated, has been taken from the author's manuscript on "Tribal Society" prepared under the Jawaharlal Nehru Fellowhip.
5. Hiralal Shukla, *Bastar Ke Van Vasi Geeton men Gandhi*.
6. I.P. Desai and B.L. Choudhry, *History of Rural Development in Modern India*, vol. II.
7. Ibid., p. 47.
8. Ibid., p. 53.
9. Ibid., p. 139.
10. See S.V. Thakar, *Bhilla Sadhu Sri Gula Maharaj Charitra Wa Karya*, in Marathi.

11. Godavari Parulekar, *Advasis Revolt.*

12. C. von', Furer-Haimendorf., *Tribal Hyderabad.*

13. Encounter with Gonds on the 6th Aban 1349F, File No. 5, Judicial and Police Department, Hyderabad.

14. Nityanand Das, "Martyr Lakshman Naik; A Hero of the Freedom Movement", *Adibasi*, vol. ix, no. 1, 1967-8, pp. 22-8.

15. Rampa disturbances. See Hapell's report, G.O. no 572, 23 July 1923, Public Deptt., Govt. of Madras (Hyderabad Archives).

16. See *Jadunang: A Freedom Fighter of Manipur, A Commemorative volume on the occasion of the 41st death annversary of Jadunang, 29th August*, 1971, (Imphal, 1971); A. Kumar Nag, *Rani Gaidinliu: Study of the Jadunang Movement of the Nags* ; and R. Mahadevan "Zeliangrang Naga Uprising of 1930-32: a brief summary", *Proceedings of the Indian History Congress, Thirty-fifth Session* (Calcutta, 1978), pp. 253-9. The Anthropological Survey of India conducted a field study of this movement, which is published in a volume on contemporary tribal movemen's edited by the author of this paper. See two papers in K.S. Singh, (ed), *Tribal Movments in India*, vol. i, one by Gangmumei Kabui "The Zeliangrong Movement: An Historical study", and the other by D.P. Mukherjee, P. Gupta, and N.K. Das, "The Zeliangrong or Haomei Movement".

17. J. Nehru, *Unity of India* pp. 187-8.

18. See File No. 226-P(S) 43, 1943, Political Deptt., Political Branch, "Criminal activities in Tripura State of Ratanmani Naotia" (National Archives of India); T.M. Das Gupta, "Riang Vidroh 1943", *Tripura Prasanga.* pp. 36-50; and T.C. Sen, *Tripura in Transition* (1923-1957). Tarit Mohan Das Gupta contributes an eyewitness account.

19. The Riangs are a small tribe; according to the Census of 1951 they numbered 38,556. See also B. Mukherjee, "The Riangs", *Bulletin of the Department of the Anthropological Survey of India*, vol. 7, January 1959.

20. Asso Yonuo, *Rising Nagas*, pp. 132-40.

21. A. N. Dyakov, *The National Problem in India Today*, p. 167.

9

Mahatma Gandhi, Nationalism and the Tribal Question

In this chapter we discuss, in depth, the political perception of the tribal question revealed by Mahatma Gandhi's attempt to understand it and by the interaction of various view-points within the parameters of the nationalist movement and its programme of social reform. The Mahatma's pre-occupation was with the development of a technique of social action based on non-violence (satyagraha). He took up only a few major issues, such as national freedom, untouchability, communal unity and rural reconstruction and sought to develop through the implementation of the programmes revolving around them the people's collective will, *lok shakti*, as the supreme solvent of social ills. The tribal (adivasi) problem, as such, did not claim his attention until the early 1940s, but he exercised the imagination of the tribal people, as of other segments of the rural community, and his life and mission became known through the adivasi welfare programmes implemented by a number of organizations. A number of social movements among the tribes were influenced by him. Two key figures, Amritlal Thakkar, popularly known as Thakkar Bapa, and Verrier Elwin, who shaped free India's tribal policy, came in close contact with him. Thakkar Bapa was a life-long collaborator, and he in a way influenced the Mahatma's interest in the tribal problem.

In the 1930s the Mahatma was exercised over the problem of untouchability; his chief concern was the welfare of the harijans, "God's chosen", who constituted a sizeable section of the Hindu community, numbering about five crores (1931 census). The tribals, in contrast, were about half the number of the harijans (2.24 crores), a bare 6.2 percent of the total population. More importantly, harijans had been victims of discrimination and labelled as untouchables. Not so the tribals.

In consonance with this line of thinking, he reminded Thakkar Bapa,[1] who was preoccupied with the tribal problems, of the Hindus' duty towards the harijans rather than the tribals, and persuaded him to accept the secretaryship of the Harijan Sevak Sangh:

> There is no limit to your greed. By all means satisfy it to the top of your bent. Your secretaryship surely is no hindrance.... You can give as much of your time as you like to the Adivasis while discharging your duty as Secretary of the Sangh. You do not want to tell me that you want to resign even after that latitude....But the eradication of the sin of untouchability calls for the moral force of the pure in heart. Do not forget that the irreligion of untouchability is today being sanctioned as religion. *That is not so in the case of Adivasis* [italics mine]. I do not mind therefore your dedicating yourself to the service of the Adivasis, but it must not be at the cost of the Harijans.[2]

Bapa yielded to the Mahatma's advice. He would, however, often yearn to go back to his first love, the tribals. Gandhiji, who did not "depreciate the service of the Adivasis" but thought that the "service of the Harijans must have the first claim on the Hindus", reminded him:

> Our ancestors have sinned grievously by putting Harijans virtually out of the pale of Hindu society. It is our sacred duty to give them once again an honoured place amongst outselves. The work is nothing less than that of reforming the current Hindu religion. No, Thakkar, while you and I live, that must be our primary duty.
>
> Everything else must come after, however important it may be in itself. All you can do is to leave a large part of the actual work to your colleagues and confining yourself to general supervision, give as much time to the Adivasis as you can spare, but the responsibility for the Harijan Sevak Sangh will lie on you. Neither of us can divorce ourselves from that work.[3]

The Mahatma was sensitive to the social and moral aspects of conversion among the illiterate rural masses including the tribals. He believed that there was no such thing as conversion from one faith to another. Religion was a personal matter between an individual and his God :

> It is a conviction daily growing upon me that the great and rich Christian Missionaries will render true service to India if confine their activities to humanitarian service without the ulterior motive of converting India, or at least her unsophisticated villagers, to Christianity, and destroying their social superstructure, which notwithstanding many defects has stood now from time immemorial the onslaught upon it from within and from without....Every living faith must have within itself the power of rejuvenation, it if is to live.[4]

Gandhi was not so much against conversion, as against the methods of it. "The methods of conversion must be like Caesar's wife, above suspicion. No nationalist government will antagonise Christians but only oppose insidious ways of undermining it".[5] There was no point in the missionaries weaning away the tribals from their animistic faith and supersititions; they should be allowed to develop according to their laws and compulsions. C. F. Andrews, on the other hand, justified proselytization as a means of conferring on tribes freedom from primitive terrors and savageries. He wrote to Elwin, a supporter of Gandhiji's views on conversion :

> And I cannot at all agree with Bapu that most forms of "religion" which are really evil in their essence, are not to be condemned, and those who practise them are not to be converted. I believe in South India the devil worship is absolutely hideous in some of its forms and utterly unworthy of man made in the image of God.

And he warned Elwin:

> Have you not gone too far in following Bapu about "conversion"? I fully accept that these hill tribes must be free from the suspicion and fear that you must have some ulterior motive. But the joy which we have in our own hearts owing to the love of Christ must find its expression, because it is the one motive power in our own lives. Bapu would seem to suggest that even to wish in one's own heart to give to another

> that joy, which has been the strength and stay of one's own life, is itself wrong.[6]

Andrews was perhaps as logical as Gandhi, but to the latter the right of the individual to shape his destiny according to his own will and judgement was an article of faith. Gandhiji, however, admired the missionary spirit. Speaking in the vastly different context of what one could do with the tribal people of the north-west, he said in 1946:

> I would accept a challenge of conquering tribal areas, but as a non-violent man I would not bribe them nor kill them: I would serve them. Have not the missionaries allowed themselves to be eaten by cannibals?[7]

In contrast, he commented upon the Congress's fitness to rule in the late thirties, and asked wryly:

> Why have the Congressmen been unable to reach these tribes (criminal tribes) and make them proof against the blandishments of those who would exploit their traditional violent tendencies, so-called or real?[8]

In the early forties, Gandhiji showed an awareness of the tribal problem, and he was the first and foremost of the national leaders to have done so. The tomes of the Congress resolutions did not contain a word about the tribal issue; probably there was no attempt to identify the issues in the times of the all-consuming struggle for independence, when the tribal issue was considered a minor part of the wider social and economic challenge.

In December 1941, Gandhiji drew up the 13-point reconstruction programme. In January 1942, it was enlarged to include tribal welfare as the fourteenth item, reportedly at the instance of Thakkar Bapa. But Gandhi was no less with it; for in the meanwhile, he had come to realize that tribals were materially no better than the harijans, that the former constituted a sizeable segment of the population, and that the danger of their neglect and de-nationalization was real. This was a departure from his old point of view:

> The Adivasis are the original inhabitants whose material position is perhaps no better than that of the Harijans and who have been long victims of neglect on the part of the so-called high classes. The Adivasis should have found a special place in the constructive programme. Non-mention was an oversight. . . . The Christian missionaries have been more or less in the sole occupation of the field. Great as his labour has been it has not prospered as it might have because of his ultimate aim being the Adivasis' conversion to his fold and thus becoming de-Indianised. Anyway ,no one who hopes to construct *Swaraj* on the foundation of non-violence, can afford to neglect even the least of India's sons. Adivasis are too numerous to be counted among the least.[9]

Soon there followed the most disarming admission to have come from the foremost national leader, and in a vein so characteristic of him. He laid stress on the interdependence of various elements in the composite life of the nation and on the unity of all sections and all communities of this vast land of ours. As he said:

> Adivasis have become the fourteenth item in the constructive programme. But they are not the least in point of importance. Our country is so vast and the races are so varied that the best of us, in spite of every effort, cannot know all there is to know of men and their condition. As one comes upon layer after layer of things, one ought to know as a national servant, one nation whose every unit has a living consciousness of being one with one another.[10]

Nothing hurt the nationalist in Gandhi more than the segregation of various communities, particularly the tribals, under the dangerous spell of the policy of the 'isolation and status quo'. The Act of 1935, he recalled, separated tribals from the rest of the inhabitants. The excluded areas were placed under the government's direct administration; the adivasis were put into water-tight compartments and classified as tribal people by the government. "It was a shame", he told social workers, "that they had allowed them to be treated like that. It was up to them to make the Adivasis feel one with them".[11] In strategically situated Assam, in 1946, he reminded the people that "it was their shame, that the Adivasis should be isolated from the rest of the nation of which they were an inalienable part". Assam was a vast field for the constructive programme, which could serve as an effective instrument for bringing the tribals into the national fold. If a social worker was "prevented from rendering silent service to the Adivasis, he should prefer to go to prison because prison going would ever in itself advance their cause".[12] In fact, prison-going for a worker engaged in the service of the adivasis would be a "most auspicious beginning for his work"; this would "enshrine him in their hearts".[13]

Impact on Tribal Movements

Though the Mahatma's interest in the tribal problem crystalized at a late stage in his life, his influence on tribal movements was wide. In the course of his itineraries through the length and breadth of the country, he came in contact with the tribes and spoke to them in a language that was familiar to them. In September 1925, he passed through the tribal regions of Bihar, and made the first acquaintance of the Hos at Chaibasa and of the Mundas at Khunti (Ranchi); he was impressed with the colony of the *bhaktas* (Tana and Birsait bhagats) who believed in khaddar and nearly four hundred of them plied their *charkhas* most assiduously and sang their *bhajans* in a chorus.[14] The spinning wheel had preceded the Mahatma. This was repeated seventeen years later at the Ramgarh Congress (1941). The visit made a profound impression on social movements among the Chotanagpur tribes.

It would be pertinent at this point to recall in brief the development of the tribal bhagat movements (bhagatism). A few of these movements arose in the medieval period under the impact of the Hindu *bhakti* movements spearheaded by Chaitanya who had passed through Jharkhand and by Kabir. In the wake of the growing contacts with Vaishnavism and socio-reform movements among the tribes, many bhagat cults came into existence, particularly among the Oraons, Santals, Mundas and Bhils. The bhagats attacked spirits and witchcraft, preached devotion to a personal God (often a Hindu deity), enjoined the observance of cleanliness and laid down a new code of moral conduct. In this sense tribal "bhagatism" served as a bridge between the tribal and non-tribal Hindu societies.

To the Hindu peasantry steeped in the medieval *bhakti* tradition, the Mahatma appeared like a *bhakti* preacher, and to the tribals like a bhagat. He spoke in predominantly *bhakti* idioms of *Ram rajya*, of the efficacy of *Ram nama*, of the service of the *Daridranarayan* (God in the shape of the poor) at his evening prayer meetings. Did he not also speak, a tribal bhagat would nod approvingly, of temperance, purity and of a personal God, as one of their own bhagat leaders (cf. Birsa Munda to the Mundas)? But the Mahatma also spoke of something more, of independence and freedom (swaraj), of a new order, of a new moral idiom. So new dimensions were added to tribal movements.

We may describe in brief three movements, the Tanabhagat movement among the Oraons, the Haribaba movement among the Hos and allied tribes, and the Rajmohini movement among the Gonds, which reflected the impact of Gandhi.

The Tanabhagat movement among the Oraons started as a reformative movement after the First World War, but it assumed a political overtone when it came in contact with the Congress movement in Chotanagpur. To traditional bhagat idioms of purity, temperance and teetotalism were added new ones such as swaraj, Gandhi raj, non-payment of taxes, *ahimsa*, etc. The tribals seized upon these idioms to express their agrarian "hunger". The Tanabhagats refused to pay land tax, because Gandhi raj had arrived and the land belonged to them. They lost in consequence their land, but they remained, above twenty thousand of them or so—a small fraction of the Oraon community—a solid phalanx of the followers of the Congress and Gandhi, in the most unfavourable circumstances, pitted against the missionaries and the establishment. Large numbers of them courted imprisonment, trekked long distances to attend the sessions of the Congress held in different parts of the country, propagated the message of the spinning-wheel and the National Flag, all the while hoping that when swaraj would come, they would not pay rent, and would get back all the land they had lost to the aliens, a familiar cry of the Sardar movement among the tribes in the 19th century.

The Mundas' reaction to Gandhiji's Chotanagpur tour in 1925 who saw a similarity between their own Birsa and the Mahatma was understandable. A Santal leader in 1928-29 in Hazaribagh proclaimed himself as a disciple of Gandhi, exhorted his people to eschew meat and drink and wear the sacred thread like the Hindus. He declared that Gandhi raj would replace British raj and that Gandhi raj would bring ease and comfort and that the bullets of the Government soldiers would become harmless like water. The Santals refused to pay the *chowkidari* tax, and displayed the Congress flag. The Mahatma crept into the bhagat's rituals. Some practised a secret ceremony; the father in the family would collect some rice and a few pice, make them into three packets for Gandhi, Durga and Kali, leave the packet for a short while by the side of a tank, throw Gandhi's packet into water and pick up the remaining two. No explanation of this queer practice, which was officially reported, was available.

Among the Hos, one Duka Ho, called Haribaba in 1930, proclaimed himself as one of the "most intimate disciples of Gandhi". The reign of Gandhi had arrived, his message ran, and this was to be celebrated with dance and feasts and by shouting "The British are no more: victory to Gandhi Mahto" (*Angrezi Bahadur noy*; *Gandhi Mahto ki jai*). The movement grew into a gigantic operation against village spirits and witchcraft before it subsided with the arrest of Haribaba and his colleagues.[15]

A bhagat movement developed among the Gonds of Surguja after the Mahatma's death. In 1951 Rajmohini, a Gond woman, driven to the extremity of hunger in a famine, went out to collect roots and tubers for her starving family. Exhausted, she lay unconscious. According to one of the versions put out by the workers of the Bapu Dharam Sabha Adivasi Seva Mandal, she had a vision of Mahatma Gandhi. Returning home she went on a fast for twenty-one days. Her prayer was granted, rain fell, peace and prosperity returned to her people. She turned a preacher. She called upon her people, in true bhagat tradition, to give up eating meat and telling lies and to follow the path of truth.[16]

Among the Bhils of the Panchmahal a similar trend could be observed. The translation from Hindi of a Bhil *bhajan* by Thakkar Bapa in 1955 is as follows:

> Do you know what Gandhi tells you,
> Give up drinking liquor, eating meat, stealing, rioting,
> Spin the *charkha*;
> Let every house echo to the sound of the spinning wheel
> Thakkar Bapa says, educate your children
> Give up your false deities, and worship Ram, the true God.[17]

Impact through Adivasi Welfare Programmes

From the early 1920s a number of organizations for the welfare of the tribal people came into existence. Though they did not owe their origin to Gandhi, they were modelled on the rural reconstruction programme that Gandhi had drawn up. The Bhil Seva Mandal (1922) was organized by Thakkar Bapa in the wake of the famine in the Panch Mahal to promote the welfare of the Bhils through education imparted from a network of residential schools (ashrams), and to provide debt relief, eradication of drinking habits and inculcate cleanliness and purity in life. In the process, the Bhils came closer to Hindu Vaishnavism. In the thirties, Shakti Ashram in Assam (1931) and Barama Ashram (1936) were founded. In the forties, a number of organizations were formed on the model of the Bhil Seva Mandal: Andhra Sramik Dharma Rajya Sabha (1942); Vanavasi Seva Mandal, Mandla (1944); Adivasi Seva Mandal, Tohana; Adimjati Seva Mandal (1944), Santals and Paharia Seva Mandal (1942), etc. The apex organization, Bharatiya Adimjati Seva Sangh was established by Thakkar Bapa in 1948 firstly to promote social, economic and educational advancement of the tribal communities, including nomadic and de-notified tribes to enable them to take their legitimate place in the national life of the country as equal citizens; and secondly to co-ordinate the activities of the bodies engaged in similar activities. This body is non-political, and it does not engage itself in any proselytizing activities.

These organizations—they have proliferated since independence—have a multi-pronged programme for the welfare of the tribes: (i) education through ashram schools assisted by the grant of stipends; (ii) medical relief through ayurvedic dispensaries; (iii) village and cottage industries; (iv) promotion of khadi and spinning; (v) debt-relief; and (vi) forest co-operative societies. Items (iii) and (iv) were taken out of Gandhiji's reconstruction programme, as was the philosophy and the context. These centres projected powerfully the image of Gandhi as *disum aba* (fàther of the nation) and brought a sizeable section of the tribals, apart from the bhagats, into the mainstream of the national movement. These organizations became the channels for communication of the ideas of nationalism and freedom to the tribal people. A nationalist perspective on tribal problems thus emerged in contra distinction to the isolationist standpoint of the missionaries and the officials. In the course of time, the approach of these organizations came to be identified too closely with the stance of a political party, and this together with other constraints handicapped their secular development to some extent.

Development of Tribal Perspective

We may now discuss the interaction of the three distinct standpoints concerning tribals, the "isolationist", "assimilationist" and the "integrationist", the latter two viewpoints represented by Thakkar Bapa and Verrier Elwin who influenced the formulation of free India's tribal policy. While Gandhiji's own view could not be placed in either of the categories mentioned above, he implicity recognized the individuality of the tribals, "not the least of India's sons", and probably the need for their protection against denationalization. While Bapa and Elwin came in close contact with him, they developed independently, out of their experiences, a philosophy and programme for the tribes. It will, therefore, be pertinent to deal at some length with the viewpoints of Thakkar Bapa and Verrier Elwin and their development in interaction with Gandhiji's.

Gandhi and Bapa

Gandhiji admired Thakkar Bapa's dedication to the tribal cause:

> If we are to regard the tribesmen and the aborigines as our fellow beings, this can only be done by observing Thakkar Bapa's mode of life. It has always been his inordinate ambition to mingle with the needy and the distressed and the moment he is away from them he feels distressed.[18]

While Thakkar Bapa's heart lay with the Mahatma, his head was with the Servants of India Society, from whose ranks he rose. Though a conscience-keeper of Gandhi, he disagreed with the latter's assessment of the relative merit of the harijan and tribal positions, and continued to highlight with characteristic humility and clarity the hardships of the latter, which he thought were worse than those of the former. This could be explained by the background of his life, his life long service of the tribals and his first hand experience of their problems.

Amritlal Thakkar joined the Servants of India Society in 1914. A terrible famine that broke out in the Panch Mahal region populated by the Bhils saw him organize his first relief work. He fell in love with the people—it was love at first sight—and since then the Bhils held "primacy of place in his heart", and aroused his "tenderest concern and foremost love".[19] Another famine afflicted the object of his love in 1922, and he founded the Bhil Seva Mandal in 1923, the forerunner of the Adivasi welfare organizations to be launched from a nationalist platform. He conducted many inquiries into the social and economic condition of the tribal people. In 1925 he spent about six months investigating the problems of tribals of Central Provinces, Assam and Chotanagpur. He stayed mainly in the Bhil area till 1932, when Gandhiji asked him to shoulder higher responsibility regarding harijan welfare. With the assumption of office by the Congress Party in some states, he was called upon to draw up a programme for the welfare of the tribals. In 1939, he toured the tribal tracts of Bihar, Orissa, Central Provinces and Assam extensively, drew up schemes for uplift of adivasi/harijan communities and conducted enquiries into their condition. He also organized welfare work among the Bhils in Khandesh. In October 1940, he became a member of the Aboriginal Welfare Board which was set up in Bihar. When the Interim Government took over, he prepared a five-year adivasi welfare plan for Bihar and Central Province. He was appointed a member of the Advisory Sub-committee of the Constitutent Assembly formed to enquire into and report on the political, economic and social set-up to be accorded to the hill-people of Assam.

In 1941, he summed up his analysis of tribal problems in the Kale Memorial Lecture,[20] which he first categorized into (i) poverty, (ii) illiteracy, (iii) ill-health, (iv) inaccessibility of the areas inhabited by the tribals, (v) defects in administration, and (vi) lack of leadership. The adivasis were the poorest section of the Indian population, not excepting the harijans.[21] The harijans, for all the disabilities and discrimination they suffered, always "lived with us" and became "part and parcel of our town and village life". In contrast, we "hardly felt" the existence of our aborigines. The "kaliparaj" the dark people, were held in contempt; they were neglected for ages; they laboured under very hard primitive conditions of life, waging an unequal fight against disease and exploitation by the advanced sections of our people.

Secondly, nobody except the missionaries, least of all Hindus, took care of them; it was the love and affection of Christians that attracted him:

> True, we Hindus rarely show that love and sympathy to the distressed and semi-wild people of our country, which we human beings should show to one another. On the Other hand we shun them and even hate them as if they were not creatures of God with the same feelings and passions as ourselves. Whose fault is it if such people find consideration, love and happiness amongst people of another religion, and so embrace it?[22]

Thirdly, tribals enjoyed far less protection and were much less organized than the harijans. While the latter enjoyed representation in proportion to their population under the Act of

1935, the tribals had only a "bare modicum of representation" (only 24; Assam 9; Bihar 7; Orissa 5; and Bombay, Madras, C. P. one in each of the three[23]). In C.P. where the aboriginal population was very nearly equal to the harijan population, and one-fifth of the total population, only one seat was reserved for the aborigines against twenty for harijans. In local boards hardly any representation had been given, except by the Bombay Government. In Orissa, out of the five seats reserved, four were filled up by nomination; nomination to provincial legislatures had been discarded in all other provinces.[24]

Fourthly, the tribals required a longer period of reservation—beyond ten years—than the harijans because they were not organized:[25]

> They live on the hills and in the jungles, and are even more backward than the Scheduled Castes. They are far less organised... The Scheduled Castes have had a lead over them. . . for as long a period as. . . 25 years.[25]

Fifthly, there was no leadership:

> Lack of leadership in the Tribal communities is a great handicap. Amongst the Christianised aborigines, e.g. of Chota Nagpur, there are a few educated people, but they generally seem to be interested chiefly in Christian aborigines than in their non-Christian brethren. Amongst the latter, leaders are fewer still. This is one of the reasons why aboriginal interests fail to receive proper attention from the authorities and from the general public.[26]

Bapa joined issue with the isolationist school of policy-makers which comprised "anthropologists and British members of the I.C.S. and other Government officers". The isolationists, according to him, believed in "keeping the aborigines in their areas, untouched by the civilisation of the plains" because they feared that contact with the Hindus of the plains would (i) break the solidairty of the tribal society; (ii) spread the contagion of social evils such as untouchability, early marriage and purdah into tribal areas; (iii) expose the tribals to the temptation of imitating only the lower strata of the Hindu community of the plains, and (iv) bring about demoralization and pose danger of being eventually contained as another depressed community. As Dr Hutton, the chief-exponent of this school, wrote:

> The opening up of the communications involving contact at many points and often practical settlement of tribal country, alters the aspect of any agricultural changes that may have been taking place. Generally speaking it substitutes conflict for contact—not necessarily a conflict of arms, but of cultures and of material interests. Attempts to develop minerals, forests or land for intensive cultivation can only be made at the expense of the tribe whose isolation is thus invaded. Again, the exploitation of minerals not only involves the tribal land but generally the introduction of an alien population, usually of an extremely mixed character and not infrequently exceptionally dissolute.[27]

He further added:

> Education in itself is a doubtful blessing in so far as it is apt to unfit them (aborigines) for environment, but it is probably a necessary weapon of defence for them in the circumstances in which they are placed, perhaps the only one of any permanent value, though the real solution of the problem would appear to be to create self-governing tribal areas with free power to self-determination in regard to sovereignty or adjacent provincial units.[28]

Thakkar Bapa protested against such efforts to isolate the tribals from the Hindus. "To keep these people confined to and isolated in their inaccessible hills and jungles was like keeping them in glass cases of a museum for the curiosity of purely academic persons". He, however, reiterated that "safeguards must be instituted to protect the aborigines from exploitation by the more advanced people of the plains, as had been done with regard to non-alienation of land". He argued:

> But how can the aborigines realise their present backwardness and work for their own economic, social and political progress if there is no contact with people more advanced than ourselves? When contact is advocated, I do not for a moment suggest that large populations of the plains should be transplanted to

> aboriginal regions and made to live amidst and dominate the Adivasis. Also, I do not discountenance the need for protection of aboriginal interests against any possible exploitation by some sections of the advanced people of the plains. What I mean to say is that a healthy comradeship should develop between the aborigines and the non-aborigines and each should profit culturally from the other and in course of time work hand in hand for the welfare of India as a whole,. I am one of those who strongly advocate reservation of seats, but in a general electorate, for the Adivasis in the legislatures and Local Boards for some time to come. All the same, I feel that there is no cause for getting alarmed over imaginary evils resulting out of the contact with non-aborigines and their civilisation.

Sharply reacting to the proposal regarding the creation of self-governing tribal areas, he pleaded for unity and "assimilation":

> In fact, it is unjust and wrong to call the indigenous social workers "interventionists". It would be proper to call them advocates of the policy of assimilation. The aborigines should form part of the civilised communities of our country, not for the purpose of swelling the figures of the followers of this region or that, but to share with the advanced communities the privileges and duties on equal terms in the general, social and political life of the country. Separation and isolation seem to be dangerous theories and they strike at the root of national solidarity. We have already enough communal troubles and should we add to them instead of extinguishing the existing ones and seeing that we are all one and indivisible? Safety lies in union and not in isolation. Nationalists cannot but view with concern and regret statements like the ... one from Dr. Hutton.[29]

Energetically repudiating the charge that indigenous social workers and nationalist politicians were the "interventionists', who approached the aborigines with the feelings of a morally and socially superior person and brought with them social evils and taboo with regard to food (such as beef-eating), he reminded that these evils were dying in the plains and there was no likelihood of their being carried to the aboriginal society. Care should be taken that contagion of social evils like untouchability did not spread into aboriginal areas. He reminded the isolationists of their perfect silence over and non-objection to "Christian missionaries' close and uncontrolled contact with tribals, introduction of the Roman script for tribal dialects, spread of Christian propaganda, migration of thousands of tribals to tea-gradens from their natural surroundings on low wages".

Bapa appreciated the Salvationists' and other missionaries' good work, and modelled his own organization and programme on theirs, but he sharply differed with them in other matters. He pleaded for greater protection and for making available safeguards under the Indian Constitution for non-Christian aborigines, because there was none to look after them in the Constituent Assembly. The representatives of Christian tribals charged him with seeking to bring about a division among the tribes, between Christians and non-Christians. He also felt that the aboriginal children should be taught through the medium of provincial languages and through the medium of tribal dialects in lower classes. Introduction of the Roman script for Khasi language should be discouraged because it presented innumerable complexities and estranged the feelings of the major communities, besides having many technical disadvantages.

On economic issues, he was for a scientific and rational solution. He disagreed with Verrier Elwin, that incorrigible romanticist, who favoured continuance of the *jhum* (slash-and-burn cultivation) with some alterations and restrictions because it was almost a religious necessity for some of the tribals. "The argument" that some tribals did not "plough the land because they considered it a sin to lacerate the womb of *dhartimata*", could not justify the practice any longer. In 1945, he protested against the plan of B.R. Ambedkar under which all communities except aborigines were to get proportionate representation; this amounted to political disenfranchisement of the tribals, on the ground that they did not possess the political capacity to exercise political power for their own good. Bapa reminded people that there were 112 adivasi graduates.[30]

Thakkar Bapa thus built up the nationalist perspective on the tribal question. In doing so, he was sharply critical of the official and missionary efforts to isolate the tribals from the mainstream of national life. But the choice of the phrase "assimilation" was unhappy, because Bapa did not advocate complete absorption of the tribals at the cost of their individuality. The formulation of the concept of assimilation in contradistinction to that of isolation and separatism was liable to be misunderstood, as it indeed was.

Gandhi and Elwin

Before Verrier Elwin took up his work among the tribals, he was involved for a brief spell from 1928 to 1932 with the national movement and came close to Gandhiji who wrote to him:

> Son you have become of your own choice. I have accepted the responsible position. And son you shall remain to the end of time.[31]

This was not to be. Elwin who was earlier enamoured of working among the untouchables in Gujarat was advised by Sardar Vallabhabhai Patel and Jamnalal Bajaj to leave the harijans alone and establish himself among the adivasis. Reflecting the thinking in the nationalist circles, the Sardar said:

> The untouchables are not your problem. They are the sin of the Hindus, and it is the Hindus who must make reparations to them.[32]

Elwin saw no contradiction in the Christians associating themselves with the freedom movement under the stewardship of Gandhi without losing distinctiveness of their own religion.[33] After "long discussion and much good advice from Gandhi", he resigned from the Christa Seva Sangh, and took a "plunge in the dark". In the company of Thakkar Bapa, "the most prominent of the social workers of his day", he toured the Bhil area, and decided to settle down among the Gonds at Karanjia. To this phase belonged some of his writings in which he sought to establish that it was the right and duty of the Christians to overthrow a foreign or despotic government;[34] in a similar vein he praised khadi to the skies.[35]

Elwin's honeymoon with the national movement came to an unhappy end in 1932, when he offered, in return for the passage to India, to confine himself entirely to his work among the Gonds and to take no part in the civil disobedience and any other political movement.[36] Gandhiji called him "*naram*" (soft, gentle, yielding), and added that "these adjectives could be ap- applied to you in certain circumstances". He, however, consoled him: "It is enough for me to know, as I do know, that you regard no sacrifice too great for the pursuit of truth".[37] In response to a letter from Elwin, the Mahatma further consoled him thus,: "God has saved you for greater service.... You must cheer up. No room for idle sorrow".[38]

However, from 1932 onwards, and particularly in the forties, when the Mahatma reached the pinnacle of his career, Elwin's links with him weakened, "though his affection for him never wavered". From an enthusiast of the khadi programme, he turned into its critic. In July 1937, he wrote to Gandhiji that the utility of spinning for Gonds or other tribes was questionable; in areas where cotton did not grow spinning seemed artificial and uneconomic. Secondly, the Mahatma's view on prohibition was damaging to the tribals. Thirdly, his philosophy of sex-relations and his excessive emphasis on diet, jarred on tribal susceptibilities. These were only minor points, and yet these led Elwin to "deprive himself of the warmth of his affection and strength, when he reached his highest stature during his later years, but it was a feeling about Truth that kept me from going to see him".[39]

Yet there were two points on which Elwin's stand coincided with Gandhiji's. The first was his view that Christianity and British imperialism were not convertible terms; this was against the view of the establishment that Christianity should have nothing to do with the policies of the Congress and Gandhiji, and that deviation from this would amount to treachery to Christ and the emperor.[40] Elwin was for the grant of independence to India. The second was the attitude to conversion which has been mentioned earlier. It could also be partly explained by the influence of mystical literature on Elwin, which made him look at religion not "as a matter of saving of your and other's soul"—in times of famine many missionaries at one time undoubtedly took advantage of people's hunger to change their religion—but as a quest for spiritual reality.[41] This attitude was also strengthened by his experience in Gandhiji's ashram "which made it impossible to believe in an exclusive form of Christianity", and once exclusiveness was taken out of Christianity or for that matter any religion, a great deal goes out of it.[42] In the forties, his views on conversion became stridently polemical. In a paper called "The foreign missionary danger" (1944), he highlighted "the rapid pace of conversion of tribes and the danger of the conversion within a few years of the entire aboriginal population in to a querulous, anti-national, aggressive" minority community, with none of the old virtues and few of the new, which will be a thorn in the side of the future Government of India"; and he advocated the prohibition of proselytization as in many other free countries:[43]

> Change of religion is actually harmful to the aborigines. It destroys tribal unity, strips the people of age-long moral sanctions, separates them from the mass of their fellow countrymen and in many cases leads to decadence that is as pathetic as it is deplorable, the methods employed are questionable. There is economic exploitation, exploitation of ignorance and social exploitation. Therefore missionaries should be withdrawn from tribal areas.[44]

About the place of the tribes in Indian society, Elwin as mentioned earlier, indignantly denied having been an isolationist; he affirmed that he had only condemned the policy of isolation. But the confusion arose out of the inept pharase, "the National Park", that he coined in the late thirties to underline the need for protection of the tribes against exploitation, and the preservation of the three freedoms for them: freedom from fear, freedom from want and freedom from interference. The fact of the exploitation of tribals by money-lenders, corrupt and rapacious officials and oppressive landlords could not be denied. He admitted later that when he spoke in terms of preserving tribal culture, he thought a little statically. Later he thought in a less static way[45] and spoke about the unity of the hills and plains as essential to the general national interest. The concept of integration subsumed the need for maintaining "cultural identity" of tribals in the wider context of national unity, territorial integrity and socialistic goals. Elwin edged closer to the nationalist school in the sense: "The special care and protection given to the tribesmen must not cast shadow on the unity of India. They must be educated to feel that they are full citizens of the Republic, with real rights and still more urgent duties". Before independence, through his writings, he made the "dominant social groups conscious of the tribal problem in the national perspective". In this sense he he was a guru—as Jawaharlal Nehru called him—to him and others. After independence, he contributed to the development of integrated tribal policy, for all its drawbacks.[46]

We have sought to trace the development of the nationalist perspecttive, particularly Gandhiji's impact on the tribals and the tribal question. In the Gandhian conspectus, the tribal problem occupied a very small space. The extracts quoted above are about all that Gandhiji had to say about the tribes and the issues that bore upon them. For a long time the harijan problem, for social and political reasons, put the tribal issue in the shade; later when the facts came to be known the two were equated. This in itself was a development of great significance. The inclusion of tribal welfare in the reconstruction programme implied recognition of the primacy of putting the tribal problem in perspective for solution. A queer result of Gandhiji's impact was the emphasis that the "archaic" bhagat element in tribal social movements received; but his influence also helped to add new and wide perspectives to them, and bring a section of the tribes into the mainstream of national life. Also interesting was the interaction of different standpoints on tribals, and the emergence of a perspective and philosophy of tribal reconstruction with its nationalist, secular and integrated orientation. The tribal welfare programme, which projected his image and message, did not attempt a basic restructuring of tribal agrarian economy to provide the base for economic development. The significance of Gandhiji's later-day radicalism in agrarian matters was missed by the architects of the nationalist or assimilationist approach to tribal issues.

Recent research in tribal folklore[47] has further revealed how the Mahatma profoundly influenced the tribes living in remote areas, as he did the peasant, during his life-time and after his death. A folklorist tells us how Gandhi was looked upon in Bastar and how his influence aided the spread of vegetarianism and "teetotalism" among tribals. Here are a few specimens of the folklore from Chotanagpur :

(i) O Father, by clearing the jungle, you won swaraj,
O Father, you got it,
O Father, by digging (the earth) you won swaraj,
O Father, you got it.
O Father, by ploughing (the field) you won swaraj.
O Father, you got it.
O Father, by sowing cotton seeds you won swaraj,
O Father, you got it.
O Father, by combing cotton wool you won swaraj,
O Father, by spinning the wheel, you won swaraj:

(ii) By plying the spinning wheel,
You got swaraj.
O, Gandhi, you got it.
By spinning cotton,
You got swaraj.
O Gandhi, you got it.
By causing a tumult,
You got Chotanagpur,
O Birsa, you got it.

(iii) O Mother, like the rising sun Gandhi was born,
O Mother, like the rising moon Birsa had come up.
O Mother, Gandhi was born for swaraj.
O Mother, Birsa had come up to put the Mundas on their feet.

Notes and References

This is a slightly modified version of the paper, "Mahatma Gandhi and the Adivasis" published in *Man in India* vol. 50, no I, January-March 1970.

1. T.N. Jagdisan and Shyam Lal (eds), *Thakkar Bapa, Eightieth Birthday Commemoration Volume.*

2. Pyarelal, "Bapa of Bapu", pp. 81-82 (quoted). Ibid.,
3. S.G. Vaze, "Thakkar Bapa, a tribute", p. 87. Ibid.,
4. M.K. Gandhi, *Christian Missions: Their Place in India*, p. 78.
5. C. Winslow Jack and Verrier Elwin, The *Dawn* of *India's Freedom.*
6. Quoted in *Tribal World of Verrier Elwin* (hereafter called *Tribal World*), p. 97.
7. Tendulkar D.G., *Mahatma*, vol. 8, p. 28.
8. Ibid., vol. 7, p. 32.
9. *Harijan* 18-1-42, p. 5; quoted in the *Selected Works of Mahatma Gandhi*, chap. 80 vol. six from the *Voice of Truth.* p. 538.
10. *Harijan*, 15-2-42, p. 38; ibid.
11. Tendulkar, op. cit., vol. 7, p. 32.
12. Ibid., p. 41.
13. Ibid., p. 34.
14. Suresh Singh, "The Haribaba Movement in Chotanagpur 1931-32".
15. Ibid.
16. S.L. Kalia, "The Raj Mohini Devi Movement in Surguja".
17. A Bhil Bhajan from *Thakkar Bapa*, op. cit.
18. *Commemoration Volume*, op. cit.
19. Ibid., p. 28.
20. "The Problem of Aborigines in India", Gokhale Institute of Politics and Economics, R.R. Kale Memorial Lecture, 1941 (hereafter called Kale Lecture), pp. 354-377 Ibid.
21. Ibid., pp. 359.
22. Thakkar Bapa, "Aborigines of Orissa,,' *Modern Review*, Sept. 1938; quoted in the footnote of the *Commemoration Volume*, p.78.
23. Ibid., "Protection of Minorities" (*Hitavada*, Dec. 4, 1948), *Commemoration Volume*, pp. 339-340.
24. Kale Lectures, pp. 369-370.
25. "Protection of Minorities", op. cit., p. 349.
26. Kale Lectures, p. 370.
27. Ibid.,
28. Ibid., p. 372.
29. Ibid., pp. 371-372.
30. A.V. Thakkar, *Aboriginals' Cry in the Wilderness.*
31. *Tribal World*, p. 56.
32. Ibid., p. 58.
33. Ibid., p. 59.
34. Ibid., p. 77.
35. See one of Elwin's earlier works, *Religious and cultural aspects of Khadi.*
36. *Tribal World*, p. 82.
37. Ibid., p. 84.
38. Ibid., p. 85.
39. Ibid.

40. Ibid., pp. 86 and 97; also see Elwin, *Truth About India Can We get it?*, p. 56.

41. Ibid., p. 96.

42. Ibid., p. 99.

43. Elwin, *The Foreign Missionary Danger.*

44. Ibid.

45. *Tribal World,* op. cit., p. 291.

46. For a tribute to Elwin, see Pradhan *et al* (ed.) p. 170. *Anthropology and Archaeology, Essays in Commemoration of Verrier Elwin.* (quoted from *A.A.S.*, vol. I, No. 2, 1966: 162)). "Elwin contributed to one of the fundamental ideals of modern India "the development of Indian nationhood. His massive scholarly studies enlightened the minds of dominant social group as to the essential oneness of the peoples of India, notwithstanding their social and cultural diversities or particulars of social life. His liberal and imaginative approach to tribal development enabled the Government of India to fromulate a tribal policy which combined the quality of idealism and realism in the contemporary social and cultural life of India, thereby helped to bring about a synthesis of the traditional and modern elements of India's life and thought in the new Indian nation".

47. Hiralal Shukla, *Bastar ke Van Vasi Geeton men Gandhi.* The *Adibasi*, published from Ranchi carried compositions eulogising Gandhi, and the message of nationalism to tribal people.

10

From Ethnicity to Regionalism

This chapter seeks to explore the dynamics of the separatist movement among tribes. The autonomy movement among the Bhils in Gujarat is a much later development and, in a way, "artificial". Elsewhere, outside Chotanagpur, tribal politics, as revealed by the election results from 1952 to 1985, has been assimilated into the all-India (the Congress, Socialist, Jan Sangh or the Bhartiya Janata Party, Communist and Swatantra) or regional (the Gantantra in Orissa) political system and programme. We will now discuss in depth the rise and fall of the autonomy movement in Chotanagpur,[1] its passage from ethnicity to regionalism as an ideology, a catalyst and the changing facets of its structure and programme (1920-85).

I

There was a combination of reasons that explained why Chotanagpur became the centre of the separatist movement. First, Chotanagpur was the most advanced of the tribal regions in point of literacy, political consciousness, and industrial progress. Secondly, the major tribal communities were concentrated in a geographically distinct region: they were not split up like the Bhils and the Gonds into different political and territorial systems. Thirdly, Christianity came in a big way to Chotanagpur; the major tribes of Chotanagpur were very effectively influenced by the missions. In fact, there was no other region of tribal middle India which witnessed such a spread of Christianity. As Christianity spread it performed many roles: it gave them a history and a myth; it accentuated the notion of private rights in land; it promoted education and medical care; it also emphasized a sense of separateness from the rest. Fourthly, the

Chotanagpur tribes had a tradition of militant and organized struggles going back over a hundred years. The struggles were organized more around land and less around forests. The incidence of proletarianization was small when compared with that among the Bhils. The tribal system had survived relatively intact in this region. Fifthly, there was a rich corpus of anthropological literature to draw upon in order to create a new sense of history, which could legitimize the tribals' search for identity. Sarat Chandra Roy, the father of Indian anthropology, was not a closet anthropologist, but also the first ideologue and active protagonist of the demand for tribal autonomy. He gave an eloquent expression to the tribals' demand for separation; his ideas and draftsmanship left their imprint on the memoranda submitted by tribal organizations before different government bodies. Lastly, Chotanagpur was exposed to the operation of many interests. The Bengalis formed a sizeable professional and land-owning community, and the Muslims were a significant trading interest. The Bengali-Behari controversy over employment in the late 1930s and the Muslim League politics also affected the development of the tribal separatist movement.

We shall briefly describe the phases through which the separatist movement was transformed into a regional movement.

The Formative Period (1912-49)

The initial phase starting at the turn of the present century saw the rise of the institutions designed to introduce reforms and stimulate development among the tribes mainly along denominational and even interdenominational lines. The leadership came from the missionaries and students. The missionaries pioneered temperance movements to check the evil of drinking habits among tribals and formed cooperative societies to free them from the clutches of moneylenders. Of the latter the most notable was the Roman Catholic Cooperative Society, founded in 1906, which had a considerable effect in "civilizing" the aboriginal and raising his standard of life generally. Societies were also formed for the promotion of education. Led by the Christian teachers and students they constituted the matrix of the political movement which was to be spearheaded by educated Christians later. As early as 1898, the Christian Association had been formed by the Lutheran graduates for the promotion of education. In 1918, the Catholics joined it to form the Christian College Union. In 1912, J. Bartholomew of the Anglican Mission, on his return from the Students' Conference at Dacca in 1911-12, founded a branch of the Dacca Students Union with the objective of raising funds for the education of poor Christian students. The Munda-Oraon Education Conference (Siksha Sabha) founded by a non-Christian leader and the Ranchi Union did the job of promoting education among urban tribals.

There were institutional manifestations not only of interdenominational but also occasionally of pan-tribal solidarity for the socio-economic uplift of the region, as a whole. In 1912, the Chotanagpur Charitable Association was organized by all aboriginals, Christians and non-Christians, to raise funds to provide scholarships for students. Voices were raised for forging unity of the people of Chotanagpur and for abolition of differences among Christians and non-Christian tribals, as also among all tribals, Munda, Oraon, Tamaria, Mahali, Lohara and Panre. A new sentiment was in the air: "All Adivasis are one, Adivasis of lower category such as Lohara, Panre, Bhuiya and Tamaria should not be looked down upon", etc. The pan-tribal sentiment was, however, weak.

When the era of constitutional reforms dawned after 1918 and demands for promotion and protection of regional and sectarian interests grew, the educated Christian tribals, mostly students, belonging to the German and Anglican missions, took a hand in organizing the Chotanagpur Improvement Society at the instance of the Anglican bishop of Ranchi. A Munda led this interdenominational (Anglican-Lutheran) body, which voiced its concern in 1916 over the "absence of security for tribals and stressed the need for the preservation of tribal identity in the changing political context". "Whatever may be done in the way of reform elsewhere", it urged, "the aborigines of Chotanagpur may be left to the administration of European officers".[2] The

Society also offered various suggestions for economic advancement of the tribal community, but it became moribund.

The phase from 1920-38 was dominated by the activities of the revived Chotanagpur Improvement (Chotanagpur Unnati Samaj) Society (1920). A tribal urban middle class was gradually forming. The society embodied interdenominational unity of the missions for political purposes, and unlike the first phase set up a sustained operation. It was led by tribal teachers and catechists and sought to secure employment for educated tribals, reservation in the services and legislative bodies, and formation of a sub-state joined to Bengal, or Orissa. Though it sought to spread its activities to villages, it remained essentially an urban movement. This period also witnessed the development of mini-revivalism among tribes, very much on the lines of the Indian renaissasance, which stressed return to the golden age of the community and formulated an individualistic approach to reform and service of the community. It is to this phase that we can trace the revival of *parha*, tribal assembly, and the discovery of lost "scripts" said to have been used by the tribes in their heyday. The society was able to focus the attention of the authorities on the problems of the tribes. The Simon Commission and the government responded to the tribal problems, and sought their solution within the framework of the then existing political structure.

The period from 1938-47 saw the rise of a militant movement under the Adivasi Mahasabha. The immediate cause of the formation of the Mahasabha was the experience of the first elections held in 1937 under the Government of India Act of 1935. The Congress had swept the polls. This persuaded mainly Christian as also some non-Christian tribals to close their ranks, and form a joint body. The Chotanagpur Improvement Society led by members of different denominations and non-tribals merged to form the Adivasi Mahasabha. In this respect this new body represented an advance on the earlier movement, commanded a wider political base, and possessed pan-tribal composition and objectives. Two other sources of influence on the Mahasabha, as mentioned above, were the Bengali-Behari controversy and the Muslim League politics. The Bengalis felt that their interests in Bihar were not safe and, therefore, they could combine with the tribals to form a separate state. The Muslim League during the mid-1940s toyed with the idea of forming a corridor passing through the tribal areas to link East and West Pakistan. They sympathized with the tribals and gave financial support to the Adivasi Mahasabha. Both the Samaj and the Mahasabha were "loyalist"; the latter remained outside the maintestream of the nationalist politics and the freedom movement. Its president, Jaipal Singh, gave support to the British war effort to which the Congress was opposed and played a prominent role in recruiting tribals for the British army. The Mahasabha was led by professional political workers, some of them highly educated and articulate. It became a Chotanagpur movement extending over both urban and rural areas. It involved tribals other than the Ranchi tribals. It demanded not the formation of a sub-state but complete separation from Bihar. A series of violent incidents occurred during this period which underlined the militant nature of the movement. But by 1947 the militancy had failed to pay off. The Sabha was routed by the Congress in the elections held in 1946. The link with the Muslim League was broken, and the Bengali-Bihari controversy died down.

The Peak (1949-58)

The period from 1949-58 saw the rise of the Jharkhand Party. The Adivasi Mahasabha was wound up (except in its cultural aspects), and a new regional party created. Behind it were the experiences of the failure of the militant movement and of the framing of the constitution for India. The tribals had been recognized as a special category, and the fifth and the sixth schedules had given them more than the anthropologists and the British administrators had prepared them for. The "exclusion" had been ended. The framers of the constitution were giving the country a secular system, which reassured the missionaries and the minorities. Further, it was discovered that the census of 1941 had given an exaggerated figure of tribal population in Chotanagpur, which sustained the Adivasi Mahasabha movement. The census of 1951, like the census of 1931 showed that the tribals were not a very large community. In fact they had never been a majority in the Chotanagpur region. Therefore, the Jharkhand party was thrown open, at least, in principle, as embodied in its constitution to all Chotanagpuris. There was thus a transition from ethnicity to regionalism as a formative factor in the movement. This was, partly, in keeping with the larger political and secular stance current in those days that language or "region" and not ethnicity should determine the formation of a province. Some elements of the Congress Socialist Party and quite a few members of the non-Bihari money lending community who could be identified as the *dikus* (the aliens) joined the party. The concept of the Jharkhand was enlarged to include all the regions that once formed part of the Chotanagpur administrative division. Thus the tracts inhabited by the Chotanagpur tribals which formed part of Bengal, Orissa and Madhya Pradesh were included in the Jharkhand. The method adopted by the party was constitutional. Though Christians dominated the movement and provided the leadership there was an unmistakable tribal core to it. This will be evident from the fact, as described later, that the party polled nearly 750,000 votes in the 1952 and 1957 elections (Chart I).

The period from 1952-57 which cut across the two elections was in many ways, the peak period for the Jharkhand movement. The Jharkhand had emerged as the major party in the Chotanagpur-Santal Pargana region. The second general elections had seen it extend its influence in Orissa, where it captured five seats, and held the balance of power in the state politics plagued by instability. It displayed remarkable unity, laid down the law in the tribal region, could mobilize thousands of people and take out mammoth processions at short notice.

The Decline (1958-63)

The phase from the late 1950s saw the decline of the party, which could be attributed to many factors. Firstly, there was the growing impact of development programmes on Chotanagpur and the increasing involvement of the tribals in developmental processes. Secondly, the spilt between the advanced Christian and relatively backward non-Christian tribals arising out of the competition for better educational facilities, employment opportunities, and control over development inputs and resources, deepened. The non-Christian tribals started looking to the Congress and the Jan Sangh for support by the late 1950s. Many all-India parties appeared on the scene and strengthened their presence (Congress, Jan Sangh, Swatantra, CPI). Thirdly, the experience of Madhya Pradesh and Orissa, which had given representation to tribal interests in the government and the council of ministers, had made it clear that all the tribals needed was a share in power to protect their interests, which could as well be secured by joining the Congress or by coming to some kind of understanding with it, as in Orissa. Fourthly, the Jharkhand party, as mentioned elsewhere in this chapter, did not have any agrarian programme. Its leaders were town-based professionals, who had little feel for rural problems. Its ally was the Janata Party which represented the zamindars of the Chotanagpur. In 1962 it admitted as its member the foremost zamindar of Chotanagpur, and it appointed a secretary from the moneylending community. The situation after 1963 had become critical and it demanded a radical programme for the tribal masses which the Jharkhand Party could not afford. Part of the Congress success later could be explained by its *garibi hatao* programme. Lastly, there was dissidence within the party arising out of the style and performance of leadership, particularly at the time of the reorganization of states, when the Jharkhand had not only failed to press its demand at a higher level, but also seen a sizeable chunk of the "Jharkhand" being given away to West Bengal. The party had always been handicapped by want of funds which alone could sustain an organization which never efficiently functioned at the higher level. The search for money led to strange alignments with elements such as the *dikus*, the traditional enemies of the adivasis. The non-Bihari *dikus* had a vested interest in the movement to keep the Bihar *dikus* away. Party support was also given to many "outsiders". All this had created strains within the party. This became evident when the party was wiped out in the mid-term elections in Orissa. But a greater blow was in store.

The elections in 1962 slashed the number of votes polled by the Jharkhand to almost half of that registered in 1957 and reduced its seats to twenty in the Bihar assembly. This was a sharp reminder to its leaders that its stance of isolation, either ethnic or regional, could no longer be maintained. The merger of the Jharkhand Party with the Congress, effected in June 1983, was thus a natural corollary of the operation of the above-mentioned forces.

Split and Radicalization (1963-76)

We enter upon another phase (1963-76) after the fourth general elections, when though the objective conditions of a movement were present and there were spurts and there was even a sustained rhythm of movements, there was no unified political system. The structure of the Jharkhand Party had been fragmented: the parent body had broken up into smaller parties formed by tribal sub-ethnic groups. The Jharkhand was like a splintered glass. There was a movement, but no composite party.

This phase had many interesting features. There was a distinct radicalization of politics. This came about as a result of the articulation of the agrarian factor in the tribal situation. The Jharkhand in its constitutional role as a regional party, had played down the agrarian issue. During the intervening years the agrarian situation had become worse. Incidence of alienation of land belonging to tribals had shown an upward trend; more and more educated tribal youths were seeking employment; construction of industrial complexes had resulted in the displacement of tribals from their land, and their absorption into industrial culture was slow. Though there was some development in tribal regions, it was on a smaller scale than elsewhere, and it was outstripped by rising aspirations among the new generation of the tribal community. The participation of a section of tribal leadership in the government, no doubt, resulted in distinct improvement in some matters: more tribals were employed in the government than before, the quotas reserved for them were, by and large, filled, more attention was paid to their region, and there was also a larger flow of funds. But evidently, this was not enough. The census of 1971 disclosed an alarming state of affairs. The percentage of the scheduled tribes in the population of the districts of tribal Bihar had fallen sharply during the 1961-71 decade: in Ranchi from 61.61 to 58.08, in Singhbhum from 47.31 to 46.12, and in the Santal Pargana from 38.24 to 36.22. This was not only because of the slow growth rate of the tribal population, which was, in fact, among the lowest but also because of the heavy influx of people from other parts of Bihar.

Secondly, this radicalization was also due to the influence of the Naxalite movement, infiltration by extremist elements of tribal organizations and the entry of the leftist parties in the region, in a big way. The latter had generally kept themselves out of tribal politics, and their interest had thus far been limited to the sections of the workers engaged in mining and industries. The leftist orientation to tribal politics meant a greater stress on the political education of workers and agrarian issues, a linking up of local and all-India politics, violence and militancy of means, and a better organization. There was also a commitment by all-India leftist parties to the concept of tribal autonomy as distinct from that of the formation of a tribal state. Thirdly, as the political character of the Jharkhand movement receded in the background, the agrarian aspects came into prominence. The formal political slogan of a separate state was not given up, but it weakened, and there was greater stress on the nature and consequences of exploitation, isolation and neglect. There was a better articulated demand for a more dominant role for the tribals and Chotanagpuris in regional administration and better educational facilities and more employment opportunities. There was also a demand for restoration of alienated land and provision for legal and institutional safeguards to protect tribal interest and end all forms of exploitation. All parties were united in stressing the regional rather than the ethnic factor.

We may conceptualize the developments during this phase in terms of (1) fragmentation of the tribal party and factionalization of tribal Politics, (2) rise of urban pressure groups, and

(3) political extrcmism, agrarian radicalism and cultural revivalism.

The merger of the Jharkhand with the Congress shocked the hard core of the Jharkhandis who were keen to maintain a separate political identity, and some sections of the dominant Christian elite and missionaries who feared loss of the leverage they could exercise. It was also stated that the merger had not been ratified by the general body of the party and was, therefore, technically defective. In fact, no sooner was the merger effected than it began to be criticized by the rump. The behaviour of the leadership which had sought the merger and benefited from it did not help. Mutual bickerings and personal rivalries delayed the implementation of the terms of the merger and its consolidation. The attitude of those leaders who went out of office became ambivalent. Though technically members of the Congress party, they encouraged criticism of the merger and worked secretly against it. Towards the close of 1966, Jaipal Singh, encourged by the formation of the separate states of Haryana and Punjab, called upon his people to act in the following words :

> The days of begging are gone. We shall now have to act in the Birsa Munda fashion to get our legitimate demands. Tribals should raise their heads against the wrong-doers and if necessary use bows and arrows.

Nothing came of it. Reviving the old Jharkhand, as Jaipal Singh himself said, was like whipping a dead horse. There was a proposal to revive the old Adivasi Mahasabha, but this could not be done.

The absence of the old guards and of a charismatic leadership which had held the Jharkhand party together created confusion, and threw the political forces into disarray. As many as nine groups or parties sprung up to fill the vacuum created by the merger, and the rump body of the Jharkhand split up into four factions.

We could briefly describe the processes of the split within the split. During the first phase (1963-68) as many as three groups claimed to represent the Jharkhand party. After the fourth general elections had decimated the party many attempts were made to unify the factions. But further split could not be averted. A faction of the party refused to recognize the seventy-one-man executive committee of the central party. On 28 December 1967 the All-India Jharkhand Party was formed. One of its first acts was to declare the merger with the Congress effected in 1963 unconstitutional and void as it was not approved by the general body. This party began to split again in 1969-70 owing to the temperamental incompatibility and conflicts between its two leaders. One faction moved closer to the Congress (O) and the Jan Sangh and the other to the Congress (R). The latter enjoyed the support of the church, which went to the length of cooperating even with non-tribals in order to checkmate the growing influences of the Jan Sangh on non-Christian tribals. The first faction lost against the second in the Khunti parliamentary by-elections (1970) caused by the death of Jaipal Singh and the Torpa Assembly by-election. The split became permanent in 1971, the first faction retaining the name of the party and the second reverting to the old name, the Jharkhand Party. At the same time both tried to extend their influence in neighbouring states by setting up candidates during election. There was hardly any difference of programme-content between them. One concentrated its activities among and drew support from the Hos of Singhbhum and the other from the Mundas of Ranchi. They contested elections separately and won ten seats in 1969 and eleven in 1972 in the Bihar Assembly and captured two parliamentary seats in 1971.

A major split in the old Jharkhand Party occurred in 1968 when the Santals separated themselves from the Chotanagpur tribals and formed their own party, which was named after the Santal Insurrection (locally called *hul*). The Santals always nursed a grievance that though they were more numerous than the Mundas and Oraons, they did not command adequate influence in the Jharkhand movement. This simmering discontent had expressed itself in a demonstration against the Jharkhand leader, Jaipal Singh, in 1957. This explains why despite the attempts to widen the political base of the party to include parts of Singhbhum and Hazaribagh, it became essentially a Santal organization. The Bihar Prant Hul Jharkhand Party was formed on 28 December 1968, In the mid-term elections of 1969 it fielded eighteen candidates out of which six won in the Santal Pargana. It voiced demands of a local nature such as introduction of the Roman script for the Santal language, creation of a separate division for the Santal Pargana, far-reaching agrarian reforms to end tribal exploitation and provide security for tribal people. In the last aspect it was a step ahead of its counterpart in Chotanagpur. The party also secured adequate representation as ministers of the changing coalition governments at state level. It split up into two factions in 1972 for the same reasons as the All-India Jharkhand Party did: personal differences and rivalries among leaders. The break-away faction called itself the Progressive Hul Jharkhand party. The result of the factional rivalries was that the two groups could capture only three seats in the 1972 elections.

Apart from differences of a personal nature among its leaders there was also a growing cleavage on communal and denominational lines among members behind the split. Paradoxically, the fragmentation of the party and factionalization of politics intensified radicalism. The language of the pamphlets issued by different groups, the nature of the demands, the mobilization of the people through processions and demonstrations were not in the least affected. In fact the processions were larger and the demands became more strident.

Another aspect of this phase was the rise and development of the urban pressure groups led by the educated tribals, mostly Christian and centred at industrial complexes to demand jobs for tribal youths in administration and industrial undertakings. This, in fact, was the core of the demands shrouded in familiar political verbiage. The process of the formation and the development of the pressure groups was epitomized in the Birsa Seva Dal (BSD) which emerged as the most important, if not the only one of the urban groups. It was essentially a socio-political organization and not a political party as it did not contest any elections until 1980. Formed with the objective of securing a better deal for tribals in matters of employment, it functioned mainly at the two industrial centres of Jamshedpur and Ranchi, and only occasionally at others. Behind its formation there were two influences at work. First, the missionaries of different denominations had been shocked by the fragmentation of the political structure of the Jharkhand Party and were dismayed at the erosion of Christian leadership as revealed by the election results. Therefore, a new organization had to be established to safeguard the interests of the educated tribals in urban areas. Secondly, the extremist elements were fairly active seeking to establish a base of their influence and operation in the tribal region. They managed to influence the BSD ideology, programmes and methods considerably. The co-existence between the pro-missionary and pro-CPM-(L) was not always happy, and subsequently there was a split. But the two worked together for some time. The name of the tribal hero Birsa Munda who led the uprising of 1899-1900 against the missionaries and the British Government borrowed by the Dal was therefore a little ironical, but it served as a draw.

Though the idea of forming an organization had occurred as early as June, 1966, an ad-hoc body could be set up only after the fourth general elections in 1967. Later an organization with field level functionaries came into existence. The constitution of the organization spoke generally of the commonalty of interests of tribals, backward classes and other "exploited sections" of the Indian population. However its objectives were primarily geared to securing the interests of tribal people. It demanded action to :

(i) bring about a wide awakening among tribal people to secure their deliverance;
(ii) remove fear, inferiority complex, sense of isolation and correct the habit of silent submission to tyranny and expolitation;
(iii) organize tribals to secure the fundamental rights and democratic/regional rights;
(iv) end and expose colonial exploitation which is the root cause of all sufferings;

(v) secure priority in the matter of providing employment in administrative and private institutions;
(vi) prevent loot of the land and secure restoration of the alienated land;
(vii) establish the rights of tribals to secure admission to educational institutions on a priority basis;
(viii) organize workers and students to secure their demads;
(xi) instil love and devotion for tribal culture; and
(x) forge unity among the people and teach them how to exercise their collective will to secure their rights.

The action-programme however, was restricted to securing employment and admission to educational institutions, amidst the slogans for the regionalization (even tribalization) of the local administration.

The BSD constitution[3] stressed the role of collective leadership to guide the people through the struggle. This was not achieved. Factional rivalries broke up the organization. The number of its members fluctuated around 2,500.

There were two phases in the development of the BSD movement. The first, from 1967 to 1969 was a militant phase. Violent methods of struggle to secure tribal rights were advocated. Meetings, processions of the youth armed with bows and arrows, gheraos and celebrations of the Birsa Day were the modes of mobilization. BSD demanded creation of a separate state, expulsion of the non-Chotanagpuris, agrarian reforms and measures against moneylenders.

There was a series of violent incidents involving grabbing of urban land[4] (at Jamshedpur), clashes between tribals and non-tribal "outsiders", which culminated in two major incidents in 1968. The first occurred at Chiri (Ranchi) on 2 June 1968. A tribal crowd surrounded a moneylender's house to protest against the moneylender's encroachment on a piece of land belonging to a tribal Christian. The moneylender's son panicked and opened fire. When the mob returned, it ran into the police who opened fire, killing six persons. The BSD leaders were arrested. An impressive procession, fifteen thousand strong, was taken out on 9 June 1968 at Ranchi. Demand for an enquiry into the incident was conceded. The commission which went into the incident blamed the police for its failure to take preventive measures to forestall the clash.

The second incident occurred at Chainpur (Ranchi) on 27 October 1968. This area was heavily populated by tribal Christians, and BSD had been fairly active, holding meetings and staging demonstrations in support of local demands. A small incident involving ill treatment of a tribal by a doctor sparked off the agitation. A large militant crowd asaulted the doctor, drove him out of the hospital, and attacked the police station. The police opened fire, killing three persons. There were minor repercussions of this incident in Ranchi and elsewhere.

The situation became worse in 1969. In March of that year the CPM-(L) launched a Naxalbari type of movement. Some elements of the BSD supported its pro-Mao slogans which appeared on the walls in Ranchi town and elsewere. But the movement failed to strike any root among the Ranchi tribals.

After 1967 the second phase of the BSD movement began. The influence of CPM-(L) and the missionaries waned. BSD pledged itself to play a constitutional role and adopt peaceful methods of struggle. Violent incidents ceased. The organization was undermined by conflicts between two factions. Some of the BSD leaders sought refuge in the Jharkhand splinter groups. The BSD has almost ceased to exist except in Jamshedpur where it shows some activity, now and then.

The Naxalite movement started in the heavily forested regions of Chotanagpur in 1969. The movement continued for two years. There were 183 incidents involving murder, dacoity, bomb explosions, and violent clashes. By the middle of 1971 the Naxalite activity had been contained, their topmost leaders arrested, and their party headquarters liquidated. There was a lull for about a year and a half. From mid-1973 another phase of a Naxalite movement began. There were nearly eighteen incidents involving murder, and dacoity. The Naxalites were seeking to influence the tribals who formed a joint front with another semi-aboriginal or detribalized community, the Mahtos, in Hazaribagh and Dhanbad which were not among the strongholds of the Jharkhand movements.

The Mahto were among the first communities to resist British rule in Chotanagpur; later historical accounts mention conflicts between the Munda and Mahto. From 1920[5] onwards the Mahto of Chotanagpur sought an identity with the Kurmi of other parts of Bihar and, later, an all-India identity through the Kurmi Mahasabha. The Maratha Kunbi were discovered as the lost kinsmen, and so the name of Shivaji, supposed to be a Kunbi, was given to the Samaj. The Shivaji Samaj (1969) highlighted the backwardness[6] of this sturdy peasant community and sought to remove it by forging a political alilance with the Santals.

The Mahto and Santals have been traditional enemies: the former, as a relatively well-to-do peasantry have exploited the latter. Their political alliance was not without opposition, doubt, and fear voiced by some sections of the two communities. Nevertheless, the leaders of the two communities were able to bring them together. The Mahtos thought that by placing the Santals in the forefront they would be able to protect their interest. A result of this alliance was the formation of the Jharkhand Mukti Morcha (1973) with the objectives of forming a separate Jharkhand state, ending exploitation of tribals by non-tribals, and securing preferential treatment for the sons of the soil in the matter of employment. The Shivaji Samaj merged with the new organization.

The Morcha combined in its operations elements of agrarian radicalism and cultural revivalism. As mentioned earlier the Jharkhand had no programme of agrarian action. BSD despite its attempt to establish a rapport with the tribal peasants remained essentially an urban party. The Santals were more sensitive to the agrarian question. The agrarian movement among the Santals—other tribes were also affected—had been erupting at harvest time in all those areas of Bihar (particularly Purnea and the Santal Pargana) where the Santals were engaged as labourers and crop-sharers. The Santals were politically-oriented, they were better organized and more militant than other tribes. The most important series of incidents occurred in 1968 in the Santal Pargana, when the Santals forcibly harvested crops standing in their land, illegally occupied by moneylenders. Yet it was striking that there was little bloodshed. From then on, such incidents became part of the agrarian landscape of Bihar.

The Morcha then launched an operation to recover alienated land from moneylenders and big peasants. There were 120 violent incidents including 48 of looting of crops or forcible harvesting of crops standing on lands in illegal possession of moneylenders, 29 attacks on "explotiers", 2 of arson and 28 murders. In the process there were five incidents of clashes with the police. The largest number of incidents (69) occurred in 1974. Later the number of incidents declined and the Morcha came out in support of the Prime Minister's 20-point programme.

Though the Mahto's alliance with the Santals gave the movement an extra ethnic dimension, the movement also developed into a pan-Santal awakening. The Hul Jharkhand supported it. The Santals of Hazaribagh, Giridih and Dhanbad formed a common front with those of the Santal Pargana.

The Santal leader, Sibu Soren, acquired something of a charisma, which was so typical of the nativistic movement:

> Through a systematic campaign, all sorts of stories are spread among the gullible tribals about Sibu Soren's supernatural powers. It is said that he crosses rivers on a motor-cycle, is not burnt by fire, dives into a pond and comes out through some hole somewhere in the land, bullets cannot pierce his body and so on. It is propagated that Sibu Soren is "Chando Bonga" (the Greatest God) and Indira Gandhi has granted him a licence to rule this part of Jharkhand territory. Surprisingly, not only some Adivasi officers of the state government, but also some others are very soft towards this extremist leader and let him have his way.[7]

Elements of the ancient tribal self-government were revived. The Baisi (courts) functioned a court without fees or pleaders and dealt out simple justice. A volunteer force was raised. Subscriptions were locally collected. Tribal traditions of collective farming and preservation of jungles, pastures, and common land were revived; a common grain pool was created. A study provides further information:

> The poor peasant movement (as this movement is described) at Tundi (Dhanbad) has successfully defied the state power as yet. It has not only retrieved the illegally alienated land redistributed it among the poor peasants but has launched joint cultivation and community irrigation programmes thereby raising the gross area sown and the agricultural production. Until the agricultural year 1973-74, they were having only one crop, i.e., kharif paddy, in the villages. This year they jointly cultivated and harvested wheat on 15 acres of land, there is standing sum-summer paddy on 75 acres of land. The activists in the movement now propose to go ahead with the reclamation of land for cultivation. The various measures which have been undertaken have not only improved the economic condition of the poor peasants and transformed them to the category of poor-middle peasants but have given them something more—a fresh and free air to breathe. The jungles are being preserved. The stocks are being raised with enthusiasm and devotion. They now know what freedom and democracy really means. It is now an area which knows no scarcity but it knows no peace either.[8]

There was yet another model of cultural revivalism among the Santals of the Santal Parganas. A Sidhu-Kanhu Baisi, named after the two heroes of the Santal *hul* was formed in February, 1966 to :

(i) speed up tempo of education among the Santal, the Paharia and the other tribes;
(ii) improve tribal economy; and
(iii) end tribal exploitation.[9]

The Baisi also exhorted the Santals to expel the *dikus* and prevent them from cultivating land. Plays were composed and staged highlighting *diku* tyranny. The ancient system of village headmanship was sought to be revived. There was an attempt to purify the Santal religion of the so-called Hindu influences which included participation in the Durga and Kali *puja*. The Baisi subsequently split up along communal lines. An All-India Sidhu Kanhu Baisi was formed in February 1970 in opposition to the parent body.

Present Trends (1977-85)

Erosion of the electoral bases of the Jharkhand Party and its fragmentation, growing impact of the all-India political parties particularly the Congress, the Jan Sangh (as a constituent of the Janata Party and later as Bharatiya Janata Party) and the Communist parties, and militancy arising out of despair mark the tribal scene from 1977. Jharkhand parties, instead of aligning themselves with one another have preferred to align either with the Congress or leftwing parties. Ethnicity has receded in the background, and Chotanagpur has been sucked into the maelstrom of national politics becoming as prone to "election waves", as any other part of the country, but the local factor in its regional rather than ethnic aspect has crystalized.

The Jharkhand parties did not contest the Lok Sabha poll as a party in March 1977. In the election to the Bihar Assembly in May 1977, all four splinter groups of the Jharkhand party polled 81,227 votes as against 3,61,187 votes in 1972. The Janata wave swept the tribal regions. In spite of this, a militant phase of the Jharkhand movement started in October 1977.[10] It originated in the statements made by Jayaprakash Narayan, about the advisability of the formation of small states, and by the Home Minister, Charan Singh, about the reorganization of the states. These triggered off developments at two levels in Chotanagpur. First, all parties, including the Janata but excluding the Jharkhand Party, came together to demand a separate state for the Chotanagpur-Santal Pargana region. Second, the Jharkhand Party demanded the formation of the Jharkhand state consisting not only of the Chotanagpur-Santal Pargana region of Bihar, but also of the adjoining areas of Orissa, West Bengal and Madhya Pradesh. The movement, which lasted from October 1977 to June 1978, centred in South Chotanagpur. There were demonstrations, *gheraos* and strikes. Ultimately, the omnibus body, Jharkhand Prant Samyukt Morcha, constituted to lead the movement, collapsed under the weight of its own contradictions, its constituents having deserted it. The movement came to an end in 1979.

The Jharkhand parties remained fragmented. In the parliamentary elections (1980), the all-India Jharkhand Party, which moved closer to the Janata Party, won one parliamentary seat, while the Jharkhand parties won another in Ranchi and the Marxist Coordination Committee of Dhanbad, the third. The Jharkhand Party boycotted the State Assembly elections in 1980 in protest against the denial of the cock symbol, but its candidates remained in the field as independents. The Bharatiya Janata Party and the Congress (I) continued to dominate the strongholds of the old Jharkhand Party. The Jharkhand Mukti Morcha emerged as a major political force in the industrial and mining belt of Chotanagpur, and in state politics, particularly after the 1980 general elections. It captured 13 seats and polled 3.38 lakh votes, while the old Jharkhand party or Parties could win only one seat and poll 33,469 votes. The Jharkhand Mukti Morcha had earlier reached an electoral understanding with the Congress (I), which helped it enormously in the elections but caused deep strain in its relations with its constituents. As Jharkhand Mukti Morcha moved closer to the Congress, its alliance with the Marxist Coordination Committee weakened and the backward Mahtos walked out of it. The All-India Jharkhand Party broke up with its leaders joining the Congress. The Jharkhand parties were wiped out for the first time since 1952 in the parliamentary elections of 1984 losing all the seats captured during the previous elections. The "sympathy wave" could be a factor in their debacle because it was widely believed that Indira Gandhi tried to help the tribes. An Oraon for the first time won from the Munda belt, which made news. The Congress continued to be the major force in the tribal region. The four Jharkhand parties polled 3,36,797 votes. The newly formed Jharkhand Mahasabha cut into the traditional votes of the Jharkhand Party. The results of Assembly elections that followed in 1985 showed that the two Jharkhand parties hardly managed to retain their strength, while the Congress improved its position. Out of 28 seats reserved for the scheduled tribes, the Jharkhand Mukti Morcha captured seven, just about its strength in 1980, and the Congress fourteen. The Communist Party of India and Dalit Mazdoor Kisan Party drew a blank while Bharatiya Janata Party had its strength halved.

As far as the total number of seats for Chotanagpur-Santal Pargana (82) were concerned, Jharkhand Mukti Morcha and BJP bagged 11 seats each and the Congress 41.

These results confirm the trends that emerged in the early 1960s. The all-India parties, particularly the Congress, have dominated the political processes, pushing the local parties in the background. This has happened because of the deep division among the tribal people, sharpened by growing stratification in tribal society, with their new middle class joining hands with their non-tribal counterparts in the Congress Party and elsewhere. The two Jharkhand parties that remain in the fray, surviving around their leaders, are confined to the Munda and Santal (also partly Ho) area. Their electoral base since 1952 has almost been halved during the period from 1952 to 1980 while the total electorate has grown in size from 18 million to 35 million. The Jharkhand parties (excluding independents) have polled as low as eighty thousand votes at their worst, and as high as about four hundred thousand votes, which is far below the peak they occupied in the fifties. This shows the extent of the erosion of their political base and the ground they have lost to the all-India parties. While the "tribal ethnicity" has receded in the background the regional factor has come to the fore, with almost every all-India party including the Congress having or trying to form a "regional set-up" and supporting overtly or covertly the concept of political or cultural autonomy of Chotanagpur.

II

Ethnicity, Regionalism and National Politics

Few ethnic movements can remain in a state of absolute political isolation. As mentioned earlier, the Adivasi Mahasabha enjoyed the support of the All-India Muslim League; the former also claimed the support of the Forward Bloc (the name of Subhas Chandra Bose was dragged in), and the Congress Socialist Party, a few local members of which were to join the Jharkhand Party later. The Congress rejected the Mahasabha demand to concede ethnicity as the basis of the formation of provinces. After independence the Jharkhand Party allied itself with the Chotanagpur Santal Pargana's Janata Party, formed in 1949, which had emerged as a strong rival of the Congress in northern Chotanagpur. The Janata Party commanded considerable support from the peasantry on account of the popular measures introduced by its founder-zamindar such as remission of land revenue, settlement of lands with raiyats on very advantageous terms and throwing open the forest for their use. He had also managed to rally round the party ex-zamindars by promising restoration of their zamindaris. This party had captured 11 seats in 1952 and 23 in 1957 in Chotanagpur, emerging as the second biggest party next to the Jharkhand Party. In 1962 it merged with the Swatantra Party and improved its strength by capturing 22 seats in the region at the expense of the Jharkhand. The compulsion to seek fresh alliances became evident to the Jharkhand Party. A resolution forming an opposition block with the Praja Socialist Party was adopted on 8 July 1962. Negotiations were started with the CPI for evolving a strategy on the labour and industrial fronts. The Jharkhand's relations with the Congress were close in Orissa in the mid-1950s. The Congress had also weakened in 1962. While the Jharkhand needed strong alliances, a faction in the Bihar Congress needed its support too, in the power game being played. The Jharkhand leaders thought that they could press for the formation of a separate state from the Congress platform by joining it. The Congress, on the other hand, was ready to concede the need for accelerated regional development in return for the support and merger of the Jharkhand Party. The agreement on merger, mentioned above, finalized on 20 June 1973 stipulated:

(i) Constitution of a Development Board for Chotanagpur and the Santal Pargana and parts of Bhagalpur, Monghyr and Shahabad districts for the purpose of economic, industrial, agricultural and educational development of the people and the general development of this area as a whole; and

(ii) Merger of the Congress and the Jharkhand Party and constitution of a sub-committee of the Bihar Pradesh Congress to coordinate political and organizational activities in the region.

Despite the fragmentation of the Jharkhand Party the splinter groups sought the support at the all-India level for the formation of a separate state in the context of a national re-organization of states. On 10 September 1974, three regional parties, namely, Maha Vidarbha Sangharsha Samiti, the Vishal Haryana Party and the Jharkhand Party jointly proposed to hold a convention of all regional political parties in India to chalk out a programme for reorganization of the states. The splitting up of bigger states became necessary, according to the spokesmen of this party, to eliminate regional imbalances and economic backwardness. The creation of smaller states would strengthen the country economically and politically, it was stressed.

None of the all-India parties committed itself to the formation of a Jharkhand state. The Jan Sangh saw behind the move the inspiration of Christian missionaries and anti-national forces:

> The separate Jharkhand State movement which was encouraged and abetted by Christian missionaries in the fifties, is in a sense no longer a sectarian movement. It has found new advocates from diverse sections of the populace. The movement which appeared to have collapsed a couple of years ago, gathered momentum in recent times and the creation of Meghalaya to satisfy the aspirations of the Hill people of Assam, emboldend the separatist political forces to launch the movement with renewed vigour for securing, in a constitutional way, a full-fledged state or an autonomous state within the state of Bihar.[11]

The Congress party never accepted ethnicity—except in the case of the creation of north-eastern states—as the basis for the formation of states; it favoured language as the factor determining the reorganization of states. The Prime Minister rejected the demand for the Jharkhand state on the ground that it was not practicable and would have repercussions in the country.[12] The President of the Bihar Pradesh Congress described the movement as "politically motivated, inspired by a parochical approach, a sinister move raised mainly by northern Biharis settled in the region, which would perpetuate the north Bihari settlers' exploitation of the tribals.[13] The Communist party rejected the demand and instead set forth in explicit terms the objective of regional autonomy for predominantly tribal areas of Chotanagpur and Santal Pargana and of economic and cultural upliftment of the adivasis. In a resolution adopted in May, 1975 it was stated:

(i) The existing organisations of the Adivasis like the Jharkhand party, Hul Jharkhand party, Jharkhand Mukti Morcha, Birsa Seva Dal, Chotanagpur Plateau Praja Parishad lack clear political perspective of tribals;

(ii) If a separate Jharkhand state of their conception comprising Chotanagpur plateau and some areas of Madhya Pradesh, Orissa, and West Bengal was set up, it would reduce the tribals to a state of perpetual minority of one-third in population. As a result, they would not be in a position to solve any of the political and economic prolems facing the tribals, instead this would enable reactionary forces to secure firmer stranglehold for plundering both the tribal and non-tribal people; and

(iii) Tribal regional councils ,according to the constitutional provisions, should be formed, for the two compact tribal majority areas in Bihar, consisting of namely (a) the major parts of Latehar Subdivision of Palamau, the Ranchi district (except six anchals), Singhbhum and Hazaribagh district and (b) the Santal area consisting of parts of the Santal Paragana and the Dhanbad district.[14]

The CPM was opposed to the division of West Bengal. The CPI(ML) parties were in favour of the tribal state.

Electoral Politics and Erosion of Ethnicity

Nothing illustrates more graphically the transition from ethnicity to regionalism than the electoral processes (Charts I—IV). The first general elections marked the zenith of the popularity of the ethnic movement. The size of valid votes polled by the Jharkhand Party remained an all-time record: 7.66 lakh; so did the number of seats captured by it, namely, 33 in the Bihar Assembly, three in the Bihar council and five in the Parliament. The Jharkhand had been able to capture not only the reserved but also a few general seats. The second general elections held after the recommendations of the States Reorganisation Commission resulted in a slight erosion in the popularity of the Jharkhand Party because its demand had not been conceded. Despite a rise in the number of voters, the votes polled by the Jharkhand was smaller in 1957, though the total number of seats bagged by it in the Bihar Assembly remained almost intact. The Party had also cast its net wider and won five seats in the Orissa Assembly and polled three per cent of the votes. The third general election, following the mid-term poll in Orissa in which the Jharkhand Party had been wiped out, came as a shock to its leaders. The number of votes polled plummeted to 4.67 lakh in 1962 as against 7.51 lakh in 1957; the number of seats captured by it was reduced to 20. The party had lost not only some general seats but also many reserved seats to its erstwhile ally the Janata Party (later Swatantra), the Jan Sangh, the Congress and the CPI which had made significant inroads into its strongholds. Following the merger with the Congress in 1963 the splinter groupsc ontested the fourth general election as independents. The result was a disaster. The trends noticed in the third general elections developed further: the Jan Sangh, Congress, Swatantra and CPI gained while the splinter groups could capture only eight seats and 1.72 lakh of valid votes. This was the lowest performance so far. A reason for this was the splitting of votes. For example, there were as many as 119 candidates contesting 15 seats in Ranchi as against 73 in 1962, 69 in 1957, and 59 in 1952.

There was some compensation, however, in the gains which the party later registered in Orissa and West Bengal. The state of political instability which supervened with the formation of the coalition governments in the eastern states after 1967, enabled the Jharkhand splinter groups to play a significant role in power politics and wrest some gains. They were able to regain lost ground in the mid-term elections in 1969. The pendulum swung back to the 1962 position. The Jharkhand groups captured 17 seats and 3.17 lakh of valid votes. The advantage thus gained was pressed home by the different groups in the state of continuing uncertainty to gain further concessions. Even so there could be no return to the 1957 position. The decline continued. While the Jharkhand crumbled in its heartland, it registered a significant advance in the adjoining areas of Orissa and West Bengal, winning four and two seats respectively in the 1971 elections. It was a creditable achievement indeed because in West Bengal the Jharkhand had never won a single seat before, and in Orissa it had staged a comeback after 1961. The Jharkhand also became the third constitutent of the United Front in Orissa, the two others being the Utkal Congress and the Swatantra Party, and Siddhilal Murmu was appointed a minister. In Bengal too, one of the two Jharkhandis became a minister in the non-Marxist United Front government, which assumed office on 2 April 1971. In Bihar the representatives of the different Jharkhand parties were always represented on the coalition governments. The 1972 elections to the Bihar Assembly witnessed the Jharkhand suffer its greatest setback: it could capture only seven seats and poll 3.6 lakh votes while the Congress captured 47 out of the 79 seats in the Chotanagpur-Santal Pargana region. As The *Statesman* observed: this "clearly indicated repudiation by the Adivasis of the Jharkhand party's demand for a separate state of the Chotanagpur with the Santal Parganas".[15] The party was also routed in the Orissa elections in 1974; the Congress swept the polls in the tribal areas which were the strongholds of the Gantantra (later Swatantra) and the Jharkhand. This underlines the growing integration of the tribals into the all-India political systems. But this statement must be qualified by the rider that election results are only one of the many indicators of the integrative process. These trends have however persisted.

Politicization of the tribes was rather slow. A study of the electoral politics in the tribal region underlined this as well the "regional" characteristics of tribal voting:

(i) Voter participation in tribal constituencies is lower than in non-tribal constituencies in almost all the states of India, though the turn out has been increasing—in Bihar from 43% to 54%—albeit at a slower rate seen in the second;

(ii) Tribal parties won their victories with a wide margin in the core (resolved) constituencies, showing cohesive backing by tribal supporters;

(iii) Tribal preferences have not yet stabilised though the pro-Congress trends since 1967 are clear; and

(iv) Tribal and non-tribal constituencies situated in the same zone almost act in a similar manner, and there are "distinct regional patterns in the sectoral behaviour of tribal constituencies reflecting not only differences between regions but also important differences among tribes themselves, their demographic distribution, levels of modernisation, intensity of self-awareness and their relationship with State and Central authority".[16]

Between the scheduled tribes and other communities, the first have always shown a greater enthusiasm for participation in the elections. This was noticed even in the first general election:

> The election symbol of the Jharkhand Party was the cock and they convened their meetings by the sound of crowing. Hundreds of people gathered whenever they heard human beings crowing. Even the illiterate, old and shortsighted women made sure that the ballot box had the symbol of cock before casting their votes. They stood in long queues exactly in the same order in which their names occurred on the electoral rolls. The tribal people showed far greater cohesiveness and civic sense than the high caste of people of other regions.[17]

The report on the first general election also observed:

> The Jharkhand along with the Socialist and the Congress was the best organised party—their policies and programmes were well-known. The methods of canvassing were personal contact, distribution of leaflets and public meetings.[18]

It further reads:

> Voters from the Scheduled Tribes and backward classes, generally, recorded votes at a higher rate than voters from others sections of the people. The punctuality, discipline and orderliness displayed by the Scheduled Tribe voters have been

particularly mentioned by several presiding officers. A parliamentary returning officer reports that the percentage of electors who recorded their votes is 30 to 35 in urban areas and 40 in rural areas, while among the Scheduled Tribes electors it is 70 to 80.[19]

Interdenominational and Inter-tribe Equation within the Tribal Movement

The foregoing account should not create the impression that the ethnic movement has been monolithic without any strains of interdenominational competition among its Christian members or inter-tribe rivalry. The semblance of unity forged and maintained for about two decades barely concealed the currents and cross-currents of differences arising out of the consideration of tribal and denominational interests. In the first phase of the tribal movement the denominational inspiration behind the political demands was only too evident. In the second phase, the Anglicans and Lutherans dominated the Unnati Samaj movement and provided its leadership; the Roman Catholics kept themselves out of it and formed their own Catholic Sabha to present their case before the government. The Catholic Sabha continued to maintain its identity even after all other bodies had merged to form the Adivasi Mahasabha. The latter organization maintained a delicate balance among the three denominations by providing suitable representation to their interests in the organization and leadership. If the president was an Anglican, the secretary was either a Lutheran or a Catholic. This equation was continued into the Jharkhand Party, even though the Party was dominated by the Protestant Christians. In 1962, following the reconstitution of the party its Catholic secretary was dropped, which caused resentment among the Catholic supporters of the Jharkhand. The latter were always suspected of maintaining an ambivalent attitude towards the tribal movement. It was stated that the Catholics were guided by global considerations in their crusade against Communism; they preferred order to chaos in India and so they lent indirect support to the Congress candidates in elections. In the 1974 Orissa elections, the Roman Catholic Church was reported to have issued secretly a "fervent" appeal to the electorate to give "mass support" to the Congress; the local branches issued a "pastoral letter" quoting the secret circular to the Christian Adivasis who consituted an overwhelming majority in Sundargarh, Mayurbhanj and Keonjhar. This was a windfall for the Congress which swept the polls.[20]

The Protestant missions, Lutherans and Anglicans, who were almost Indianized, encouraged and practised grass-root democracy in electing their church bodies (*mandlis*). This explains their consistent support to the tribal movement. They still form the core of the Jharkhand groups.

The militant movements in Chotanagpur were led by the Kolarian tribes, the Munda, Ho and the Santal, who have been dominant communities, less exposed to external influences and more cohesive. The Oraon have lived longer in exposed regions, and have been less militant and more resilient. Both the Munda and the Oraon joined the Sardar movement which sought to establish the peasant rights of the tribal people but the Oraons broke off in mid-1880s. The Munda provided the leadership for the students' movement in 1915-20. The Oraon constituted the leadership of the Unnati Samaj Movement; the Munda kept out of it and formed their own Munda Sabha. Except in the early phase of the Adivasi Mahasabha, the Munda remained the dominant element in it. The Jharkhand Party had its strongholds in the Ho, the Munda and the Santal regions. Some sections of the Oraons had become a little lukewarm in their support later, and with pro-Congress Tanabhagats in their ranks, they switched their support to the Congress and the Jan Sangh (now Bhartiya Janata Party) the popular 1967 votes polled in favour of latter went up from 17.2 in 1967 to 33.2 per cent in 1969—and continued to support the Congress since. The Jharkhand parties have had their bases among distinct sub-ethnic groups: the Hul-Jharkhand is entirely Santal (and partly Ho) now; the All-India Jharkhand Party (Bagun group) as mentioned earlier, draws its support mainly from the Hos of Singhbhum; and the Jharkhand Party relies on the Munda.

An interesting sidelight is provided by the fact that the major tribes have generally dominated the elections while minor tribes have played a smaller role. For example, out of 32 seats captured by the Jharkhand Party in the 1952 elections the Santal accounted for seven, the Munda three, the Ho five, and the Oraon seven, while the smaller tribes such as the Kharia and the Kharwar got only two seats and one seat respectively. In 1967, again, while the Santals had captured ten, the Oraon seven, the Ho six, and the Munda five, the Chero could get only one seat out of the 29 reserved seats. The parliamentary seats have always been captured by major tribes. A reason for the dominant role of the major tribes could be their relatively strong economic base and cohesive social organization. They are settled peasants while minor tribes are primarily artisans, small cultivators and craftsmen, or are engaged in shifting cultivation.

In the first three general elections Christian candidates were mostly elected from Ranchi and Santal Pargana, while non-Christian candidates won mainly from Singhbhum and Palamau. The Christian candidates has been gradually declining. In 1967 while non-Christians captured 75.8 per cent the Christians could capture only 24.2 per cent of the reserved seats in the Bihar Assembly. A similar pattern also emerged in the parliamentary elections. This trend has persisted since. The erosion of Christian leadership has had its repercussions elsewhere.

While the major tribes first supported the Jharkhand Party and later the Congress, some of the minor tribes have always been pro-Congress. For example, the Santal's neighbours, the Paharia who benefited from the welfare schemes spearheaded by Congress-supported voluntary agencies, the Asurs of Ranchi and the Kharwars of Palamau have generally voted for the Congress. The Paharia had even organized a Yugavasi Sabha against the Adivasi Mahasabha. Even among the major tribes, the hinduized bhagats, the Sapha Hor among the Santals, the thread-wearing Santals in Hazaribagh and Tanabhagats among the Oraon have always been pro-Congress.

A change in the ideology is also noticeable. While the Jharkhand Party or parties remained committed to the concept of a Jharkhand state, the JMM projected a radical ideology. The Jharkhandi is described as a producer irrespective of caste, tribe or nation residing in the Jharkhand. The Jharkhand is described as an internal colony which is being exploited by outsiders. Even though the region accounts for 28 per cent of minerals, it avails itself of only 15 per cent of the state's budget for development. The development process itself is exploitative of the local inhabitants and outsiders have moved in to seize all opportunities of employment. There is a Jharkhand nationality and as in all nationality questions, self-determination is the key element in the social formation. It is only with a separate state of Jharkhand that the nationality question can be satisfactorily resolved for the benefit of the exploited and depressed working classes. The Jharkhand must therefore turn into a *lalkhand*, that is, the movement of political separatism and struggle of the working classes should go together, according to its protagonists.[21] The JMM has emerged as the most effective of various Jharkhand parties (Chart IV).

The map of the Jharkhand has undergone a change. At the outset of the movement the Jharkhand state was to include the old feudatory states of Orissa and Madhya Pradesh, two districts of West Bengal, parts of Bihar Arrah district (Bhabhua), Bhagalpur (Banka) and Monghyr (Jamui) adjoining Chotanagpur and inhabited by its tribes, and of course, Chotanagpur. In recent years, adjoining parts of Bihar districts have been left out. The Jharkhand map now shows three districts of West Bengal, four of Orissa, two of Madhya Pradesh and seven districts of Chotanagpur in Bihar. The Chotanagpur-Santal Pargana belt of Bihar was the epicentre of the movement; while the parent organizations are located in Bihar, the adjoining areas of Orissa, West Bengal and Madhya Pradesh, peopled by Chotanagpur tribes, were marginally influenced by the movement. For instance, in the Lok Sabha elections in 1980, the party could poll only 50,192 votes in West Bengal and 61,881 in Orissa. The assembly election figures for Orissa were 25,002 in 1977 and 34,782 in 1980. It was only in Bihar that it was able to recapture its 1971 performance of polling about four lakh votes. Thus the Chotanagpur-Santal Pargana region of Bihar remains the centre of the movement.

III

It is paradoxical that what the old Jharkhand Party with its impressive electoral achievements could not gain in its heyday from 1949 to 1962, the fragmented Jharkhand parties and urban pressure groups achieved after 1967. There was no participation of tribal elements in the Bihar Government from 1950 to 1959. A tribal minister was inducted in 1960. Since 1963 and particularly since 1967 the tribal leaders have played their cards skilfully; there have been adequate representation in the government not only of the two major tribal regions, Chotanagpur and the Santal Pargana, but also enthusiastic participation by both Christian and non-Christian elements in them. At one time, in the 1970s, tribal leaders headed as many as eleven corporations set up by the government. A major demand of the tribals has also been met by setting up the Chotanagpur-Santal Pargana Development Authority, which embodies the concept of regional development and provides for a separate pool of resources of which tribals will be the main if not exclusive beneficiaries. The widespread unrest in tribal regions also influenced the passage of a number of agrarian measures including many pieces of legislation, which place stringent curbs on alienation of tribal land and provide for debt redemption, credit support, allotment of homestead sites. Restoration of land alienated during the period of thirty years, which was a major demand of the tribal movements, has been made possible through an enactment. There has also been impressive progress in providing employment to tribals in administration and industrial undertakings. Almost all tribal groups including the radical elements welcomed the Prime Minister's 20-point programme as an instrument for accelerated development and radical transformation in the tribal area.

The failure of the Jharkhand movement to develop into a full-fledged regional movement may be explained by many factors. Firstly, its appeal to the non-tribal sections of the Chotanagpuris was small, because it was essentially a tribal party, and the tribals and non-tribals were not on the best of terms. Secondly, its past record of alliances with the forces which had worked against the national movement and remained "loyalist" cost it the sympathy and support of a large section of the ruling elite. Thirdly, its structure contained many contradictions which sharpened and multiplied as the cleavage between the Christian and non-Christian tribals deepened. Lastly, the region had always been exposed to the operation of pan-Indian forces. The ethnic movement therefore could not remain in a state of political isolation. The impact of development and macro-political system and the merger with the Congress considerably weakened the demand for a separate state. The slogan of Jharkhand state was, however not given up. But the possibilities of the Jharkhand Party capturing its pre-1962 position of strength appear to be remote. Moreover, as the election results show, there has been a gradual erosion of ethnicity as a factor in regional politics.

Thus, tribal ethnicity in a multi-ethnic society characterized by economic interdependence among different communities struck out a different course of development in Chotanagpur from that of the north-east. Separatism in this tribal region did not develop into secessionism. Recently a section of extremists demanded the formation of a sovereign nation for a part of Singhbhum known as the Kolhan conquered by the British in 1837 on the ground that this part of the country had never merged with the Indian Union during or after the transfer of power in 1947. Two representatives of their organization went abroad to seek support for this claim, and there was a violent confrontation between its members and the police on 26 October 1981.[22] However, this move was not supported by the people and parties. Secessionism was neither feasible in the current circumstances nor warranted by socio-economic developments.

All tribal parties speak of a set of regional objectives and programmes of action. This has been due to the realization that tribals do not form the majority in Chotanagpur as a whole and that there are backward communities in this backward region which could also be brought together on a common political platform to demand their share in the control of economic resources and exercise of political power. Now, almost all political parties have their regional units for Chotanagpur, which has acquired the attributes of a sub-state, a mini-secretariat to formulate and supervise the implementation of sub-plans of five year plans and a bench of the high court. This has no doubt been due to the articulation of the tribal factor by the Jharkhand and other parties over the years.

Notes and References

1. I started my study of tribal autonomy movements in Chotanagpur as part of Jawaharlal Nehru Fellowship project. On 28 March 1973, I presented a paper entitled "From Movement to Party, A Study of the Tribal Politics in Middle India 1920-63" at the Nehru Memorial Museum and Library. (K.S. Singh, "The Freedom Movement and Tribal Sub-Movements 1920-47" in B.R. Nanda (ed) *Essays in Modern Indian History*, Oxford University Press, Delhi, 1980). In 1976 I presented a paper on "Tribal Ethnicity in a Multi-Ethnic Society: A Study in the Process of Confflict and Integration in Colonial and Post-Colonial Chotanagpur" at a UNESCO Seminar in Manila; it was later published in *Trends in Ethnic Group Relatiohs in Asia and Oceania, Race and Society*, UNESCO, Paris, 1979. Earlier in September 1975 I had presented another paper "From Ethnity to Regionalism: A Study in Tribal Politics and Movements in Chotanagpur from 1900 to 1975" at a seminar held by the Indian Institute of Advanced Study which has been published in S.C. Malik (ed). *Dissent, Protest and Reform in Indian Civilization*, Indian Institute of Advanced Study, Simla, 1977. In December 1980, I presented yet another paper on Tribal Unrest partly updating the earlier studies at a seminar on tribal development organized at Bhubaneswar in October 1980 by the National Commission on Backward Areas. In my Devraj Chanana Memorial Lecture, delivered at the Delhi University, on Tribal Transformation on 8-10 December, 1981, I referred to some recent aspects of the Jharkhand movement. All the material were put together in my article "Tribal Autonomy Movements in Chotanagpur", *Tribal Movements*, Vol. II, Manohar, 1983. The present paper brings the story uptodate.

Also see, *Jharkhand Andolan me Videshi Missionarion aur Videshi Paison ki Bhumika* (year not given). Further see for a brief overview K.L. Sharma, "Jharkhand Movement—Bihar", *Economic and Political Weekly* (*EPW*), 10 January 1972. For the radical phase of the movement, see Arvind Narayan Das, "Peasants Struggle in Chotanagpur", *EPW*, March 1, 1975 and Arun Sinha, "Bihar's Resurgent Adivasi", *EPW*, 9 September, 1978. Also see Nirmal Sengupta, "Class and Tribe in Jharkhand", *EPW*, April 5, 1980, Nirmal Sengupta, "Class and Tribe in Jharkhand", *EPW* April 5, 1980, and Hiranmoy Dhar, "Split in the Jharkhand Mukti Morcha", *EPW*, 2 August 1980.

2. "Address not formally Presented", Appendix XI presented in India *to Hjs Excellency the Secretary of State for India, East vol. XVIII.*

3. *The Constitution of the Birsa Seva Dal* (in Hindi), December 10, 1971.

4. In Jamshedupur, for example, the BSD volunteers grabbed large chunks of valuable urban land. sold it in pieces to non-Bihari businessmen who in fact abetted this operation. Colonies named after tribal leaders were established, where only a minority of tribals lived, the majority being the non-Biharis connected with the industries.

5. See for example *Census of India* 1931, *Bihar and Orissa*, pp. 263 and 268. The Kurmi or the Mahto in Chotanagpur were originally recognized as a scheduled tribe; in 1931, they were descheduled as a tribe as they claimed the status of ksatriyas. In Palamau, like the Kahar they wear the sacred thread and say that they belong to the 'karo bans'. See "The Kurmi of Chota Nagpur", Appendix V, Bihar and Orissa, vol. VII, Part I, Report, pp. 291-94.

6. *The Searchlight*, Patna, June 1, 1975, reported that the Chotanagpur and Santal Pargana Kurmi Mahasabha had met at Ramgarh and called upon the Governor of Bihar to (a) fix by an ordinance the lowest marriagable age of a Kurmi girl at 14 and that of a Kurmi boy at 18 and make violation of these age-limits a congnizible offence; (b) include all the communities figuring in Annexure I of the backward classes in the State of Bihar in the tribal list; and (c) rehabilitate the persons displaced by the construction of the Subarnarekha and Kherkai dam near Chandil.

7. *The Economic Times*, May 13, 1975.

8. Pradhan H. Prasad, "Agrarian unrest and Economic Changes in Rural Bihar: Three Case Studies", *Economic and Political Weekly*, June 14, 1975.

9. *The Searchlight*, Patna, September 10, 1974.

10. For further details, see the author's "Tribal Autonomy Movements in Chotanagpur", op. cit.

11. *The Organiser*, July 29, 1972.

12. *The Indian Nation*, Patna, April 25, 1975.

13. *Ibid.*, January 12, 1975.

14. *The Patriot*, New Delhi, May 11, 1975.

15. *The Statesman*, March 21, 1972.

16. Myron Weiner & John Osgoodfield, *Electoral Politics in the Indian States: Three Disadvantage Sectors*, vol. II, pp. 78-119.

17. *Report of the First General Elections under the Constitution of India in Bihar*, 1951-52 p. 13.

18. S.V. Kogekar and R.L. Park (ed), *Report on the Indian General Elections*, 1951-52 pp. 29-30.

19. *Ibid.*, p. 14.

20. *The Indian Express*, February 18, 1974.

21. A.K. Roy, *Jharkhand aur Lalkhand*, Marxwadi Coordination, Dhanbad, July 1981. For a detailed exposition of this theme see Nirmal Sengupta (ed), *Fourth World Dynamics : Jharkhand.*

22. *Ravivar*, 20 December, 1981; *The Sundary Observer*, Bombay, 27 December, 1981.

CHART IA

PERFORMANCE OF THE JHARKHAND PARTY/PARTIES

		1952	1957	1962	1967	1969 (B.H.A.)	1971 (H.P.)	1972 (B.H.A.)	1974
(A) *BIHAR*									
Candidates set up	1 House of people	6	14 (2 retired)	11	(As independents)		19 HJ 3 AIJ 16	106 BPHJ 16 PHJ 5 AIJ 44 JP 41	
	2 Bihar Legislative Assembly	44	96 (16 withdrew or retired)			75	NA	24 HJ 13 Ind. 11	
Candidates who forfeited their deposits	3 House of people	NA	4	3	NA	NA	NA	NA	
	4 Bihar Legislative Assembly	NA	27	36	NA	NA	13	NA	
Seats won	5 House of people	3	5	3	1	—	1	—	

	6 Bihar Legislative Asesembly	83	32	20	8 (As independents)	17 (HJ- 7 Ind-10)	—	8
	7 Bihar Council	3	—					
Valid votes polled	8 House of people	749,702 (14.76)	751,830 (14.79)	467,338 (4.70) ..	143,470	x	191898 343,314 (1971)	x
	9 Bihar Legislative Assembly	766,366 (15.21)	726,936 (13.75)	432,044 (4.39)	172,123	229,327	—	361,187
	10 Percentage of valid votes to the total.	3.3	7.34	4.00	NA	NA	0.46	2.09
	Variation	—	29.5(+)	17(—12.5)	—	—	—	—
(B) Orissa	11 Orissa Assembly	x	25; contested all lost (1961 Jan)	x	—	—		4 (out of 15) 16 contested all lost

NB One difficulty in compiling the statistics has been to identify the independents put up by the Jharkhand parties which were not "registered parties". Part the of statistics about the Jharkhand parties' performance is therefore hidden under "independents". For purposes of computation data regarding the performance of all Jhakhand Parties have been clubbed as for as possible though a few discrepancies remain.

Source : Reports of the First, Second, Third, Fourth and Fifth (typed) general elections in the Bihar; *Report of the mid-term Elections in Bihar* 1969. (office of chief electoral officer, Patna)

Chart (contd.) Bihar

	1971	1977	1980	1985
Bihar Assembly				
Contesting candidates	—	30	58	NA.
Candidates who lost their security deposit	—	22	40	—
Candidates won	—	1	11	13
Valid votes polled	—	81228	399574	
Percentage in relation to Election	—	0.31	1.02	NA.
Percentage in relation to total valid votes	—	0.45	1.170	NA.

Chart I C Bihar (contd.)

(Lok Sabha)

	1971	1977	1980	1984
Seats contested	19	Nil	12	NA
Lost	18	Nil	11	NA
Won	1	Nil	1	NA

Sources : Bihar state: A statistical Analysis; Lok Sabha General Election 1977. 1980; Bihar Legislative Assembly 1980.

CHART II A

PARTYWISE BREAK-DOWN OF THE ELECTED SCHEDULED TRIBE CANDIDATES IN THE RESERVED CORE CONSTITUTENCIES IN BIHAR.

	1952		1957		1962		1967		1969	1971	1972
	HP	BLP	HP	BLP	HP	BLP	HP	BLP	(Mid-term elections to BLA) BLA	(Part)	(BLA)
1. Congress	2	7	1	6	1	3	4	14	6	3	17
2. Jharkhand	3	25	3	21	3	18	(Contested as independents)		10	2	AIG (B) 4 JP (H) 1 BPIIJ 2 PHJ 1
3. Socialist or S.S.P.	—	3	x	x	x	1	x	1	—	x	8
4. Janata	x	1	x	3	—	—	—	—	—	—	—
5. Lok Sevakh Sangh	1	2	—	—	—	—	—	—	—	—	—
6. P.S.P.	x	x	x	x	x	1	—	—	—	—	—
7. C P I	x	x	x	x	x	1	x	x	—	—	1
8. Swatantra	x	x	x	x	1	8	x	1	—	—	—
9. Jan Sangh/BJP	x	x	x	x	x	x	x	5	6	—	—
10. Independents	x	x	1	2	x	x	1	8	17 HJ7 Ind.10	1(H)	3

6(6)	38(38)	5(5)	32(32)	5(5)	32(32)	5(5)	29(29)	29(29)	5(5)	29

HP—House of People
BLA—Bihar Legislative Assembly
( )—Reserved seats

AIJ (B)	All-India Jharkhand Party (Bagun)
JP	Jharkhand Party (Horo group)
BPHJ	Bihar Prantiya Hul Jharkhand Party
PHJ	Progressive Hul Jharkhand Party
HJ	Hul Jharkhand.
JMM	Jharkhand Mukti Morcha

Chart II B Bihar (contd.)

	1977	1980		1984	1985
	Parliament		Bihar Assembly	Parliament	Bihar Assembly
Congress	—	2	12	4	14
Jharkhand	—	2	7	—	11
CPI	—	—	1	—	—
Jan Sangh/BJP	—	—	6	—	3
Lok Dal (DMKP)	—	—	2	—	—
Independents	—	—	—	—	

Source : *Bihar State Assembly General Election 1980. A Statistical Analysis.*

Chart III

Performance of the Jharkhand Party/parties in Bihar
(An Overview)

	Votes polled for the State Assembly	*Seats won in the State Assembly*	*Seats won in the Parliament (No. of votes)*
1952	766,366	33	3
1957	726,939	32	5
1962	432,644	20	3
1967	172,123	8	1
1969	229,327	17	nil
1971	343,314	—	(191,818) 2
1972	361,187	8	1 (1,95,880) (1971)
1977	81,227	1	×
1980	399,574	14	1 (1,40,778)
1984*			(nil) (3,36,797)
1985*	438,300*	9	—

*JMM

Chart IV (Bihar)

	1971 (LS)	1972 (BA)	1977/1977 (LS)	(BA)	1980 (LS)	1980 (BA)	1984 (LS)	1985 (BA)
All India Jharkhand	1,32,026	1,48,731 (00.86)	11,133—		(as independent)	—	2,415	—
Jharkhand (Horo)	—	89,591 (00.52)	—	66,832	1,40,778	34,523	77,094	—
Bihar Prantiya Hul Jharkhand	—	93,594 (00.54)	—	3,262	—	—	—	—
Hul Jharkhand	58,872	—	—	—	—	—	—	—
Progressive Hul Jharkhand	—	29,271 (00.17)	—	—	—	—	—	—
Jharkhand Mukti Morcha	—	—	—	—	—	3,64,991	3,36,797	4,38,300
Chotanagpur Bhumi Rakshak Sangh	4,982	1,274 (00.01)	—	—	—	—	—	—
Jharkhand Mahasabha	—	—	—	—	—	—	21,537	—

Sources (i) *Lok Sabha General Election*, 1977, *Bihar State: A statistical Analysis.*
(ii) *Lok Sabha General Election* 1980. *Bihar State : A statistical Analysis.*
(iii) *General Elections* 1977, *Bihar*—office of the Chief Election Officer, Patna, Bihar.

House of People/LS Lok Sabha/Parliament
BA Bihar Assembly.

11

The Post-Colonial Scenario

Social Anthropology has moved away from the stereotype of a tribe as an isolate, and has focused on interaction and interdependence of tribes and peasants.[1] Recent literature has delineated the process of the assimilation of tribes into the caste-peasant base of Indian civilization through the adoption of agricultural technology and linguistic and cultural norms of the peasant castes. The varna-jati model of absorption has now given way to the search for political status as an ethnic minority within the constitutional framework informed with an egalitarian and democratic ideology. This has inspired the rise of ethnic-based solidarity movements led by an educated elite, there being a broad correlation between the intensity of the separatist solidarity movements and the degree of spatial and cultural isolation from the regional caste/peasant society.[2] The social historian has seen this process of integration within the framework of the political economy of feudalism and colonialism.[3] As mentioned earlier, the jati model of integration is inadequate.[4] This process of integration has sometimes been oversimplified; the transition of tribes into peasants and of peasants into a depeasantized working class is generally described as a unilinear process.[5] Such studies of a tribe as a class or an ethnic community overlook the complexities of tribal social formations and the pull of ethnicity amidst growing differentiation. G. S. Ghurye, who had propounded his anti-isolation and pro-assimilation viewpoint regarding tribals in 1942, has recently not only reiterated his views but has also questioned the social anthropologists' commitment to the concept of integration instead of assimilation of tribes into the larger society.[6] What irks him is that the American model of ethnic-cum-cultural pluralism has been unabashedly applied to the Indian situation, even though it has failed in relation to the American Indians. Ghurye notes that while the

Russians have set out to Russianize their nationalities, the Chinese have Sinified their minorities and the Americans did try to Americanize their ethnics once upon a time, there is also a case for the assimilation of the scheduled tribes, a process which has been held up by the faulty policies of the government out to appease the tribals.

Therefore, it will be appropriate to set the post-colonial processes of the tribal transformation in a wider perspective. We will first deal with the perspective and ideology, economic transformation and social stratification in tribal society in India. We will then discuss how these processes are reflected not only in ethnic-based solidarity movements but in a whole range of movements.

I

We are by now familiar with the stories of the annihilation of indigenous peoples and the formation of the reservations for the "Red Indians" in the New World, under various treaties concluded between their chiefs and the colonizers' governments, continuing encroachment on reservations and restriction of the natives' rights in them, etc. The encounter with the white settlers and Christianity gave rise to many a movement, the study of which has generated a good deal of information and stimulated a lot of theoretical model-building. In the United States which has an Indian population of 800,000 divided into 300 tribes living in 300 reservations, about 40 per cent of them are living below the poverty line. This is in spite of the fact that the Federal Government spends an incredibly large amount on their welfare and the Indians enjoy full rights as American citizens. The Indians have refused to be assimilated and to give up their identity in spite of the Americanization of their life-style. The process of grabbing of the Indian land continues. In a "damning" indictment, the World International Tribunal at Rotterdam (Holland) in November 1980 held the governments of the United States and Canada guilty of "stealing" the land of the Indians and "charged them with following a systematic policy of genocide against the Indians". of having illegally deprived them of the lands and of unleashing violent repression against their protest movements". The tribunal also condemned the activities of various multinational corporations in the Indian settlement areas which have resulted in reckless mining. deforestation, despoiling of the land and utter callousness in waste disposal on the part of the multinational corporations and have caused serious environmental and health hazards leading to innumerable diseases and, in the long run, physical deformities and deaths.[7]

The North American model of reservations travelled to Latin America. A recent study of the policy, legislation and administration of welfare measures for these people, conducted by the International Labour Organisation revealed that they were still governed by the 19th century attitude of complete assimilation and denied rights to a share in the administration of their affairs. In Brazil the Indians who are not integrated with national life are held under tutelage and thus denied the exercise of full civic rights. Of the 180,000 Indians under tutelage none has applied for emancipation. In Columbia the general law of the state does not apply to the "savages" who are being reclaimed to civilization by the missions. In general the picture which emerges is dismal.[8]

In Australia, too, the aborigines were pushed off their ancestral land and herded onto reservations, and they continued to be exterminated until 1928 when the last official killings were reported. Their number fell from 300,000 in the late 18th century to 67,000 in 1901, but has been slowly increasing since then, having reached 161,000 today. It was not until 1967 that equal citizenship rights were given to the aborigines, their languages were recognized, and the Commonwealth assumed concurrent jurisdiction over matters relating to them which earlier fell within the purview of the state regimes. Other administrative changes are a creation of the Department of Aboriginal Affairs, an Aboriginal Development Commission and an elected National Aboriginal Conference. The aborigines' customary law is being integrated into Australian jurisprudence. The ownership of land however remained the key issue and it was not until 1977 that the government enacted a law whereby the aborigines could lay claim to any crown land not already occupied. It is reported that about 25,000 aborigines acquired freehold title to roughly 28 percent of Northern Territory's 523,620 square miles of rock and shrub. Similarly the Government of South Australia handed over to the Pitjantiatiara tribe title deeds to about 40,000 square miles of territory.[9] Complications have, however, arisen in this regard as Australia has struck rich oil and mineral deposits in the aborigines' homeland.

Alongside the reservations, there is also the model of incorporations established for indigenous people. There are Maori incorporations in New Zealand in which the Maori landowners have become shareholders, farming is determined by a managing committee and profits are disbursed annually as dividends. While these have carried out expensive farming operations, which have contributed significantly to the overall growth and productivity, they hardly claim to be a vital link of New Zealand's economy.[10]

Against the capitalistic models of reservations and incorporations based on the concept of the assimilation of indigenous peoples could be pitted the socialistic concept of self-determination of nationalities which was formulated as part of the debate on the national question in the second and third decades of the present century. Soviet ethnographers recognize ethnicity as a process of social consolidation working at a level lower than nationality and as a key element in socialist reconstruction. At the time of the foundation of the USSR the right of the nationality and national minority to determine its political and economic status was recognized and their union into the great family was considered a voluntary act. In consonance with this principle the ethnic boundaries were rigorously demarcated and made coterminous with the administrative boundaries of republics and autonomous territories. The policy has been to promote the full development of cultural autonomy of the nationalities while integrating them fully within the politico-economic system of socialism. While describing this process the Soviet ethnographers have noted that the pre-Revolution social system of many of these national minorities was characterized by the rise of private property and social differentiation, alienation of the upper crust from the working populations, etc. With the growth of the socialist economy, the primitive communities have been generally urbanized and their pastoral or agrarian economics have been integrated into the macro-level industrial complexes leading to a phenomenal rise of productive forces.[11] At the same time there have also been strong centralizing influences at work, for example, the widespread use of the Russian language as the medium of communication. Once the choice of self-determination has been exercised at the time of the formation of the state or the nation-state, secessionism is out of question and is seen as the handiwork of neocolonial forces.

The third world under the colonial system was generally spared the traumatic experiences of the reservations. The colonial encounter with the indigenous population was not as direct and as bloody. The colonial system, in the countries of tropical Africa and South Asia, preferred a system of direct or indirect rule or a combination of both for the indigenous population. These countries shared the experiences of national oppression, ethnic conflicts and contradictions, of the role of the ethnic factor or factors in their freedom struggles. After attaining independence, many of the African states faced the task of forming a nation out of myriad tribes, and the euphoria over the unity of ethnic communities forged in the course of the freedom struggles gave way to a mature understanding of interethnic relationship and the need for its development in the process of national consolidation. Although many African states had passed the stage of tribal formation, tribal forms and prejudices survived. Therefore while ethnic goups were exhorted to give up their tribalism it was generally understood that the solution of ethnic problems is linked with the socio-economic transformation of nation-state.

Secession has no place in the system. As Jomo Kenyatta said: "Nationhood and familyhood must and can be contrived out of our many tribes and cultures".[12] This is also echoed in one of the objectives of the Tanganyika African National Union, which is "the creation of a nation out of more than 120 tribes, out of peoples of different religions and different social groups, and a nation in which race is of less importance than a record of service and an expected ability to give service".[13]

Of particular interest is President Julius Nyerere's socialistic experiment in a tribal milieu:

> In the past, when our population was divided into different tribal groups, the land belonged to the particular tribe living on it. In future, however, our population will be united as one nation, and the land will belong to the nation. And today just as one man cannot prevent another man from his tribe from using land, so also tomorrow one tribe will not be able to prevent another tribe from using land that is actually the property of the nation as whole.[14]

Many of these countries are grappling with the colonial backlog of discrepancies between ethnic and political boundaries, inter-tribe conflicts, and movements of separatism and secessionism.

The African experience is relevant because we too are faced with the problem of consolidating a nation-state and have inherited the colonial backlog of ethnic conflicts which have sharpened as the process of development has intensified. Our founding fathers too sought to create and consolidate a nation-state out of a congeries of communities including tribes. However, India is not the best example of a plural society, because while pluralism stresses cleavages and discontinuities among the sections of people differentiated by race, ethnicity, religion or culture, there has been an all pervasive sense of cultural unity, a wide ranging sharing of its idioms and symbols, in spite of diversities in our country. Tribals were not aliens; their isolation was relative, never absolute; they have been part of the Indian civilizational universe. However, as a nation-state in the process of consolidation, we too are confronted like others with ethnic problems.

To go back to the colonial experience of the subcontinent, unlike Africa which adopted the system of indirect rule, namely, rule through the traditional chiefs of territories, a large part of the tribal region and most of the tribal population in India were integrated within the administration of the province of British

India or within that of the Indian states where the British Resident kept a watch on the tribal situation and, in some cases, even acted as the agent for the tribal regions. The colonial system ended the relative isolation of the tribal society; brought it into the mainstream of the new administrative set-up, policy and programmes. As elsewhere, it followed the dual policy of strengthening the feudal crust of the tribal societies, formed by the rajas, chiefs and zamindars and simultaneously created conditions in which their economy and political system were undermined by the rampaging market forces.[15]

That the normal laws should not automatically apply to the tribal areas was the principle that underlay the passage of the Scheduled Districts Act (1874) and shaped the concept of the backward areas in the Government of India Act of 1919. Whether or not this principle should continue to be applied was a matter that figured in a most lively debate in the early 1930s. While one school contended that the aborigines formed a distinct element in India and should be placed in charge of the British Government, the nationalists saw in this proposition the continuation of the imperial policy of divide and rule. However, the tribal and non-tribal areas were both partly and fully "excluded" in the Government of India Act of 1935. Gandhiji reacted sharply to the segregation of various communities, particularly the tribals, under the dangerous spell of the policy of the "isolation and *status quo*".[16] On the eve of the transfer of power the most scathing indictment of the colonial policy of isolation and *status quo* for tribals came from the last Biritish Governor of Bihar, T. G. Rutherford, who said that the British had only provided a certain amount of protective legislation which functioned effectively when the officers responsible were really sympathetic and in largely with the aid of missionaries. On the whole the tribals were treated as delightful primitives.[17]

The need to provide adequate safeguards for the tribals was again extensively discussed in the Constituent Assembly, and the nationalist opinion favoured incorporation of far more radical provisions for safeguarding of the tribals' interests in the forms of the Fifth and Sixth Schedules of the Indian Constitution. This appreciation of the uniqueness of tribal factors within the framework of Indian nationalism and the extension of political rights to tribals was beyond the expectations of the colonial administrators and anthropologists.

Short of providing a measure of protection for tribals in middle India under the Fifth Schedule and of autonomy in the north-east under the Sixth Schedule, it was neither possible nor practicable to create a tribal state out of the adjoining tribal majority areas of the provinces at the time of the transfer of power. India had inherited the boundaries of the provinces fixed with an eye on administrative convenience. Language and not ethnicity determined the reorganization of states in the 1950s. It was within the political and cultural system of the states that the tribals in middle India were sought to be integrated, even though they were divided between more than one state. Ethnicity influenced the formation of states in the north-east in the 1960s and 1970s, even though certain ethnic areas remained to be integrated. However the application of the principle of tribal ethnicity elsewhere in middle India is fraught with difficulties because nowhere except in two districts and a few *taluqas* are the tribals in a majority. The Chotanagpur Development Authority presents an interesting model of regional autonomy in planning and develop ment. Its performance deserves to be watched for some time before the concept of regional autonomy is examined for application elsewhere in middle India.

The process of decolonization which began after the transfer of power involved enfranchisement and grant of full citizenship rights to tribal communities and setting up of democratic institutions. This resulted in the curtailment and abolition of the power of the tribal chiefs who had acted as the natural leaders of their community. The chiefs enjoyed a great deal of power in the Mizo hills and therefore, when threatened with loss of power they joined hands with the anti-national forces while the educated tribal elite favoured union with India. In middle India, tribal chieftainship was abolished with the zamindari and intermediary interests in the first flush of land reforms. As a corollary to this a new leadership came up through elections and as agents of development process which controls the apparatus of political power and corners a good bit of development benefits today. Almost all over the country this class of tribal elite exploits the stereotypes of tribal society to secure benefit and acts as the mediator with the government; it has more in common with the middle class elsewhere than with its own people.

Secondly, while isolation was equated with the *status quo* in the colonial society, a new strategy of development was drawn up combining the twin elements of protection and development. Seen in the perspective of the third world, the Indian strategy of tribal development, in spite of its limitations, could be described as a unique experiment.

Jawaharlal Nehru's philosophy and vision shaped the tribal policy in the 1950s, particularly in the north-east. He avoided the extremes of the two standpoints; namely, the anthropological approach which sought to treat the tribals as museum specimens to be kept apart, for study and observation; and the other approach which sought to destroy their individuality, distort the process of their development, and absorb them in a culture and way of life that was alien to them. That they should be "engulfed by the masses of Indian humanity" was a prospect that appalled Nehru:

> I am alarmed when I see not only in this country but in other great countries too--how anxious people are to shape others according to their own image or likeness, and to impose on them their particular way of life....I am not at all sure which is a better way of living. In certain respects I am quite certain theirs is better. Therefore, it is grossly presumptuous on our part to approach them with an air of superiority or to tell them what to do or not to do. There is no point in trying to make them a second-rate copy of ourselves.[18]

Therefore, while tribal identity should be preserved, tribals should develop in their own way without let or hindrance. As Nehru admitted, these reactions were, to begin with, instinctive and not based on any knowledge or experience. Gradually and towards the close of the 1950s, outlines of a policy emerged:

(i) People should develop along the lines of their own genius and we should avoid imposing anything on them. We should try to encourage in every way their own traditional arts and culture.

(ii) Tribal rights in land and forests should be respected.

(iii) We should try to train and build up a team of their own people to do the work of administration and development. Some technical personnel from outside will, no doubt, be needed, especially in the beginning. But we should avoid introducing too many outsiders into tribal territory.

(iv) We should not over-administer these areas or overwhelm them with a multiplicity of schemes. We should rather work through, and not in rivalry to, their own social and cultural institutions.

(v) We should judge results, not by statistics or the amount of money spent, but by the quality of human character that is evolved.

In consonance with this philosophy a strategy of tribal development was framed. The Nehru era laid the foundation of tribal policy. The Scheduled Areas and Scheduled Tribes Commission (1961) evaluated the working of constitutional safeguards for the tribals and tribal development programmes. It noted the changes of far reaching character introduced in tribal areas by the development process. The Commission while endorsing Nehru's approach made wide ranging recommendations involving protection of tribals' land, of their right in forest, their rehabilitation, etc. all within the framework of the Nehruvian policy.

The framework of policy and strategy imbued with Nehru's humanism held the ground for about fifteen years. It still provides the sheet anchor of India's tribal policy though in recent years there has been a considerable broadening and deepening of the structure of the policy and programmes in spite of many shortcomings. We enter upon a more intensive phase from the mid-60s. The formulation of the Fifth and Sixth Five Year Plans showed perception of (a) the deleterious effects of the disturbance of the environment consequent upon the intensive exploitation of the natural resources of tribal regions on the tribal communities, (b) the growing incidence of exploitation of the tribal people, their loss of land, their indebtedness, their transformation from peasants into labour, particularly in the zones of intensive industrial activities, and (c) the diversities of tribal situations, which called for a more area specific approach to planning and development. This means a gradual moving away from the schematic pattern of the earlier plan and formulation of a more integrated approach to the tribal problems. More backward communities have been identified as tribes. Uttar Pradesh appeared for the first time on the tribal map of India. Areas of tribal concentration were enlarged to bring within the ambit of planned development the populations ranging from 50,000 to 100,000. Each tribal region prepares its own sub-plan, which forms a part of the plan of the state. Each project in the sub-plan region—there are 180 intensive tribal development projects—prepares its own project report with reference to the special needs of the areas; these are compiled into the sub-plan, which is a part of the plan prepared by the state. A plethora of legislation has been enacted to prevent alienation of land, regulate moneylending, abolish the bonded labour system, and organize labour. The new package of programme seeks to tackle more effectively on a wide front the programmes of credit and marketing, application of a simple and relevant technology to agriculture, development of a programme of social forestry under which the tribals could become the owners rather than remain workers in forests, and further development of communications, health and education, which have already made an impact. The resources being mobilized for the development of the tribal regions from many sources, outlay in the state plan, investment of the central government ministries, institutional finance and the special central assistance for development of tribal areas have reached an all time high. The funds allocated for tribal development by successive governments since independence might not have been commensurate with the proportion of the tribal population and they were very low up to the Fourth Plan, but they did rise to 3.01 per cent in the Fifth

Plan and to 4.37 per cent In the Sixth Plan, thus inching very close to their share in the plan efforts. In fact this plan ended up by registering a spectacular investment in tribal development, of the order of Rs. 5535 crores i.e. 5 percent of the plan outlay. About 40 lakh tribal families were assisted under poverty alleviation programmes. The Seventh Five Year Plan, in continuing with these programmes, seeks to bring up a substantial number of about 85 percent of the scheduled tribe families living below poverty line and to reduce their number to less than 10 percent by 1994 by raising levels of productivity and creating income generating assets. Protection of tribals' land against alienation and of tribals' interest in forest is as much required as development, and therefore the protective laws and their implementation mechanism are to be strengthened. Tribal women, shifting cultivators and primitive communities deserve special attention. Today a vast infrastructure exists: there are 181 Integrated Tribal Development Agencies, 245 Marginal Areas Development Agencies and 72 projects for primitive communities. The problem is the right implementation of programmes. The development experience shows that even where ample funds are available, the administration in tribal areas has to be so reoriented and the technology of development so evolved that the tribals are able to absorb and take advantage of the development programme.

To sum up, while the Indian experiment with tribal development is comprehensive in the world perspective of the treatment of the indigenous peoples, one has to take a balanced view of its processes. On the positive side the tribals who are full citizens have, barring a couple of islandic communities, maintained their demographic growth rate. They have also maintained their identity, their distinct way of life, although they have not remained unaffected by the storms blowing around their country. They have also remained in good parts of the north-east and a large part of middle India an agrarian community in possession of their lands, even though the incidence of land alienation has sharply increased in and around urban areas. From almost the zero level in the 1930s progress in education and literacy, health care and communication has been remarkable, though critical gaps exist in the utilization of these facilities by tribals as compared to non-tribals. They have also participated in the democratic processes and have a share in the control of the apparatus of political power. In some states, such as Gujarat, Madhya Pradesh and even Bihar they have played their cards well. Therefore there is no substance in the allegation that their population has declined and that they have been prevented from acquiring real political powers.[19] On the negative side however they remain the most backward, underdeveloped and, next only to the scheduled castes, the most exploited community.

II

We now turn to an analysis of the processes of economic transformation. Both economic and non-economic criteria determine the definition of the "tribes", which is an administrative category. The traditional criteria are tribals' relative isolation, homogeneity, and settlement in a well-defined habitat. To these are added criteria influenced by administrative convenience and the compulsions of rural development: primitiveness, economic backwardness and treating the community as a whole notwithstanding the levels of advancement of its strata as a unit of development planning. Thus the more primitive groups have been distinguished from the less primitive; the former are characterized by low literacy rate, pre-agricultural technology and small population. Implicit in this two-fold division has been the recognition of the fact that there is not one tribal system but many, that there is not one but several tribal economies. Before we turn to the spatial distribution of tribal economies, it should be noted however that except for a few isolated and small communities, no tribe in India today subsists on a single techno-economy of production. The primitive technology of hunting, foodgathering, shifting and terrace cultivation is confined to the heavy monsoon zone covered by tropical forests in the north-east, parts of eastern and central regions, the Nilgiris, and the Andaman Islands. While there is historical evidence of the practice of shifting cultivation having prevailed in western India, it is no longer practised in the arid and semi-arid regions. The hunting and foodgathering tribes are the Onges and Jarawas of the Andaman Islands and the Shompens of Nicobar Island, the Sulungs in the north-east who are now taking to shifting cultivation, the Cholanaickans in Kerala and the Birhors in Bihar and Orissa. Foodgathering is now generally a subsidiary and, during the lean months, a primary source of food for most of the primitive tribes on the mainland. Shifting cultivation is being practised by 2.6 million tribals who constitute 8.7 per cent of the tribal population. Wet terrace cultivation has developed in western Himalayas, north-east India and in a couple of pockets in Bihar and Orissa. Pastoral economy which constitutes about 10 per cent of the tribal population survives in the high altitude of the sub-Himalayan regions, the arid zones of Gujarat and Rajasthan, and in a small pocket in the Nilgiris. All over tribal India settled dry cultivation has emerged as the primary mode of food production involving nearly 60 per cent of the tribals.

The major thrust of change has been from tribe into peasant. We are in a position today to trace the process of transfer of technology from peasants to tribes in the pre-colonial and colonial societies. By the end of the 18th century communities of peasantized tribals had emerged in Assam, Rajasthan, middle India, etc. The colonial period witnessed an accentuation of this trend as movement of peasants into tribal regions continued. The colonial administration built up a hierarchy of tenures for the upper crust of the tribal society which consisted of the tribal chiefs and recognized the occupancy rights of tribal peasants. The colonial system followed the policy of reclaiming the tribes to civilization through the adoption of plough culture and integration into market. The survey and settlement operations which were introduced in unsurveyed tribal regions acted as an instrument for the transformation of tribes into peasants. They identified different categories of land, determined tribals' rights in land, fixed rent and thus grafted the concept of private property in land on to the tribal system. Transition to settled agriculture was also helped by the conservation of forests resources for commercial exploitation, which pushed the tribals off their land in reserved forests.

Since independence this process of transformation has intensified. Pressure of tribal population on land has grown as the carrying capacity of land has diminished. There has been diffusion of improved agricultural technology by government agency. Of particular interest is the extension of agriculture technology into the tribal economies of the north-east because unlike middle India, there was no transfer of technology from peasants to tribes, no inter-ethnic participation in production. Separation of craft from agriculture occurred within the tribal community itself and its economy was integrated with the market system across the Inner Line. With introduction of new technology the shifting cultivation is being increasingly combined with terrace and wet cultivation in the foothills and low-lying areas, iron implements have replaced the wooden tools and a variety of new crops is grown to suit the market. The technological innovations have brought about a change in social relationships. Hunting, foodgathering and shifting cultivation technologies were associated with the system of communal or collective ownership of land and use of labour. The systems of terrace and wet cultivation are associated with the emerging trends of private ownership of land, increased use of inputs and labour, and the role of market. In the north-east while the two forms of collective and private ownership exist side by side, yet evidence suggests that the latter preponderates in areas of wet cultivation.

Much the same kind of technological changes are taking place, though on a smaller scale, in the regions of dry cultivation. As the dry farming technology is developed and applied to settled agriculture, the pace of the transformation of tribal agriculture is quickened. At present, much of settled cultivation is at subsistance level, and the majority of the tribals produce not a marketable surplus but "marketed surplus" which they are forced to do to buy their necessities. However, pockets of modernized agricultural farming are emerging among the Mundas and Oraons of Chotanagpur, the Gonds and Korkus of middle India, the Badagas and Mulu Kurmbas of the Nilgiris. Cash cropping of coconut has turned the Nicobarese into an affluent community. Incidence of cash cropping has been reported from parts of tribal Gujarat, Rajasthan, Andhra, Orissa and Chotanagpur.

This process may be discussed at some length. In Chotanagpur, particularly in Ranchi, tribals have taken up cultivation of wheat as a second crop, aided by minor irrigation. They have constructed thousands of wells helped by the voluntary agencies and government. About one-third of the area under the improved variety of crops and a substantial area under the high yielding varieties is owned by tribals. The increase in production of cereals and vegetables has not resulted in generation of surplus; it has only shortened the tribals' hunger period.

In this connection the findings of two micro-level case studies in the transformation of tribal economy are interesting. The first is based on the study of the working of the Tribal Development Agency (TDA) of Chakradharpur (1972-8), which embraces remotely situated tribal regions lying on the borders of Ranchi and Singhbhum, and peopled by the Ho and Munda communities. During the last six years the TDA spent Rs 1.80 crore, a major part of which went into developing a minor irrigation system in the undulating terrain and application of the new agricultural strategy. Over 52,000 out of 70,000 families participated in the programmes. There has been a noticeable increase in the area under cultivation, and consumption of fertilizers by farmers has gone up. There has been a rise in the production of vegetables and wheat and summer crops, the areas under which have multiplied. As tribal economy is traditionally deficit in draught cattle, their distribution helped boost agriculture. The application of the techniques of dry land farming has substantially helped agricultural development. The upland was treated for acidity and cropped with high yielding varieties which became instantly popular, covering about 30 per cent of the area. It is however in the area of wheat cultivation that the most spectacular results could be seen. Tribal peasants have taken to double, and, in some cases, even triple cropping instead of the traditional monocropping and the area under both is progressively being extended. This would not have been possible without the reorientation of irrigation policies. The emphasis has shifted from the construction of weirs and large irrigation works to the exploitation of underground and surface water resources through a chain of intake wells constructed in river beds, big diametre wells a few of which were energized with pumps in rivulets and streams. As tribal economy is starved of credit because of the legislative restriction on the transfer of land, a major innovation has been the arrangement for easy flow of credit from co-operative institutions and banks on furnishing personal or collective security by tribal farmers, thus reducing their dependence on moneylenders. Tribals have always been responsive to the programmes concerning rearing of pigs, ducks and goats; and aided by subsidies this programme has become very popular enabling a tribal family to earn an additional yearly income of Rs. 2,500 to Rs. 4,000. An evaluation of the impact of this intensive programme of development suggests (i) that the traditional lean and hunger period has been shortened; (ii) that surpluses which have emerged are being used for creating productive assets, or meeting higher consumption requirements; and (iii) that there has been visible affluence among a few middle level tribal-peasants who have benefited most from the development process.

The other project, the Indo-German Project, smaller in size, was started in April 1979. It covers 709 families in the Simadega block. They mostly belong to the primitive Kharia tribe. The project has spent Rs. 40 lakh which works out to a per capita investment of Rs. 4,000 making it an essentially capital-intensive project. It introduced the new agriculture strategy, supported by a vigorous irrigation programme. Like the TDA, it constructed big diametre wells (160) and set up lift irrigation schemes (4); there were also mobile pumping sets. Altogether they irrigated 700 hectares owned by tribal families. Thus mono crop areas were brought under double (525 ha) and triple cropping (100 ha), accounting for a total production of 26,400 quintals. The average family income has thus gone up. They have used the increased income to buy land and fancy goods, repay debt, acquire assets, etc. There is no starvation. Out-migration has stopped.

There are many such success stories which suggest that the first "green revolution" has spread to the backward tribal tracts creating pockets of affluence. The technology of the second green revolution in pulses and seeds, maize and minor millets has been developed and is being introduced. The plateau regions of Orissa have reported a substantial rise in the yield of these crops benefiting tribals. The small peasant sector in tribal areas has become dynamic, as part of the overall process of the transformation of rural society.

As a result of the introduction of the new agricultural technology, and methods of farming suited to the north-eastern region, foodgrain production rose by 16 per cent between 1972-73 and 1977-78; the area under various crops increased during the same period from 30.88 lakh hectares to 31.39 lakh hectares, while the average production rose to 1,130 kg from 989 kg in 1972-3—an increase of 14 per cent. Manipur reported the highest yield (1,626 kg per hectare) while the corresponding figures for Meghalaya and Tripura were 1,152 kg and 1,224 kg respectively. For the country as a whole about 7.44 lakh acres of tribal land was brought under various improved agricultural techniques in all eight tribal development agencies. The other dimensions of the agricultural strategy for the tribals who subsisted on agriculture and forest produce comprised (a) allotment of land for cultivation (18,253 acres), (b) land-development and soil conservation programmes (23,531 acres), (c) extension of minor irrigation (60,000 acres) through wells (5600), (d) construction of tanks, roads and arterial roads, and (e) distribution of plough bullocks (12,800 pairs) and saplings and grafts (7.3 lakh). Seventy-one per cent of the targeted beneficiaries (3.36 lakh) have benefited from these programmes. In fact, the entire thrust of the programme appears to be to peasantize the tribals, draw them closer within the network of the new agricultural policy and programme, to improve productivity of land, bridge the food gap and to increase earnings from land. Financing of the scheduled tribes/castes by the commercial banks rose from Rs. 36.78 crores to Rs. 808 crores in 1984-85. The inflow of institutional finance explains the success of the new agricultural strategy in the tribal areas. A critical study of the physical achievements of their programmes during the five year plans shows that notwithstanding a wide range of variations in performance, they have succeeded in achieving their objectives, though in a limited way.[20] Yet tribals' transition to the peasant system is not complete, their dependence on forest as a source of food and earnings is in many ways as crucial as their dependence on land.

Tribal areas in middle India have witnessed a rapid growth of urban population and industrialization. An immediate result of this has been the immigration into tribal areas of non-tribals in search of jobs. In Chotanagpur the level of immigration jumped from 4,80,000 in 1951 to 10,72,920 in 1961 and to 14,29,805 in 1971. The demographic pattern has thus been disturbed and tribal population is declining. Another result has been the displacement of tribals from lands which have been acquired for setting up industries and constructing projects. In the early phase of industrialization the tribals were paid handsome compensation for land which they did not know how to use. They became nomads. The threat of displacement still haunts them. The strategy of relief and rehabilitation therefore will have to be reoriented with the objective of recreating community settlement in appropriate environment. This means that some land will have to be given for the land to be acquired, and displaced persons will have to be assured opportunities of employment or self-employment. Absorption into industrial culture of the indigenous people through training and education should be a part of an industrial project, and a charge on it as has been the experience of socialist countries. This is all the more necessary because there has been a steep decline of village industries and traditional crafts in tribal areas.[21]

III

The political and economic processes of tribal transformation described above have been reflected in social stratification. There existed within a tribe a measure of distinction between the high and the low in terms of social and physical distance, notion of purity and pollution, prestige and status, habits and customs, etc. The colonial system created and strengthened a threefold division with the feudatory chief zamindars at the top, the well-to-do headmen in the middle and the general mass at the bottom. As mentioned earlier, a class of insider *diku* and professional tribal moneylender also grew up as the unintended result of the anti-land alienation laws, which restricted transfer of land from tribals to non-tribals. A rich stratum of tribal buyers of land emerged as suggested by the data on transactions in land and moneylending in the district settlement reports.[22]

This process has developed further in the post-colonial phase. The 1961 census reports suggest a three-tier pattern of land-holding in tribal society.[23] In a perceptive analysis of emerging stratification in tribal Gujarat, Bose identifies four distinct classes of peasants, among tribals: rich peasant, middle peasant, poor peasant, and agricultural labourer:

> In no region has a single tribe solely occupied a particular class position: but they are generally distributed among all the four classes. However, some tribes are in better position than the others. For instance, in Vadodara, none of the Nayakas are rich peasants, 30.3 per cent of them are labourers and 54.5 per cent are poor peasant, while all the rich peasants in this district belong to the Bhil tribe. But, from the same tribe we find 35.4 per cent are middle peasant, and 1.6 per cent are rich peasant, and 10.5 per cent are agricultural labourers. Again, in Sabarkantha in which 97 per cent of the district tribal population belong to Bhil tribe, we find that 11.6 per cent are agricultural labourers, 65.1 per cent are poor peasant; 21.7 per cent are middle peasants and 1.6 per cent are rich peasants. A similar pattern has also been observed in the other districts.
> At the bottom of the stratificatory system are the tribal agricultural labourers. A majority of agricultural labourers are landless, a few of them have less than one acre of land of poor quality which virtually means having no land at all and like landless labourers they also live by selling their labour power.[24]

In restudy of the Chodhras (Chaudhri) Shah tells us about the emerging differentiation based on landownership and education which reflects in political attitudes and behaviour:

> The rich Chaudhris identify their interest with those of the non-tribal rich farmers. In fact, some of them supported the Khedut Samaj (rich peasant organization) against paddy levy and land ceiling. Educated Chaudhri boys identify themselves with the urban middle-class boys. These attitudes reflected in the 1975 state Assembly elections to some extent. The majority of the poor peasants, voted for the ruling Congress, believing that it was a party of the poor. The peasants got equally divided between the Congress and Janata Morcha, and the majority of the rich peasants voted for the Janata Morcha. Similarly most of the educated Chaudhris, like the urban and rural educated youths, voted against the ruling Congress on moral issues, considering the ruling party as corrupt. This division of votes starta-wise in the tribal society also reflects the general voting pattern among the caste Hindus in South Gujarat. Thus, in perception, behaviour and life style, member of the different strata among the Chaudhris in general and educated and rich peasants in particular are becoming part of the larger society, joining hands with the similar secular strata outside the tribal society. Such process, on the one hand, disintegrates the tribal society in terms of its culture-customs, rituals, life style and economic interests and integrates some of its sections with the larger society, on the other.[25]

Mishra reports a similar process from the north-east :

> The special division of labour between tribes and the subjugation of one by the other having performed its historic role lapses into oblivion and a new phase of social karyokinesis within the members of a single tribe comes into existence. In some place, as in the Khasi hills, where private property in land is well developed, the division of labour takes a new shape. Here the first group of citizens discriminates against the second, the second against the third, and all discriminate jointly against the rest. In addition to this the law of female ultimogeniture in matters of inheritance has a built-in-tendency to create both propertied as also dispossessed sections of society. And it is through the force operating in this endogenous process that the landlord, tenant and labourer come into being to perform their roles as assigned by the great social division of labour.[26]

However it should be noted in evaluating the findings of these studies that there are also pulls in the opposite direction.

The bonds of ethnicity and the appreciation of the political advantages of the tribe as an ethnic minority are still strong. This has inhibited the development of intra-tribal contradictions which are overshadowed by the confrontation of tribals with non-tribals. An interesting aspect of stratification is the developing nexus between the "insider" and "outsider".[27] *Diku*, the alien, a creature of the colonial system, acted as the middleman, trader and moneylender. While the protective tenancy laws sought to curb this class, they had the unintended result of spawning a class of tribal moneylenders or the insider *diku*. Recent settlement operations in Chotanagpur have also revealed extensive transaction in land between tribals and tribals. This process operates in the north-east also where the business and trading communities across the Inner Line have maintained close relations with their tribal agents. Therefore, it appears that no matter how strong the sentiments against these aliens in the north-east and elsewhere may be they are far too deeply entrenched in the economic system of the region to be expelled, because their ouster will mean the collapse of the market, with which tribal economy is being increasingly linked. Even the most primitive economic system of the Cholanaickans has been drawn into the vortex of market forces.

We have described above various models of tribal transformation, the uniqueness of the Indian experiment with all its merits and shortcomings, the social impact of the transfer of agricultural technology, and the process of transformation of tribes into peasants. We have also discussed the factors which have contributed to social stratification. All these processes are reflected in a wide ranging variety of tribal movements which are discussed in the following section.

IV

A survey of tribal movements conducted by the Anthropological Survey of India (ASI) towards the close of 1976 identified 36 ongoing tribal movements.[28] Fourteen of these were concentrated in the north-east. These movements include political movements representing the transition from the politics of insurgency to that of integration, socio-cultural movements seeking new identity, script-based and language movements. Eastern India reported seven movements, the most important of them being the movement for the establishment of a Jharkhand state. There were also mobility movements among the Kurmis re-seeking a tribal status. Central India reported the continuation of the bhagat movements and a political movement of sorts among the Gonds. The northern parts of Andhra which are a part of the central Indian system witnessed a militant tribal uprising. There were four movements in western India, a bhagat movement among the Bhils, two agrarian movements among tribal peasants and halpatis and a political movement for autonomy. In the south, where there are small isolated primitive tribes, only an incipient political process could be observed among them.

These studies suggest that tribal unrest assumes an organised character only among the large homogeneous landowning tribal communities who have a relatively strong economic base such as the Munda, Santal, Bhil, Gond, etc. Very few of the primitive tribes, who have a pre-agricultural technology, have participated in movements. The major tribal communities have also a high degree of literacy and high rate of participation in democratic processes. It is these groups who react strongly to the issues concerning land and forest on which they subsist. A new middle class is also emerging from among them in urban areas who agitate about reservation of jobs. They are sensitive as well to the exploitation of their people as labourers in agriculture, mining and industries. Their demands are couched in secular idioms.

Movements in the North-East

Tribal movements in the north-east stand in a category by themselves because of the region's unique geopolitical situation and historical background. Many of these tribes living on the international boundaries traditionally acted as bridge or buffer communities until the advent of colonialism and shared ethnic and cultural affinities with tribesmen across the frontiers. Developments across the frontiers have had a profound influence on the situation in the north-east. This region was not as completely integrated within the politico-economic system of colonialism; it remained relatively isolated from the cultural systems of the mainland and the political upheavals of the freedom struggle. It is interesting to record that the entire system of the non-regulation administration had its origin in the experiences of the tribal uprising of the 1820s in the Arakan hills, which continues to be a disturbed area. Many of the elements of this system were introduced elsewhere in the country, while they tended to isolate the north-eastern region all the more from the rest of the country. Further, unlike middle India the tribals in the north-east (except Tripura) are in overwhelming majority and have never faced any threat to their identity of the kind that inspired the millenarian movements elsewhere in the country. Their institutions are relatively intact. They remain in possession of their land and forest. Therefore there were no agrarian and forest-based movements of the type that occur in middle India. Christianity has emerged as the strongest factor of modernization, and has given the tribals as it has done elsewhere a strong sense of identity. Considering the geopolitical factor and the relative isolation from the political system and cultural influences from the mainland, the dominant form of movement has been political, seeking goals ranging from autonomy to independence and relying on means ranging from constitutional agitation to armed insurgency. Even the cultural movements in this region are only a dimension of these political processes.

Political processes in the north-eastern hills picked up on the eve of transfer of power and gathered strength later as the secular and democratic system was consolidated. Old tribes assumed new names, small tribes merged with larger tribes, tribes combined to form a new ethnic-cum-territorial identity. Beyond the territorial identity states were created to accommodate tribal aspirations for autonomy. In the process the Sixth Schedule model of political autonomy for the north-east was exceeded. Nagaland enjoys more autonomy than other states as no law can apply to the Nagas unless it is approved by the state assembly. This political process extending from the merger of tribes to formation of a new territorial identity and to formation of states is a unique feature of the north-eastern situation.[29]

While the processes up to the formation of the state were almost common to all tribes, there were differences on the question of their relationship with the nation state. A section of the Nagas chose the path of insurgency, followed by the Mizos, the Meitei, and the Tripuris. Other sections of the same tribes preferred integration. For example, in Nagaland the Angami, the Ao and the Sema who had played the major role in the beginning of Naga insurgency opted for sedate regional politics. The centre of gravity shifted from the area dominated by these tribes to the area inhabited by the Konyak and Lotha and now to thei nter-national border. The insurgency is now dominated by the Hemis, and the Konyaks and Tangkhuls. In fact there has been a reaction among these minor tribes against the dominance of the advanced tribes such as the Ao, the Angami, the Chakesang and the Lotha. There is a demand for the formation of the remote and underdeveloped Mon and Tuensang districts into a union territory.

The cultural dimension of the political processes is interesting. There has been a phenomenal rise of Christianity during the decade, 1961-72, as a symbol of tribal identity, as a marker of status in all states except Arunachal where the Freedom of Religion Act has been promulgated to forbid conversion to the faiths alien to Arunachal Pradesh by force, fraud, inducement and allurement. However, there has been conversion in Lohit and Subansiri divisions.

Sanskritization has not been at work in the north-eastern hills. The Brahma movement among the Bodo Kacharis stopped short of the hills. The sanskritization process in the Manipur Valley has not only come to a stop, there is even an attempt at de-sanskritization, an impulse to go back to the pre-Vaishnava, pure forms of Meitei culture represented by the Sanamahi cult. It has secured official recognition, many members of the government being among its ardent supporters. The prevailing idea is that Vaishnavism softened the martial Meiteis by enjoining abstention from meat and drink. The Meitei now play a second fiddle to the tribals and *mayangs* (outsiders). Such feelings have been fomented by the political activists of the Manipur National Front which has been preaching a kind of cultural revivalism and invoking the common pre-Hindu Mongoloid heritage to unite not only all Sanamahis but all Mongoloid peoples of the north-east. The anti-Bengali and anti-Vaishnava thrust and orientation of the Meitei revivalistic movement have given way to the demand for severance of all cultural links with the rest of the country forged by history and cultural interaction over the past five hundred years. In 1979 a former minister presided over the burning of the holy scriptures at Kangla Fort where two and a half centuries ago the upcountry brahmins had burnt down the entire lot of Manipuri scriptures. There was even a revival of drinking to boost the martial spirit of the Meities until the *imas* (mothers) launched their drive against the boozers. The state government has recognized the 27-letter Manipuri script determined as such in 1969.

Related to this attempt to identify the Mongoloid heritage of the north-eastern peoples at the cultural level is the effort to bring together the insurgent groups under a common banner. However it is forgotten that the the Indo-Mongoloid (*Kirat*) heritage is very much part of the Indian ethos, and Vaishnavism did not prevent the Meiteis from fighting the British.

Two other nativistic movements have sought to revive the pure and pristine elements of tribal culture. The Seng Khasi, a socio-cultural organization of the Khasi had been established as early as 1889 to preserve the Khasi way of life. Through its platform the non-Christian Khasis have tried to strengthen the ancient system of clan relationship, which was disturbed by the large-scale conversion of the Khasis to Christianity. The second, the Zeliangrong movement, started as a religio-cultural movement under Jadunang, assumed a political overtone and became the only movement to have established linkages with the national freedom struggle. Under Gaidinliu it has remained strongly nationalistic, has promoted tribal solidarity and demanded creation of a separate administrative unit to be formed out of the territories inhabited by the constituent tribes in the contiguous regions of Manipur, Assam and Nagaland.

The influx of foreign nationals aroused the apprehension of the tribals, even though nowhere in this region except in Tripura did this assume the form of a movement directed not only against illegal immigrants but also against all those who are traditionally considered outsiders by tribals—*mayang* (Manipur), *dhakar* (Meghalaya), *vais* (Mizoram), etc. Acts of arson and violence involving these communities occurred from 1978 onwards in Meghalaya, Manipur and Mizoram. They reached their bloodiest culmination in Tripura in June 1980. The anti- *mayang* riots in mid-1980 in Manipur left 2,000 Mayangs homeless and 150 hospitalized. Meghalaya, for long regarded as an island of peace, stability and communal harmony in a region in ferment, witnessed serious disturbances involving tribals and non-tribals. Even though the non-tribals form a small portion of the total population and do not conceivably pose any threat to the integrity or security of tribals, a movement, apparently taking a cue from Assam and elsewhere developed against the non-tribals from mid-1978 and spread. This "sons of the soil" type of movement revived elsewhere the demand for the formation of the Uttarakhand and Gorkhaland states in north Bengal. The Assam agitation against the foreigners alarmed the plains tribals, who demanded creation of a separate state, Udayachal; later it was toned down by the Plains Tribals' Council of Assam (PTCA) to embrace the concept of regional autonomy within the framework of the present state of Assam.

Middle India

Unlike the tribal societies in the north-east, those in middle India were closely integrated with the colonial system, its economy and administration. The interaction of the peasants and tribes had led to the development of settled agriculture as the primary mode of subsistence in the pre-colonial period. This process was accentuated in the colonial phase as waves of peasants moved into tribal areas. They also carried with them their cultural systems that inspired the rise of the bhagat movement among tribes.

In the colonial phase the tribals not only faced threat to the control of their environment and resources such as land but also lost control over them. This was at the root of the long chain of tribal uprisings centering on the crucial question of the possession of land. Together with the agrarian struggle sanskritization processes were at work too. In the post-colonial phase these processes continued, except in one respect, namely, that the sanskritization process slowed down, if not actually reversed as in the north-east, as demand for implementation of the welfare measures following the recognition of the tribes as a privileged category grew. We may categorize the movements in middle India as follows :

(i) Movements for political autonomy;
(ii) Agrarian and forest-based movements;
(iii) Sanskritization processes; and
(iv) Cultural movements based on script and language.

Movements for Political Autonomy

The Gonds and Bhils voiced their demand for the formation of a separate state at the beginning of the Second World War, though it was never spelt out and sustained by an organized movement.[30] Kumra Bhimu in Adilabad, according to some, demanded a Gond raj in 1941.[31] The Raj Gond leaders such as Raja Naresh Singh demanded the formation of a separate state for the adivasis to be carved out of the tribal areas of Chatisgarh and contiguous districts of Rewa region and Vidarbha, in a memorandum submitted before the States Reorganization Commission. On 19 May 1963 Narain Singh Uikey, President of the Gondwana Adivasi Seva Mandal reiterated the demand for the formation of the Gondwana state, consisting of the Gond and other tribal regions of the Chattisgarh and contiguous districts of Vidarbha in Maharashtra to protect them against exploitation.

A movement of the Gonds of the lower strata led by Hira Singh developed in the late 1950s and reached its peak in 1962-3 before dying down.[32] Hira Singh, son of Penu Gond Manjhi belonged to Amapara (Durg) and came of the respectable ranks of the

Deo Manjhis. He chose Durg as the centre of his activities in 1948, founded an organization called Adivasi Kalyan Samiti to promote the welfare of the Gond people in their homeland and gave himself the name Kangla Manjhi in token of his identity with the poor (*kangal*), by which he is better known now. The objectives of the Samiti were to uplift the tribal people by promoting implementation of development programmes launched by the government, to encourage cultivation among the tribals who could no longer depend on forest by securing facilities for this and lastly to construct shrines to the Gond deities, Gaura Deo and Burha Deo. In 1961, he held as many as 30 meetings; his sphere of influence extended over Balaghat, Siwani, Jabalpur, Mandla, Chhindwara and Durg. There were instances of conflict with local government functionaries. He advocated non-payment of tax which could be collected only by his sarkar. He also declared formation of the Gondwana raj, which would solve all problems for 40 lakh tribals of middle India. He acquired considerable following and could mobilize one lakh tribals at one point temporarily, in the region extending up to the Bhandara district. The Manjhi and 18 of his associates were arrested for violating the laws in 1960. They were charged in four cases with committing many offences such as impersonation of public servants, forming public assemblies and cheating. They were acquitted on appeal of all offences by the sessions judge. The Manjhi continued to claim that he was a social reformer. The movement does not show any activity now. Kangla Manjhi however continues to hold meetings. Some people have described the movement as concealed insurgency. The local authorities do not agree and neither he nor his movement was taken seriously by them. For most of them the Manjhi was an eccentric person and his movement was quixotic.

A tribal autonomy (Adivasi swayat raj) movement was reported from south Gujarat. An adivasi leader (*gamit*) who represented the tribal area of the Dangs threatened to form a "Dangi Sena" and ask for a separate state if the problems of the people were not solved. A conference held at Ahwa in the Dangs in May 1969 called for the formation of an Adivasi autonomous state. There was widespread sympathy for this movement. The CPI(M) lent its support. The Adivasi Rashtriya Mahasabha stated that they would ask for the creation of a full-fledged state, separate from Gujarat, comprising adjoining tribal territories of neighbouring states if their problems were not solved. The movement is confined to the Broach district.[33]

On the larger plane the Gujarat tribes have been part of a political combination called KHAM (ksatriya, harijan, adivasi and muslim) directed against the dominant communities of brahmins and patels.

The best organized and most articulate movement for tribal autonomy is in Chotanagpur[34] which has been described at length in the preceding chapter. Here we present only a summary to put in perspective similar post-colonial movements in this chapter.

When the era of constitutional reforms dawned after 1918 and demands for promotion and protection of regional and sectarian interests grew, the educated Christian tribals, mostly students, belonging to the German and Anglican missions, took a hand in organizing the Chotanagpur Improvement Society at the instance of the Anglican bishop of Ranchi. The period of 1938-47 saw the rise of a militant movement under the Adivasi Mahasabha. The immediate cause of the formation of the Mahasabha was the experience of the first elections held in 1937 under the Government of India Act of 1935. The Congress had swept the polls. This persuaded most Christians as also non-Christians to merge with the Adivasi Mahasabha. In this respect the latter represented an advance on the earlier movement and possessed a pan-tribal composition and objective. The Adivasi Mahasabha was wound up and merged with a new regional party, the Jharkhand Party, in 1949. Behind it were the experiences of the failure of the militant movement and of the framing of the Constitution of India. The Fifth and the Sixth Schedule had given the tribals more than the anthropologists and the British administrators had prepared them for. The Jharkhand Party was thrown open, at least, in principle, to all Chotanagpuris. There was thus a transition from ethnicity to regionalism as the formative factor in the movement. The period from

1952 to 1957 which cut across two elections was in many ways the peak period for the Jharkhand movement and party, which had emerged as the major party in the Chotanagpur-Santal Pargana region. The second general elections had seen it extend its influence in Orissa, where it captured five seats and held the balance of power in the state politics plagued by instability. It displayed remarkable unity, laid down the law in the tribal region, could mobilize thousands of people and take out mammoth processions at short notice. The decline of the party which began in the early 1960s could be attributed to many factors. First, there was the growing impact of development programmes on Chotanagpur and the increasing involvement of the tribals in the development process. Secondly, the split between the advanced Christian and relatively backward non-Christian tribals arising out of the competition for better education facilities, employment opportunities and control over development inputs and resources deepened. The non-Christians started looking to the Congress and the Jana Sangh for support by the late 1950s. The elections in 1962 slashed the number of votes polled by the Jharkhand Party to almost half of those registered in 1957 and reduced its seats to twenty in the Bihar Assembly.

We enter upon an interesting phase (1963-80) after the fourth general elections, when though the objective conditions of a movement were present, there was no unified political party. The structure of the Jharkhand Party had been fragmented; the parent body had broken up into smaller parties formed by tribal sub-ethnic groups. There was a movement, but no composite party. The radicalization of politics was also due to the influence of the Naxalite movement infiltration by extremist elements of tribals' organizations, and the entry of the leftist parties in the region, in a big way. Another aspect of this phase was the rise of the urban pressure groups led by the educated tribals, mostly Christian and centred at industrial complexes, to demand jobs for tribal youths in administration and industrial undertakings. The process of the formation and the development of the pressure groups is epitiomized in the Birsa Seva Dal (SBD) which emerged as the most important, if not the only one, of the urban groups.

The most important development during the period was the formation of the Jharkhand Mukti Morcha (1973) with the objective of forming a separate Jharkhand state, ending exploitation of tribals by non-tribals, and securing preferential treatment for the sons of the soil in the matter of employment. The Jharkhand Mukti Morcha (JMM) combined in its operations elements of agrarian radicalism and cultural revivalism. The Morcha launched an operation to recover alienated land from moneylenders and big peasants in north Chotanagpur, which was not the stronghold of the Jharkhand Party. Elements of the ancient tribal self-government revived. The Baisi functioned as a court without court fees or pleaders and dealt out simple justice. A volunteer force was raised. Tribal traditions of collective farming and preservation of jungles, pastures and common land were also revived; a common grain pool was created.

The Jharkhand Party which was steadily losing ground in the general elections since 1961 did not, as a party, contest the Lok Sabha poll in March 1977. In the elections to the Bihar Assembly held in May 1977, all four splinter groups of the Jharkhand Party together polled only 81,227 votes as against 3,61,187 votes in 1972. The Janata wave swept the tribal regions. In spite of this, a militant phase of the Jharkhand movement started in October 1977. It originated in the statements made by Jayaprakash Narayan about the advisability of the formation of small states and by the then Home Minister, Charan Singh, about the reorganization of the states. This triggered off developments at two levels in Chotanagpur. All parties including the Janata but excluding the Jharkhand Party came together to demand a separate state for the Chotanagpur-Santal Pargana region.

The Jharkhand Mukti Morcha emerged as a major political force in the industrial and mining belt of Chotanagpur and in state politics after the 1980 general elections. It sought to broad-base the separatist movement by including within its ambit the peasant and working classes. "A Jharkhandi is a producer irrespective of caste, tribe or nation residing in the Jharkhand." The Jharkhand is described by its ideologues as an internal colony which is being exploited by outsiders. Even though the region accounts for 28 per cent of minerals it avails itself of only 15 per cent of the state's budget for development. The development process itself is exploitative of the local inhabitants and outsiders have moved in to seize all opportunities of employment. There is a Jharkhand nationality and, as in all nationality questions, self-determination is the key element in the social formation. It is only within a separate state of Jharkhand that the nationality can be satisfactorily solved for the benefit of the exploited and depressed working classes. The Jharkhand must therefore turn into a *lalkhand* that is, the movement of political separatism and struggle of the working classes should go together, according to its protagonists. This formulation, by bringing tribals and non-tribals together, strikes at the root of tribal ethnicity which formed the ideology of the Jharkhand party in practice. This also reflects the difficulties of transition from one ideology to another. That its protagonists are finding it difficult to put it across will be evident from the difficulties within the party with the tribal constituent particularly and in relation to other tribal communities outside. The weakening of the Jharkhand Mukti Morcha in the 1980 election and its being confined to Santal and partly Ho belt are pointers to this.

The failure of the Jharkhand movement to develop into a full-fledged regional movement so far could be ascribed to the fact the it was essentially a tribal party, and the tribals and non-tribals were not on the best of terms. Its structure contained many contradictions which sharpened and multiplied as the cleavage between the Christian and non-Christian tribals deepened. The region had always been exposed to the operation of pan-Indian forces. The ethnic movement, therefore, could not remain in a state of the absolute political isolation. The impact of development programmes and a macro-political system and the merger with the Congress considerably weakened the hold of tribal ethnicity. Tribal ethnicity in a multi-ethnic society characterized by economic interdependence among different communities struck out a different course of development in Chotanagpur unlike the north-east. Separation in this region did not develop into secessionism.

Agrarian and Forest-Based Movements

The spread of agrarian movements in tribal areas is restricted within the overall geography of tribal movements. In the north-east Tripura alone reported an agrarian movement stemming from loss of tribals' land to Bengali refugees and the rise of a political movement around this phenomenon. Few agrarian struggles were reported from the northern and southern parts of India. Though tribal discontent over various forms of exploitation was widespread, it was organized into movements only at a few places involving a few tribes, in middle India.[35]

The leaders of the freedom struggle in the tribal regions had mobilized the tribals by focusing on their rights in forest being eroded through its commercial exploitation. Forest, next only to land, was the most important resource on which the tribals subsisted. A series of forest satyagrahas were launched in the 1930s by the Indian National Congress to demand restoration of tribals' customary rights to extract timber and collect forest produce for consumption. The Kharwars of Palamau, the dominant tribal peasant community inhabiting the forest region south of the Koel river, were drawn into such a struggle led by the Congressmen from across the river.[36] The freedom movement aroused expectations among the Kharwars that days of their opression were numbered and that the era of the swaraj which would lead to the restoration of their rights in land and forest would dawn. Instead the forests vested in the state and were notified as protected forests in which the customary rights to free fuel, free timber for domestic use, free grazing and to free collection of minor forest produce were regulated, even restricted in practice, under the watchful forest guards who harassed the tribals. Independence thus brought little relief from the day-to-day worry of the tribals about making both ends meet; in fact their problems multiplied as their forest, which they were accustomed to look upon as their own, to be exploited for their benefit, was no longer their own, and their movements in it were subject to check and control.

Land which was another important resource was subjected to the payment of land revenue. Independence did not mean abolition of rent as had been promised by the Congress leaders during the freedom struggle. Restrictions were also placed on the cultivation of barren lands, which according to the tribals fell within the ambit of their traditional rights. The vision of primeval independence, which meant freedom from all fetters, all obligations to pay taxes, etc., did not materialize. The Kharwars felt cheated. A reaction against the Congress rule set in the mid-1950s. The stage was thus set for the commencement of a satyagraha concerned mainly with the free utilization of forest produce and extraction of timber without making any payment. It was only marginally concerned with non-payment of rent.

The tribes of Madhya Pradesh were the first to strike. In 1957 a forest movement developed with Khobi village (Ambikapur-Surguja) as its base, involving the Kharwar tribe, who were led by their leader, Chuni. Chuni was influenced by the Gond preacher, Rajmohini. Later, he broke away from her, advised people not to pay land revenue and forest dues, held meetings to propagate his view that '*j'ungle zamin azad hai*" (forest and land are free). A *sarkar* was reportedly established. Chuni was also influenced by the Kharwar leader Fetal of Palamau who was expected to pay him a visit. Chuni's men felled trees illegally in forests, demanded free use of land and forest, etc. With the aid of a typewriter Chuni started sending message's to the effect that the authority of the government servants was at an end. However, in an encounter with the police on 18 December 1957 two persons died and the movement fizzled out. Fetal of Palamau across the border also decided to strike a few weeks later. The reports received by the government stated that he was going to organize a raid on contractors' labourers engaged in wood cutting. The local authorities decided to arrest Fetal to prevent the movement from taking a violent turn. A bloody conflict occurred on 1 February 1958 and the movement died down.

On the face of it, the Gonds did not have traditions of militant struggle waged in defence of their right in land and forest. The Gond zamindars, however, spearheaded the 1857 rebellion in their region like the zamindars elsewhere, but the Gond peasants as a whole were not involved in any movement. From the 1940s, there have been instances of the Gonds' resistance to encroachment on their right in forests. Since independence, their territorial and political systems have broken down, and their rights in forest and land have been eroded. New settlements have been founded in their land. Peasant castes have immigrated in large numbers in the Adilabad and Chanda districts and outsiders have flocked to the industrial centres and townships which have sprung up in the Gond land.

The fact that Gond movements have centred around forest rather than land is understandable in the context of Dandakarnya ecology. In the early 1930s Gonds of Adilabad led by Kumra Bhimu started a short-lived insurerection over the forest question. Known as the "Babejheri revolt', it is still recalled in folklore and its leader, Bhimu, is held in veneration to this day. A wooden post erected in a hamlet called Jodeghat marks the place where he lies buried. The Gonds of Adilabad have since been steadily losing ground to the aliens. Restriction of their rights in forest was the burning issue in the 1940s; today it is their right to land.[37]

As the pressure of population on land grows, there is greater need for land. The tribals are asking not only for restoration of the land that they lost by invoking the provision of the Andhra Pradesh Scheduled Area Land Transfer Regulations, 1959, which came into force in 1963, but also the transfer of ownership and delivery of possession in regard to the land allotted to them. Out of 11,356 applications for restoration of land, 1,702 claims were upheld and about 7,000 cases were pending in 1981. The land records were not maintained properly and the government did not make sure before alloting lands to tribals whether they belonged to the forest department or to non-tribals. The tribals also suspect collusion between non-tribals and petty officials. Of late, they have been organized by CPI (ML) of the People's

War Group. In February 1981 there was an unusual spurt of forced harvesting on lands taken away from them by non-tribals, raiding of houses of moneylenders and decamping with mortgaged valuables. The traditional system of communication was revived to organize the tribals. Signals were exchanged by beating the drum. The Gond *durbar* held on 6 February 1981 at Keslapur declared that the problems of the tribals had come to a boiling point. The Gonds also prevented the demarcation of land for afforestation. They had earlier reacted strongly to the scheduling of the Lumbadars, a community of traders and moneylenders, as a tribe in 1977, because the Lumbadars always exploited the tribals and their status as a tribe helped them to legitimize their illegal possession of the Gonds' land. On 20 April 1981 a conference was planned by CPI (ML) at Indervalli. The meeting was banned and the tribals were persuaded not to assemble there. However, they took out a procession which came into conflict with a police force. About 15 tribals lost their lives.

The tribals constitute 37 per cent of the population of Dhulia district in Maharashtra, of which the Bhils are the most important. They have been losing land to non-tribals by legal or illegal means since the 1830s, the pace of which picked up after independence. There have been large-scale transfers of land from tribals to non-tribals who include moneylenders, rich landlords and traders. As landlessness and poverty grew the tribals sought employment on low wages. Ambarsingh Suratwanti, a Sarvodaya worker and a Bhil himself, started to organize the adivasis in 1967. He toured the tribal area, sang bhajans to educate and mobilize people, and formed a Gram Swaraj Samity to unite the Bhils against oppression. There was also another body called Sramik Sangathan wedded to Marixism-Leninism which started working among the tribals in 1971. The two organizations launched a movement in 1971 which involved organization of rallies, drawing up a charter of demands, and survey of the problem of land alienation. They demanded prevention of land transfer from tribals to non-tribals, restoration of land illegally transferred, implementation of the employment guarantee scheme and fixation of minimum wages for agricultural labourers. Between February and April 1972 their activities resulted in getting 1,872 acres of land in 31 villages restored to the tribals.

Ambarsingh died on 21 February 1974 but the movement continued. The Government of Maharashtra issued an ordinance in July 1975 to prohibit alienation of tribal lands and to provide for the restoration of lands alienated in contravention of the law. The two organizations also attended to the problems of the agricultural labourers and got hours of work and nature of work regulated. Rates of wages were fixed. The organizations took up the problems of regularization of the settlement of land reclaimed by tribals in forests. Unlike the agrarian movement, the tribal satyagraha has promoted education of tribals and anti-liquor campaigns on the social front.

The agrarian movement among tribes in Chotanagpur in recent years has taken the form of forcible harvesting of crops on the land formerly owned by them but currently in illegal possession of and cultivated by non-tribal moneylenders and rich peasants, the demand for restoration of land under the provision of tribal tenancy laws and compelling payment of remunerative prices for their produce in markets which have been the traditional plundering grounds.

However, it is not land but forest which has become the focal point of widespread disturbances recently.[38] More than land, forest is intimately connected with tribal life. It is the abode of the spirits and the place of worship (*sarna*), the seat of lifecycle ceremonies including burial (*sasandiri*). It is the source of food and employment. Under law all customary rights are extinguished in the reserved forests. In practice tribals have been reclaiming land with the connivance of petty officials, and it is a common sight to see patches of cultivation in reserved forests. Of late, as pressure on land has increased, there is demand for more land, and therefore, trees are felled in forest reserves causing loss not only to the national economy but also to the tribal economy in the long run. In 1978-9, as the Jharkhand movement was intensified the forest question loomed large. The issues agitating the tribals in this connection were (a) payment of remunerative price for lac and minor forest produce, (b) payment of compensation for the damage done to the crops by elephants, (c) payment of appropriate wages for work in the forest, and (d) recognition of their traditional rights to reclaim lands by clearing jungles in the areas outside the reserved forests. They were also instigated by the forest contractors to agitate against the operation of the Forest Development Corporation, which appears to have destroyed the traditional nexus between them and the tribals. Paradoxically both the tribal leaders demanding the Jharkhand and the traders agitating against nationalization of minor forest produce put up a joint front in August 1978. There were voilent protests against the nationalization of minor forest produce and the operation of the Forest Development Corporation even though the latter paid good wages and generated employment. In the wake of the agitation, government decided to de-schedule a few items from the list of the minor forest produce to be purchased by the Forest Development Corporation. Bands of Munda Christians obstructed the felling of trees and plantations in the Porahat region of Singhbhum district. They *gheraoed* and assaulted the forest officials; they burnt down godowns. Resistance to the plantation of teak became the symbol of the movement. Rumours were spread that teak was replacing sal, a sacred tree, and that nothing grew under teak, not even grass, roots and tubers, on which wild life and the tribal people subsist. As elephants did not eat the leaves of the teak, they destroyed teak trees and their depredations in areas under crops increased. The agitationists also contended that fruit bearing trees were cut down to establish teak nurseries, thus depriving the tribal people of a source of food. Felling of sal trees has also been justified by the agitationists on the ground that they enjoyed the traditional right to reclaim land for cultivation. They also claimed that all forest areas constituted the Jharkhand, and so they had the right to fell trees to reclaim land. The tree war has now spread into Orissa, and its splendid sal forest is being cut down.

As briefly mentioned above, Naxalite movements mobilized tribal and non-tribal peasants against oppression by rich peasants, money lenders and local officials in its two phases, the first from

1967 to 1972 and the second from 1978 onwards. The movement established the bases in north Bengal, the Srikakulam-Adilabad region of Andhra Pradesh, Chotanagpur-Santal Pargana belt and the Bhil regions of western India. A study of the Naxalite movement of the first phase undertaken by the Anthropological Survey of India revealed that the tribal participation in its leadership structure was marginal. The two Naxalite leaders, Jangal Santal from Naxalabari and Gundhar Murmu from Gopiballavpur, were both Santals, but they had been for a long time associated with the CPI(M):

> The tribals in the Naxalbari and the Srikakulam areas were primarily swidden-cultivators who faced precarious economic condition when they were forbidden by the administration to carry out their cultivation on hill slopes and in forest areas. The Naxalite leaders lumped all these tribals along with the other non-tribal cultivators within the category of 'peasantry'. Existing anthropological literature as well as field experiences suggest that tribals and non-tribals may form a local community, co-operating in day-to-day essential matters within the broad framework of agrarian economic structure, but the tribals are found at the same time to perpetuate a cultural autonomy and ethnic identity of their own and to respond differentially to any innovation of exogenous cell. The extremist movement during the period 1967 and 1972 was therefore not a tribal movement. It was, in the main, a politically motivated movement initiated and led by non-tribal individuals. As a start they stirred up the discontent of tribals, took out processions with them and held demonstrations.[39]

Contradictions between tribals and peasants notwithstanding, these political movements did bring the two together for some time and the tribals' participation in some phases was considerable. This was not without an impact. The understanding of the tribals' problems gained from these struggles helped shape the plethora of legislations to prevent alienation of land, abolish bonded labour, liquidate indebtedness, etc. The Integrated Tribal Development Agency was established in sensitive areas to quicken the tempo of development and attend to the special needs of the tribals. Two notable features of the administrative arrangements were the flow of institutional credit and a new credit-cum-marketing system.

Sanskritization Processes

In spite of the pulls of the secular advantages of the tribal status. the process of sanskritization has not come to a stop in middle India, though it has slowed down. The bhagat movements which in the colonial period acted as the instruments of sanskritization among tribals are still alive and new movements have been reported from Madhya Pradesh, Gujarat and Rajasthan.

Gahira Guru leads a Sant Samaj movement among the Kawars to promote social reform.[40] Rajmohini inspired by Mahatma Gandhi still carries on with her reform among the Gonds.[41] In Rajasthan the old bhagat sects continue to flourish.[42] In Gujarat too, an area so far little known for the bhagat movements, a number of movements have been reported, apart from the intensive propagation among the tribals by the Swami Narayan sect.[43] A *baba* has stirred up the tribals a great deal in Bastar.[44] After having developed a base of support among tribals the Baba supported the Congress in the 1972 elections. However, his activities impoverished the tribals; he was arrested during the Emergency and later externed. Early that year the *baba* sought to organize a *vanaspati yajnya* which would have enabled him to make a clean pocket of Rs. 50 lakh as the tribals were called upon to contribute their forest produce. The Baba however had to postpone the *yajnya* under the pressure of public opinion. He was charged with collecting funds and exploiting the tribals. He then returned to Bastar, demanding the articles seized from him.

While the bhagat movements are flourishing in the more backward conditions of Madhya Pradesh and Rajasthan, sections of non-Christian tribals are seeking a return to the pre-Hindu and pre-bhagat forms of tribal religion centering around the *sarna* or the sacred grove, under the new religions called *Sarna Dharam* and *Sari Dharam*.[45] Their followers numbered 4.28 lakhs and 35,000 respectively in 1961. Their number has gone up to 9.51 lakhs and 1.61 lakhs in 1971. Evidently the movement is gaining ground.

Compared to this such movements as *Adi Dharma* (1,309). Birsa cult (280), the Bonga cult (4,391), *Jah-era* (185) and Kharwar cult (7,418), have paled into insignificance. Another such attempt to return to pre-Hindu forms of tribal religion is represented by *Gondi Dharma*, established by the Gond raja of Chanda, which seeks to differentiate itself from Hinduism.[46] This remains a one-man show and has not gained ground yet.

In restudy of the Andhra tribes, Furer-Haimendorf describes the continuing spread of popular Hinduism and mentions in this context discouragement of such customs as cow sacrifice and the use of intoxicating liquor as an offering to tribal gods, besides "the undoubted tendency" to "classify members of aboriginal tribes as Hindus and to play down the distinctions between tribal religions and popular Hinduism". However, he admits that there is no "organized movement to convert tribals to sanskritic Hinduism" and the efforts of Hindu missions are "concentrated more on modifying such customs than on propagating a new doctrine". Finally, he says that while India is a secular state and the official policy is one of tolerance, "there have been instances of official interference with such tribal practices as animal sacrifice".[47] This seems to be the continuation of the non-brahminical process of acculturation.

Script and Language

The efforts to evolve a script and build up an indigenous literature in tribal languages could be seen as part of an overall movement to define and assert tribal identity.[48] This process in Chotanagpur could be traced to the 1920s when the upcoming tribal middle class started a movement to gain political autonomy, and gave a fillip to revivalism in art and literature, which sought to preserve and recreate many of the cultural symbols of the past. Probably the most dynamic of the identity movements in middle India is the one based on the Santali script, the *Ol chiki,* fashioned by Raghunath Murmu (1905). Now recognized as the great guru, Raghunath Murmu devised this script which is unlike and distinct from the *ol iurum*, the dusty writing, which comprises the scripts of Oriya, Bengali, Hindi and English languages. In devising this script Raghunath Murmu drew upon the traditional Santal practice of communicating messages through symbols on stone, cattle, etc. The new script symbolized a return to the great tradition of the past, and set off a revivalistic movement. Raghunath Murmu followed up the invention of the script by writing text books in it. Teachers were trained and schools (*itun asram*) established to popularize the new script. A whole cultural movement sprung up from these efforts. An Adivasi Cultural Samiti was formed in 1953 to build up a literature and publish a journal, *Sagen Sakam* in the *Ol* script. The Samiti was rechristened Adivasi Socio-Cultural Association in 1962. This association in its successive conferences sought to build up an all-embracing movement aimed at reforming the Santal society and reviving its pristine elements. Thus the Santals should return to the traditions of the "sacred grove". The authority of the *manjhi* the traditional community headman should be recognized to settle petty disputes; no restrictions should be imposed on the manufacture and drinking of rice beer (*handia*); the present system of Santal marriage should be reformed, etc. The *Ol chiki* has in fact become the symbol of Santal identity. In March 1981 the *Ol chiki* was recognized by the West Bengal government and arrangements to impart primary education in it were announced.

Across the border in Bihar, Lakho Bodra claimed that the lost script, *Varana Kshiti*, the shining letters of the Ho people, were revealed to him at the end of a forty-day ordeal in a cave. Himself a Ho, born in 1922 at Paseya near Chakradharpur, he comes of a relatively well-to-do peasant family; a stint as a railway clerk and a long stay at an industrial centre, Jhinkpani, exposed him to the stresses of the new situation developing in the Ho country. He brought together the pieces of marking on the rocks and inscriptions from different parts of his land and further "discovered" the script. This consists of 41 letters, each with a capital and small form, as in the Roman script. A remote influence of the Brahmi script could be seen in the forms of some of the letters of the alphabet, but many new forms have been added. A comparison with the Santal script would be necessary to confirm its influence on the Ho innovation. Like Raghunath Murmu, Lakho Bodra wrote primers and text books, trained teachers and set up schools to popularize this script. Unlike the Santal master he dabbled in politics, contested the parliamentary election in 1957 and lost. Like him, however, he tried to use the script, though not as successfully, as the starting point of a reformative movement, under the auspices of a new organization called the Adi Samaj. Of his two compositions, the *Shaar Hora* deals with the cosmology of the Hos, and the *Bonga Hora* with the rituals to propitiate the spirits. Even though they bear the imprint of Hinduism, the new religion is represented as rooted in the Ho traditional system. Sacrifice is prohibited; marriage with parent's consent is permitted. A set of Kol rules for regulating the life of the follower has been laid down, with a view to reviving the primitive culture (*adi sanskriti*) and to bringing the script of the Ho on a par with that of the civilised society. The movement showed considerable activity till the early 1960s. Bodra was also able to influence local politics and bring up political leaders. A number of centres were set up to popularise the new cult. The movement now shows signs of decline. The school at Jadopokhar does not function regularly, though his volunteers continue to visit some of the neighbouring schools to popularize the script, and to preach reforms.

A few miles away from Jhinkpani (Singhbhum) a social reform movement has developed under a Ho master named Kripa Sindhu. The supreme God, the Singbonga appeared before him and said :

> There in no religion in your society. Your society is disorganized. It will be organized through a new religion only. You are the person who can reform the society. I will show you the way, which will be propagated among your people. By this religion, you and the world will get inspiration for truth. The life of people will be happy on the basis of inspiration given by Singbonga. Through this religion there will be mutual trust and understanding among mankind.[48]

Lifecycle ceremonies were simplified, drinking was prohibited and simple prayers were prescribed. The movement has about

10,000 followers. The Singbonga spoke again to one of Kripa Sindhu's *chela*, through *vani* (inspiration), and a script was born. Primers have been written in this script. A beautiful temple has been constructed and a number of development programmes have been launched. The organization got affiliated to the All India Banbasi Girijan Samaj to seek an all India platform to popularize the script and win recognition of their demand for funds to promote development.

The tribals of Tripura have demanded recognition of Kak Barok as a state language and medium of instruction for tribal children. The Kak Barok, a tribal dialect, is a cover term for the six groups and two sub-groups of the tribal community of Tripura accounting for 4 lakh out of 4.50 lakh of tribal population. Starting as an unwritten language, Kak Barok gradually developed into a language. With the publication of a grammar, dictionary, primers in Bengali script, it became a literature. A Kak Barok Sahyitya Sabha has been formed to highlight the language issue and demand recognition of the Roman script for the language, as against the Bengali script. The movement for the adoption of the Roman script for the tribal dialect has also been supported by the Boro Sahitya Sabha of Assam, the Mizos, the Khasis and the growing Christian population among the Tripura tribals, which has nearly doubled during the 1961-71 decade. The Sabha also published books. The Bible was translated into the Kak Barok language. The language and script movement on the one hand, and the movement for tribal autonomy on the other were integrated. The language and script thus became a symbol of tribal identity.

In Manipur the ideological conflict between the Gouriya who favour the Vaishnava structure of beliefs and rituals and the continuance of the present political system and the Sanamahis who go back to the pre-Vaishnava roots of Meitei culture and support political autonomy for the state, has assumed yet another dimension. While the Gouriya support the Bengali script, the Sanamahis are for the revival of Meitei script, which had existed and was lost as the *puyas* (the sacred texts) written in it were burnt down or those kept in the royal archives were interpolated with the Bengali words. The search for the new script is on from among the families which are said to be still in possession of some old *puyas*. Naoria Pulla discovered in 1935 the "Manipuri script" with 35 alphabets. He also wrote several books in which he described the original religion of the Meitei and their customs. He was the founder of the Sanamahi movement. Later, many groups came into existence which were divided over the number of letters in the old Meitei alphabet. There were altogether three sets of alphabets in use in the different *puyas*, of 27, 25 and 18 letters each. The Manipuri Sahitya Parishad is in favour of 35 letters. The old script is being taught in 32 schools by volunteers; about 100 students are taking their examination in the old script every year. The *puyas* are being reprinted. The old script has caught the imagination of the youth. There can be no culture without a language and a script, and the old script is now an integral part of the Manipuris' search for identity.

The Chakmas claim to have discovered a script of their own. The Savaras of the Ganjam and Koraput districts are also reported to have found a script for themselves. Two more enterprising Santals, Ramdas Tudu of Ghatsila and Ramchandra Murmu of Silda, have discovered their own Santal scripts.

The process of discovery of the scripts will go on as long as the search for a new identity is on, because language is an ingredient of self-consciousness. A script, whether revealed (Ho), invented (Santal), or recovered (Meitei) is an essential complement to a language, which is indispensable to cultural identity. The objective could be the preservation of the pure and pristine elements of culture (Ho, Santal), or movement for political autonomy (Tripura and Manipur). In all cases, demand for recognition of the script is part of the demand for a new social order in the tribals' search for identity.

But though these scripts have been widely acclaimed by tribals, there is reservation about their functional relevance. Many favour the Devanagari as the script for inter-tribal communication, as adopted by the missionaries in Chotanagpur. However, there should be determined and coordinated efforts at the national level to respect the susceptibilities of these little communities, undertake a scientific evaluation of their script, build up a literature in their own language, and to ensure the observance of Article 29 of the Indian Constitution in letter and spirit, which enjoins protection of the interests of the minorities and their right to conserve the distinct language, script or culture of their own.

Other Trends

As mentioned earlier, Christianity has been an important factor of cultural change in tribal regions. The tribal Christian population in the 1961 census was 1.6 million. During the decade 1961-71 there has been a steep rise in the Christian population of the north-east, Manipur (84%), Meghalaya (75%), Nagaland (76%), Tripura (56%) and Assam (45%). In the mainland, Orissa has reported the biggest rise (88%) followed by Madhya Pradesh (52%). These trends have persisted since then. Proselytization has not been a unilinear process. There is oscillation between traditional religion and Christianity, a measure of compromise with the first while getting absorbed in the second.[49]

In recent years, there has been an endeavour to Indianize, even indigenize Christianity. Elements of tribal life which harmonize with Christianity have been accepted. In the first phase Christianity sought to Christianize paganism; now it is the other way round. There is the Indianization of the Church and its personnel, of prayers and liturgy. The second step has been 'indigenization', i.e. the acceptance of such elements of tribal region, and festivals, dance and music as do not come into conflict with the tenets of Christian faith.[50]

Islamization among the tribes has received little attention in anthropological studies for the simple reason that there are only 61,233 tribal Muslims concentrated among the Gond and Bhil communities in Madhya Pradesh. There is no evidence of conversion of tribals to Islam practised as a deliberate policy of the Islamic state. Among the Gonds only one section of the Raj Gonds embraced Islam as a symbol of the higher style of life characteristic of the Muslim aristocracy during the medieval period. The exposure of a section of the Raj Gond aristocracy to Islam did not cause any split in the Gond society. In the present day situation this Islamized group, having lost all its former power and prestige, is too small to hold its own as a separate entity. Its social structure is under stress and it is bound to merge with the local Muslim community. The Tadvi Bhils were converted to Islam, by the *pirs*. For a long period after their conversion, they remained on the borderline of Islam and animism. Their contact with other Muslim communities steadily drew them closer to Islam and weaned them away from their ancient faith, but being numerous they have been able to maintain their identity in an ethnic sense and to resist change in their social structure.[51]

We have discussed a whole range of movements extending beyond the stereotype of solidarity movements varying in their goals, organization, geography, leadership, etc. The movements in the north-east are entirely different from those elsewhere in the country because of its different socio-political background. In middle India which includes the northern parts of Andhra Pradesh we have movements for political autonomy, the most articulate and best organized of which is the Jharkhand movement. Then there are script-based movements, movements centering on the tribal's rights in forest and land. Sanskritization processes have not come to a stop but have also slowed down, as evident from the persistence of the bhagat movements. Behind all these movements lie the tribal's interminable search for identity and his urge to secure a better deal for himself. The folk heroes of the first phase of tribal movements in the post-colonial period and the more literate and less charismatic leaders who followed have only given expression to these unspoken urges of the tribal people. All movements cannot be dismissed as anti-national and dealt with as a mere law and order problem. We also cannot dismiss the tribal movements as so many bush-fires. Like peasant movements the tribal movements at this stage of social formation are bound to remain local, limited, restricted to dominant tribe or a group of tribes. This however does not minimize their importance, or detract from the issues they seek to highlight.

While no nation state can allow itself to be liquidated it is its dominant core that has to show understanding and treat tribal communities with consideration. The tribals form only 7.5 percent of our population, but they occupy 20 percent of the geographical area, which contains 70 percent of minerals and bulk of forest and water resources. The tribes are the dominant community in the great belt of the tribal territory lying across middle India and in the north-east. They constitute a sizeable section of our labour force, both industrial and agricultural, which is 38.5 per cent of the tribal population as against 32.9 per cent of the general population (1971). They are our sentinels. As Gandhiji said, they are the last but not the least of India's sons. The statement issued by the seminar on Tribal Situation in India (1969) at the Indian Institute of Advanced Study said:

> Integration must be sharply differentiated from assimilation which means complete loss of cultural identity for the weaker groups. Each group must be able to uphold its cultural heritage with dignity and a sense of achievement... Tolerance is a quality without which we can hardly survive as a nation... Integration is a dynamic and continuing process which necessarily involves give-and-take by the various sections of the national community... this process could never be complete and... it was for enlightened citizenry of public opinion to make sure that it never stops.[52]

This statement is as relevant today as it was when it was issued sixteen years ago.

Notes and References

The present paper is a revised version of my article "Transformation of Tribal Society: Integration vs Assimilation", which was based on the Eighth Devraj Chanana Memorial Lecture delivered under the auspices of Delhi University, December 10-11, 1981.

1. S.C. Dube, (ed.) *Tribal Heritage of India: Ethnicity, Identity and Interaction*, vol. I.
2. Surajit Sinha, "Transformation of Tribal Society in Modern India" Fifth Devraj Chanana Memorial Lecture, 1973 (unpublished).

3. K.S. Singh, "Colonial Transformation of the Tribal Society in Middle, India" Presidential Address, Bhubaneswar, 1977. Also see R.S. Sharma, *Indian Feudalism: c 300-1200*.

4. See Chapter 4.

5. A.B. Bardhan, *The Unsolved Tribal Problem*, Freedom Jubilee Series No. 5, Communits Party Publication, 1973. Also see, Sharit Bhowmik, *Class Formation in the Plantation System.*

6. G.S. Ghurye, *The Burning Cauldron of North-East India*; also see *The Scheduled Tribes*,

7. "Red Indians fight for the right to live on the Land of Ancestors", *The Searchlight*, September 15, 1981.

8. See, Lee Swepston, "Latin American Approaches to the Indian Problem", *International Labour Review*. vol. 117. no. 2. March-April 1978.

9. See, Sunanda K. Datta-Ray, "New Dreams for Old", *The Statesman*, December 1 and 2, 1981. Also see Rupa Chinai, "The Alienated Aborigines" *Sunday Standard Magazine*, March 8, 1981.

10. I.H. Kawharu, J.M' McEwen, and W. Winiate, "Maori Incorporations in New Zealand", New Zealand National Commission for UNESCO (unpublished).

11. *Theory and Practice Problems of the Contempory World*, in *Social Sciences Today*; Also see, Yu V. Bromley, *Soviet Ethnography: Main Trends. Problems of the Contemporary World, in Social Sciences Today.*

12. Quoted in R.N. Ismagilova, *Ethnic Problems of the Tropical Africa: Can they be solved*? p. 122.

13. Ibid p. 126.

14. Ibid.

15. K.S. Singh, "Colonial Transformation of the Tribal Society" op. cit.

16. K.S. Singh, "The Mahatma and the Adivasis", *Man in India*, vol. 50. no. I, January-March, 1970.

17. Quoted in K.S. Singh, "Colonialism, Anthropology and Primitive Society: The Indian Scenario (1928-47)", Second Indo-GDR History Seminar, University of Delhi, December 1981. See chapter 6 of this book.

18. Quoted in K.S. Singh, "Jawaharlal Nehru, Tribals and their Transformation", Seminar on Nehru and Village, Madras, February 22-27, 1980.

19. Steve Jones, "Tribal Underdevelopment in India", paper presented to UN Institute for Economic Planning and Development, Environment Training Programme, Seminar on Environment and Poorly Integrated Societies in Africa (Mauritius April, 1976). Also see a rejoinder by Bhupender Singh, *Planning Strategy for Tribal Development in Retrospect and Prospect, A Mid-Term Appraisal, Occasional Papers on Tribal Development*, 29, Government of India, Ministry of Home Affairs, New Delhi 1981.

20. K.S. Singh, "Tribal Economy in India", Indo-Soviet Symposium in Social Sciences, February 22-26, 1977, Visva-Bharati, Santiniketan. Also see

by the same author, "Transformation of Tribal Economy: Two Case Studies" (unpublished), 1978; and "Pattern of Agricultural Changes in Tribal Chhotanagpur", *Trends of Socio-economic Change in India* 1871-1961, *Transactions of the Indian Institute of Advanced Study*, volume VII,

21. N. Prasad, and A. Sahay, *Impact of Industrialisation on Bihar Tribes*, 1961; *Census of India, 1961 : Social Processes in the Industrialisation of Rourkela* 1968; L.P. Vidyarthi, *Industrialisation in India. A Case Study of Tribal Bihar* . Also see Pradhan, H. Prasad and N. Sengupta, "Regional Distribution of Economic Benefits arising from a Steel Plant: A Case Study of Rourkela Steel Plant" (*mimeographed*).

22. K.S. Singh, "Colonial Transformation of the Tribal Society", op. cit.

23. *Land Tenures in India, Census of India 1961*, Volume 1, India, Part XI-A (i) 1968.

24. Pradip Kumar Bose, "Stratification among Tribals in Gujarat", *Economic and Political Weekly*,, February 7, 1981.

25. Ghanshayam, Shah, "Socio-Economic Condition of Chodhras: A Restudy", Centre for Social Studies, Surat (unpublished).

26. Bani Prasanna Misra, "Kirata Karyokinesis: Modes of Production in Tribal Societies in North-East India", in Arvind N. Das and V. Nilkant (ed) *Agrarian Relations in India.*

27. K.S. Singh, "Tribal Ethnicity in a Multi-Ethnic Society: A Study in Colonial and Post-Colonial Chotanagpur", UNESCO Seminar on Trends in Ethnic Group Relations in Asia, Manila, March 1976.

28. The papers presented at the ASI Seminar are published in two volumes by Manohar, New Delhi.

29. See S.M. Dubey, "Inter-Ethnic Alliance, Tribal Movements and Integration in North-East India", K.S. Singh, (ed.), *Tribal Movments*, vol. I.

30. A.M. Dyakov, *The National Problem in India Today.*

31. Christoph von Furer-Haimendorf, "Aboriginal Rebellions in the Deccan", *Man in India, Rebellion Number*, volume XXV, December 1945.

32. K.S. Singh, "The Gond Movements", in K.S. Singh, (ed.), *Tribal Movements*, vol. II.

33. See I.P. Desai, "The Tribal Autonomy Movement in South Gujarat", *Ibid*,

34. K.S. Singh, "Tribal Ethnicity in a multi-ethnic Society: A Study in the processes of Conflict and Integration in colonial and post-colonial Chotanagpur", UNESCO Seminar on Trends in Ethnic Group Relations in Asia, Manila March, 1976. Also see, by the same author, "From Ethnicity to Regionalism: A Study in Tribal Politics and Movements in Chotanagpur from 1900 to 1975" in S.C. Malik, (ed), *Dissent, Protest and Reform in Indian Civilisation.*

35. K.S. Singh, "Agrarian Dimensions of Tribal Movements", A.R. Desai, (ed), Agrarian Struggles in India after Independence, Oxford University Press (forthcoming).

36. K.S. Singh "A Forest Satyagraha", *Tribal Movements* vol. II.

37. K.S. Singh "The Gond Movements', Ibid.

38. K.S. Singh, "Tribal Unrest", paper presented at Seminar on Developmental Aspects of Tribal Areas, Novmber 11-13, 1980, Bhubaneswar, National Commission on Backward Areas, Government of India.

39. Ashim Kumar Adhikary, and Ranjit Kumar Bhattacharya, "The Extremist Movement: An Appraisal of the Naxalite Movement with Special Reference to its Repercussion Among Tribes", K.S. Singh *Tribal Movements*, vol. II.

40. A.K. Danda, "Gariha Guru and His Sant Samaj Movement", Ibid.

41. Ekka, Willian, "Reform Movement of Rajmohini Devi", Ibid.

42. R.S. Mann, "Structure and Role Dynamics among the Bhils of Raiasthan", Ibid.

43. B.B. Lal, "Socio-Religious Movements Among the Tribals of South Gujarat", Ibid.

44. Vikas Bhatt, "A Baba in Bastar", *ibid.*

45. P.C. Hembram, "Return to the Sacred Grove", Ibid.

46. K.N. Thusu, "A Political Movement of the Gonds," Ibid.

47. Christoph von Furer—Haimendorf , *Tribes of India, The Struggle of Survival*, p. 318.

48. K.S. Singh "Tribal Identity Movements based on Script and Language", *Man in India*, vol. 62, no. 3, September 1982.

49. K.N. Sahay, "Impact of Christianity on the Uraon of the Chainpur Belt in Chotanagpur : An analysis of its cultural processes", *American Anthropologist*, vol. 70, no. 5, October 1968.

50. K.N. Sahay, "Indigenisation of Christianity in India", *Man in India*, March 1981.

51. M.K.A. Siddiqui, "Islamization Among the Tribes of Central and Western India", *Bulletin of the Anthropological Survey of India*, vol. xxii, nos. 3 & 4 , 1976; also see by him "Impact of Islam on Some Tribes of Central and Western India", *Man in India*, vol. 59, no. 3, July-September 1979.

52. K.S. Singh, *Tribal Situation in India*. (*ed.*)

12

Conclusion

This work started by investigating the conceptual framework developed by the colonial administrators, ethnographers and missionaries for the study of tribal society and found it inadequate. They had chosen to describe the tribes as isolated, and attributed the ills which overtook them in the colonial phase to the non-colonial factors such as the corrupting Hindu influence on the tribal chiefs, and to the naivety of tribal character. They ignored the impact of colonialism in its totality upon tribal society. With their exclusive concern with the tribes they overlooked the operation of pre-colonial historical processes such as the migration of many communities and the penetration of cultural and religious influence which led to the formation of a composite society in middle India region. The portrayal of the tribesmen as the Noble Savage, was therefore naive but this simplistic model served to justify the presence of the British raj as the guardians of the tribes, even though there were tribal rebellions directed against it.

In presenting an alternative model of the transformation of tribal society, it has been argued that tribal society in India like other segments of Indian society has been part of the universe of Indian civilization and of its dominant social formations through history; that the autonomy of its unique social structure has been subjected to similar historical processes, and that its isolation has been relative and never absolute, at least in middle India. In this connection we discussed the relationship of history and anthropology and of colonialism and anthropology. It would be appropriate to recall that the roots of such change went back to the pre-colonial phenomenon of state formation and allied formations which tended to integrate, no matter how loosely, such of the tribal communities as were involved in them into the pan-India or regional systems. The beginning of change in tribal society was conceptualised in terms of state formation, which appears to be the crucial factor in tribal situations. In this connection the emigration of peasants and artisans, among others, to tribal regions deserves to be investigated further. The peasants not only generated agricultural surplus for the new state, they also interacted with tribes in many fields, and the interaction of peasants and tribes holds the key to the understanding of many processes in the exposed tribal regions. This part of the story is not fully told because it has to be reconstructed out of a mass of evidence, both historical and anthropological. The process of diffusion of technology and dissemination of culture therefore cannot be understood only in terms of the brahminical model, for there is nothing in anthropological literature to suggest that the brahminical settlements today are functioning as the centres of diffusion of technology. Only a multilinear model of change can bring out the interaction among various communities, which could be seen in terms of transfer of technology, rise of link languages, absorption and recreation of epic traditions, and many other processes within an autonomous social formation emerging in tribal regions.

The tribes severely remained outside the varna system. The process of their integration with peasant-jati has been so far explained largely in cultural terms. This model has its merits, but this does not go far to explain the multiplex processes of the integration of tribes, particuarly such of them as stand outside the economic and cultural system of jati, with the agrarian and economic system of a region as peasants of various categories, and as small producers, landless labourers and artisans producing for market. The projection of the cultural system of the jati swallowing up the tribes also deserves to be corrected from yet another angle. The tribes as the dominant community in some regions laid down the law and set the model for emulation by incoming communities. Tribalization is a complex phenomenon that deserves to be critically investigated.

Colonialism not only marked the continuation of many of these pre-colonial processes of change, but also strengthened them. Colonialism produced profound changes in the tribal society in all its aspects, its political system, social structure, economic and agrarian institutions and relationship through direct intervention (or ambivalence) and market processes. Middle India witnessed the most radical transformation of tribal society. Tribal areas were opened up. Large scale influx of aliens began. Tribals' control over environment and resources declined, as pressure on their land and encroachment on their rights in forest, mounted. When the tribals reacted sharply through their rebellions a new set of laws protecting their land and a new administrative system were designed for them in some areas, while others were effectively integrated into the political, administrative and agrarian systems of British raj. However, there was a great deal of ambivalence in regard to the tribal affairs in princely India, where the *status quo* was allowed to continue. In fact conditions in the native states were considered even congenial for tribes. The colonial administrators-turned-anthropologists recognised the tribes as a distinct element in Indian society, which was to be excluded from the Indian political system. They pleaded that the British should continue to retain control over tribal affairs even after the transfer of power. This suggestion was considered impracticable, and one of the last colonial administrators went so far as to say that they had done little more than preserve the tribals as delightful primitives. However, the framework of a protective policy, which was the legacy of colonialism, was incorporated into the Constitution of India.

Tribal rebellions were the product of the colonial system, even though some of the colonial administrators tended to comfort themselves with the thought that these were directed more against local functionaries than against themselves. This illusion was shattered many times. Nor does the characterisation of such movements as defensive help in their understanding, because this ignores the internal dynamics of a tribal society and the interaction of various elements which hold it together. These factors come into play in rebellions. All tribal movements cannot be clubbed together; nor are many of them linked with peasant and freedom movements either. They have to be studied as part of the tribal system, and the change in their structure and ideology has to be related to the transformation of tribal society. Thus a wide range of tribal movements emerges. This study discusses the range and type of primary resistance movements including the "baronial resistance" led by their chiefs in an upsurge in which many communities other than tribes participated lending the crusade against "outsiders" or the agents of colonialism a class or even a regional character. It then passes on to the second phase of tribal movements, in which the tribals articulate their problems regarding land and forest, and their urge for social reform. When the struggle for freedom develops some of the tribes seek accommodation within its parameters, and also voice their demands for security and autonomy. In this context the role of Mahatma Gandhi and the interaction of various viewpoints on the assimilation vs integration of tribes is relevant to the understanding of the tribal situation. The Mahatma profoundly influenced tribals, as their folklores reveal, brought some of them within the ambit of the political movement and reconstruction programmes, and his impact strengthened the sanskritization processes. However there were also tribals who kept out of them and sought political autonomy. Development of tribal autonomy movement in Chotanagpur has to be seen in terms of the internal dynamics of tribal society and also exogenous processes.

The post-colonial phase witnessed on the one hand the incorporation of the provisions for the safeguard of the tribes in the Indian Constitution and on the other the decolonization of the political system, including the dismantling of the system of protection for tribes at some places. Influx of non-tribals in search of land and employment went up, and the process of the tribals' gradual loss of control over their environment and resources continued. Thus while tribes participate in democracy, control the apparatus of political power in some states, and influence policies and programmes in a few others, large sections of them are still engaged, as their wide-ranging movements reveal, like other sections of our people, in the struggle to achieve the objective of "growth with equity".

Bibliography

(A) Primary Sources

India Office Library, London:
(i) IOR L/P & J/7/6787 Backward Tribes.
(ii) IOR : L/P & J/3712 & 343.
(iii) IOR : L/P & J/9/51.
(iv) IOR : L/P & J/4077 C.
(v) IOR : L/P & J/9/343.
(vi) IOR : L/P & J/(C) 8712.
(vii) IOR : L/P & J/6/1488.

Andhra Pradesh State Archives/State Government Hyderabad:

Hapell's Report G.O. 572 July 1923 Public Deptt., Government of Madras

File no 15 P. A/497, Judicial and Police Department, Nizam Government Hyderabad 1940.

National Archives of India, New Delhi:

File No. 226-P(S) 43, 1943, Political Department Political Branch "Criminal Activities in Tripura State of Ratanmani Naotia".

Foreign Political Department 1932 no 643.

(B) Secondary Sources: (*i*) *Books:*

"Address not formally presented", *Appendix XI, Presented in India to His Excellency Secretary of State for India, East,* vol. XVIII, London, 1918, British Museum.

Adhikary, Ashim Kumar and Bhattacharya, Ranjit Kumar., "The Extremist Movement : An Appraisal of the Naxalite Movement with Special Reference to its Repercussion Among Tribes" K. S. Singh (ed) *Tribal Movement, Vol. II,* Delhi, Manohar, 1983.

Aitareya Aranyaka with the comn. of Sayanacarya, Anandashram Sanskrit Granthawali No. 38, Poona, 1959.

Ambedkar, B.R., *The Untouchables: Who were They and Why They Became Untouchables,* 1948.

———*Who were the Shudras: How They Came to be the Fourth Varna in the Indo-Aryan Society* Reprint, 1970.

Amin, Samir, *Unequal Development, An Essay on the Social formations of Peripheral Capitalism,* New York, Monthly Review Press, 1976.

Asad Talal (ed), *Anthropology and the Colonial Encounter*, London: Ithaca Press, Reprint, 1975.

Askari, Syed Hasan, "A Shuttari Saint of North Bihar", *Journal of Bihar Research Society* March, June, 1981.

Baden-Powell; B.H., *The Indian Village Community*, London, 1896.

Bailey, F.G., *Tribe, Caste, and Nation : a study of political activity and political change in highland Orissa*, Bombay, Oxford University Press, 1960.

———*Politics and Social Change, Orissa in* 1959, University of California Press, 1963.

Bardhan, A.B., *The Unsolved Tribal Problem*, Freedom Jubilee Series no. 5, Communist Party Publication, 1973.

Basu, Jogiraj, *India in the Age of the Brahmanas*, Calcutta, 1960.

Bhadra, Gautam, "The Kuki (?) uprising (1917-19) : Its Causes and Nature", *Man in India*, January-March 1975.

Bhaduri, Manindra Bhusan, "The Astronomy of the Mundas and Their Star Myths", Paper read in the Ethnology and Folklore Section of the Second Oriental Conference held at Calcutta in 1922.

Bhatt, Vikas., "A Baba in Bastar", K. S. Singh (ed) *Tribal Movements, Vol. II*, Delhi, Manohar, 1983.

Bhavishya Puran, Venkateshwar Press, Bombay.

Bhowmik, Sharit, *Class Formation in the Plantation System*, New Delhi, People's Publishing House, 1981.

Bloch, Maurice (ed), *Marxist Analyses and Social Anthropology, ASA studies*, London, Malaby Press, 1975.

Bodding, P.O. Rev., "The Kharwar Movement among the Santals", *Man in India, Vol. I*, 1920.

Bodra, Lakho, *Shaar Hora*, Part I-II, 1956, *Bonga Hora, Kol Rule* 1961.

Bombay District Gazetteer, Panch Mahal, Gujarat.

Bose, N.K., "The Hindu Mode of Tribal Absorption", *Cultural Anthropology and other Essays*, 1953.

———*Cultural Anthropology*, Bombay, Asia Publishing House, 1961.

———*Culture and Society in India*, Bombay, Asia Publishing House, 1967.

———*Problems of national integration*. Simla, Indian Institute of Advanced Study, 1967.

———*Tribal Life in India*, New Delhi, National Book Trust, 1971.

———*Some Indian Tribes*, New Delhi, National Book Trust, 1972.

———*Anthropology and Some Indian Problems*, Calcutta, Institute of Social Research and Applied Anthropology, 1972.

———*The Structure of Hindu Society*, trans. by Andre Beteille, New Delhi, Orient Longman, 1975.

Bose, Pradeep Kumar, "Stratification among Tribals in Gujarat", *Economic and Political Weekly*, February 7, 1981.

Brett, E.A., *Colonialism and Underdevelopment in East Africa, The politics of economic change* 1919-39. Heinemann, 1973.

Bromley Yu. V., "*Soviet Ethnography: Main Trends, Problems of the Contemporary World*", Social Sciences Today, Editorial Board, USSR Academy of Science, Moscow, 1978.

Buhler, G., *The Laws of Manu*, translated with extracts from Seven Commentaries, 1881.

Campbell, James M., *Gazetteer of the Bombay Presidency: Khandesh*, vol. 21, 1880.

Carmichael D. F. (ed), *Manual of the District of Vizagapatnam in the Presidency of Madras*, Madras, 1869.

Carnegy, P., "The Bhars of Oudh and Banaras", *Journal of Asiatic Society of Bengal*, 1876.

Carr, E.H., *What is History?*, 1967.

Census of India, 1931, *Bihar and Orissa*, Report, Vol. VIII, Part I, 1932.

Census of India 1961, *Social Processes in the Industrialization of Rourkela*, 1968.

Centre for Social Studies, Surat, *Caste, Caste-conflict and Reservations*, 1985.

Chatterji, Suniti Kumar, *Kirata Jana-Krti, The Indo-Monogoloids: Their contributions to the History and Culture of India*, Royal Asiatic Society of Bengal, Calcutta, 1951.

Chauhan, B.R., "Tribalisation", in Vyas, N.N., Mann, R.S. and Chaudhary N.D. (eds), *Rajasthan Bhils*, Manikyalal Varma Tribal Research and Training Institute, Social Welfare Deptt., Govt. of Rajasthan, Udaipur, 1978.

Chevalier, Francois, *Land and Society in Colonial Mexico, the Great Hacinda*, trans. by Alvin Eustis, University of California Press, 1973.

Choudhary, S. B., *Civil Disturbances in India* 1757-1857 Calcutta, 1972.

The Constitution of India, Government of India, 1983.

The Constitution of Birsa Seva Dal (Hindi) 1971.

Chinai, Rupa, "The Alienated Aborigines", *Sunday Standard Magazine*, March 8, 1981.

Cobden-Ramsay, L.E.B., *Feudatory States of Orissa*, 1910.

Culshaw, W.J. and Archer, W.C., "The Santal Rebellion", *Man in India, Rebellion Number*, December 1945.

Dalton, E.T., *Descriptive Ethnology of Bengal*, Calcutta, 1872.

Danda, A.K., "Gahira Guru and His Sant Samaj Movement", K. S. Singh (ed), *Tribal Movements Vol. II*, Delhi, Manohar, 1983.

Das, Arvind Narayan, "Peasants Struggle in Chotanagpur", *Economic and Political Weekly*, March 1, 1975.

Das Gupta, T.M., "Riang Vidroh 1943", *Tripura Prasanga*, Govt. Printing Press, May, 1977.

Das, Veena, *Structure and Congition, Aspects of Hindu Caste and Ritual*, Delhi, Oxford University Press, 1977.

Datta, K.K., *Anti-British Plots and Movements before* 1857, 1970.

Das, Nityanand, "Martyr Lakshaman Naik: A Hero of the Freedom Movement", *Adibasi*, vol. 11, no. 1, 1967-8, Bhubaneswar.

Datta-Ray, Sunanda R., "New Dreams for Old", *The Statesman*, December Delhi, 1 and 2, 1981.

Desai, A. R. (ed) *Peasant Struggles in India*, Oxford University Press, 1979.

Desai, I.P., "The Tribal Autonomy Movement in South Gujarat, K. S. Singh (ed) *Tribal Movements*, Manohar, Vol. II, 1983.

Desai, I.P. and Choudhry, B.L., *History of Rural Development in Modern India*, vol. II, New Delhi, 1977.

Dhar, Hiranmoy, "Split in the Jharkhand Mukti Morcha", *Economic and Political Weekly*, 2 August 1980.

Directorate of Social Welfare, Rajasthan, Jaipur, *Scheduled Tribes of Rajasthan and their Welfare* (year not given).

Dube, S.C. (ed), *India since Independence: Social Reforms in India*, 1947-1972 New Delhi, Vikas Publishing House, 1977.

———*ed. Tribal Heritage of India, Ethnicity, Identity and Interaction.* vol. I, Delhi, Vikas, 1977.

Dubey, S. M., "Inter-Ethnic Alliance, Tribal Movements and Integration in North-East India", K. S. Singh (ed), *Tribal Movements*, Vol. I, New Delhi, Manohar, 1982.

Dumont, Louis, *Homo Hierarchicus: The Caste System and its Implications*, London, Granada Publishing Ltd., Paladin (Paper back), 1972.

Durga Saptshati, Geeta Press, Gorakhpur.

Dyakov, A.N., *The National Problems in India Today*, Moscow, 1966

Ekka, William., "Reform Movement of Rajmohini Devi" K. S. Singh (ed) *Tribal Movements, Vol. II*, Delhi, Manohar, 1983.

Elwin ,Verrier, *Loss of Nerve*. A comparative study of the result of the contact of peoples in the aboriginal areas of Bastar State and the Central Provinces of India, Essay submitted for the Welcombe Medal.

———*Truth about India, Can we get it*? George Allen Unwin, 1932.

———*The Agaria*, Humphrey Milford, London, Oxford University Press, 1942.

———*The Aboriginals*, Oxford University Press, July 1943.

———"Saora Fituris" *Man in India, Rebellion Number*, 1945.

———*Myths of Middle India*. Oxford University Press, 1949.

———*The Foreign Missionary Danger*, published by H.C. Vidyarthi, Ranchi, All India Dayanand Mission, 1962.

———*Religious and Cultural Aspects of Khadi* Sarvodaya, Prachuralaya, Thanjavur, 1964.

———*Tribal World of Verrier Elwin*, Oxford University Press, 1964.

Eschamann, Anncharlott, Kulke, Hermann, and Tripathi, Gaya Charan (ed), *The Cult of Jagannath and the Regional Triditions of Orissa*, South Asia. Interdisciplinary Regional Research Programme, Orissa Project, Research New Delhi Manohar, 1978.

Firth, Raymond "The Sceptical Anthropologist, Social Anthropology and Marxist views on Society" Bloch, Maurice (ed) *Marxist Analyses and Social Anthropology*, ASI study 2, London Malaby Press, 1975.

Forbes, L.R., *Report on Ryotwari Settlement of the Government Farms in Palamau*, 1872.

Francis, W., *District Gazetteer of Vizagapatnam* 1907.

Frank, Andre Gunder, *Capitalism and Underdevelopment in Latin America*, 1969.

———*Latin America, Underdevelopment or Revolution*, 1970.

———*Capitalsim and Underdevelopment*, 1975.

Furer-Haimendorf. C. von, "Aboriginals Rebellions in the Deccan", *Man in India*, Rebellion Number, vol. 25, December, 1945.

———*Tribal Hyderabad, Four Reports*, 1945.

———*Raj Gonds of Adilabad*, London, Macmillan, 1948.

———"The Position of the Tribal Population in Modern India", Philip Mason (ed), *India and Ceylon, Unity and Diversity*, London, Oxford University Press, 1957.

———"Tribes and Hindu Society", *Contributions to Indian Society* (NS) no. 4, Dec., 1971.

———"The changing position of Tribal population in India", *Royal Anthropological Institute News*, no. 22, Oct., 1977.

———*Tribes of India. The Struggle for Survival*, Delhi, Oxford University Press, 1982.

Gait, E.A., *History of Assam*, (Revised), Calcutta, 1963.

Gandhi, M.K., *Hindu Dharma*, Ahmedabad, Navajivan Press, 1950.

———*Christian Missions : Their Place in India*, Navajivan Press, Ahmedabad, 1941.

Ganguly, P.C., "Separation in the Indian Polity: A Case Study", in Pradhan M.C., Singh, R.D., Mishra, P.K. and Shastry, D.B. (ed.) *Anthropology and Archaeology: Essays in Commemoration for Verrier Elwin*, 1902-64, London University Press, 1969.

Gazetteer of the Bombay Presidency, Poona District, Vol. XVIII Part II, 1985.

Ghurye, G.S., *The Scheduled Tribes*, Bombay: Popular Book Depot, 1969.

———*The Aborigines-so-Called and Their Future*. 1943, Popular Prakashan.

———*Caste and Race in India*, Bombay, Popular Prakasan (Reprint), 1979.

———*Indian Acculturation : Agastaya and Skanda*, Popular Praksan, 1977.

———*The Burning Caldron of North-East India*, Bombay, Popular Prakashan, 1980.

Godelier, Maurice., *Perspectives in Marxist Anthropology*, *Cambridge Studies in Social Anthropology*, Cambridge University Press, 1977.

Goswami, M.C., "Tribe-Peasant-Caste Relations in North-East India", Presidential Address, Section on Anthropology & Archaeology. Fifty Eighth Indian Science Congress, Bangalore, 1971.

Gough, Kathleen, "Anthropology: Child of Imperialism", *Monthly Review*, April, 1968.

———"New Proposals for Anthropology" *Current Anthropology* Vol. 9, 1968.

Government of Bihar, Chief Election/Electoral Officer, Patna

———*Report of the First General Election under the Constitution of India in Bihar* 1951-2, 1953.

———*Report of the Second General Elections in Bihar* 1957, Patna 1958.

———*Report on the Third General Election in Bihar* 1967, Patna 1963.

———*Report on the Fourth General Election in Bihar* 1967, Patna, 1968.

———*Lok Sabha Am Chunao Ka Prativedan,* 1971.

———*Bihar Vidhan Sabha Ka Am Chunao* 1972 *Ka Prativedan.*

———*Lok Sabha General Election* 1977, *Bihar State, A Statistical Analysis.*

———*General Election* 1977 *Bihar Legislative Assembly, A Statistical Analysis.*

———*Bihar Legislative Assembly General Election* 1980, *A Statistical Analysis.*

———*Lok Sabha General Election* 1980, *Bihar State, A Statistical Analysis.*

Grant, Charles, *The Gazetteer of the Central Provinces of India,* 1870.

Griffiith, R.T.H. (trans.) *Sam Veda,* Banaras, 1893.

Grigson, W.V., *The Maria Conds of Bastar,* Oxford University Press, 1938.

Guha, A., "Ahom Migration, its impact on rice economy of medieval Assam", *Artha Vijnana,* vol. ix, no. 2, June, 1967.

Guha, Ranjit, *Elementary Aspects of Peasant Insurgency in Colonial India,* Delhi, Oxford University Press, 1983.

Gupta, Murari, *Chaitanya Charitamrita,* Amrit Bazar Patrika Office, 1931.

Haldar, R.D., "An Abstract of the Annals of the Nagbansi Raj family of Chotanagpur", *Man in India,* vol. vii 1928.

Harris, Marvin, *The Rise of Anthropological Theory. a history of theories of Culture,* Columbia University, 1968.

Hembram, P.C., "Return to the Sacred Grove" K. S. Singh (ed) *Tribal Movements,* Vol II, Delhi, Manohar, 1983.

Hemingway, F.R., *District Gazetteer of Godavari,* Madras District, 1907.

Hobsbawm, E.J., *Primitive Rebels,* The Norton Library, 1959.

Huizinga, I., *Homo Ludens, A Study of the Play-Element in Culture,* London, Routledge & Kegan Paul, 1949.

Hunter, W.W., *A Statistical Account of Bengal, Hazaribagh and Lohardaga* Vol. XVI, London, Trubner & Co., 1877.

———*The Annals of Rural Bengal*, London, 1883.

Hutton, J.H., *Census of India* 1931, Vol. I Report, Delhi, 1933.

Indian Statutory Commission, Vol. 3 *Reports of the Provincial Committees appointed to confer with the Indian Statutory Commission*, Calcutta, Government of India, Central Publication Branch, 1930.

Ismagilova, R.N., *Ethnic Problems of the Tropical Africa: Can they be solved*? Moscow, Progress Publishers, 1978.

Jack, C. Winslow and Elwin, Verrier, *The Dawn of India's Freedom*, London, George Allen and Unwin, 1931.

Jagdisan, T.N. and Lal, Shyam (ed), *Thakkar Bapa, Eightieth Birthday Commemoration Volume*, Madras, 1949.

Jaiswal, Suvira, "Studies in Early Indian Social History: Trends and Possibilities", *The Indian Historical Review*, vol. 6, no 1-2 July, 1979-January 1980.

Jarret, Colonel H.S., (trans.) *Ain-i-Akbari of Abul Fazl-i-Allami*, Vol II, Calcutta, 1949.

Jarvie, I.G., *The Revolution in Anthropology*, 1976.

Jha, A.P., "Nature of the Santal Unrest of 1871-75 and the origin of the Sapha Hor Movement" *Indian Historical Records Commission Proceedings*, Vol. XXXV Part II 1960.

Jha, J.C., *Kol Insurrection of Chotanagpur*, 1963.

———*The Bhumij Revolt*, 1832-33, 1967.

Jharkhand Andolan Men Videshi Missionarion aur Videshi Pasion Ki Bhumika (year not given).

Jones, Steve, "Tribal Underdevelopment in India", Paper presented to UN Institute for Economics Planning and Development, Environment Training Programme, Seminar on Environment Africa, Mauritius, April, 1976.

Kabra, Kamal Narayan, "Notes towards a theory of indicators of development", *The Indian Journal of Public Administration*, Special Number, Development of Backward Areas, vol. 23, no. 3, July, 1971.

Kalia, S.L. "Sanskritization and Tribalization", *Bulletin of the Tribal Research Institute*, Chhindwara, M.P., vol. 2, no. 4, April, 1959.

———"The Raj Mohini Devi Movement in Surguja", *Bulletin of the Tribal Research Institute*, Chhindwara, vol. 2, no. 1. June, 1962.

Kane, Pandurang Vaman, *History of Dharmasastra, Ancient and Medieval Religious and Civil Law*, vol. 2, Part I, 1941.

Kaviraj, Narhari., "The Santhal Agitation over the Rent Question", *Problems of National Liberation*, Vol. I, No. I November, 1974.

Kawharu, I.H., J.M. MCEwen, and W. Winiate, "Maori Incorporations in New Zealand", New Zealand National Commission for UNESCO (unpublished).

Keith, Arthur Berriedale, (ed), *The Aitareya Aranyaka*, Oxford, Clarendon Press, 1909.

Kogekar, S. V. & Park, P. L., (ed), *Report on the Indian General Election* 1951-2, Bombay, Popular Book Depot, 1956.

Kosambi D.D., *The Culture and Civilization of Ancient India in Historical Outline*, London, 1965.

Ku., Samar and Hansda "Amar Shahid Baba Tilka Manjhi", *Adivasi* 9/16 August 1984, Ranchi.

Kulke, Hermann, "Kshatriyaization and Social Change, a study in Orissa Setting", in Pillai, S. Devadas (ed.), *Aspects of Changing India, Studies in Honour of Professor G.S. Ghurye*, 1976.

Kunju, A.P., Ibrahim, "The Kuricciyar and the Palassi Rebellion" (unpublished).

Lal, R.B., "Sons of the Aravallis: The Garasias", (mimeographed), Tribal Research and Training Institute, Gujarat Vidyapith, 1979.

———"Social and Cultural Life in the Dangs", *Adivasi Gujarat* (year not given).

Land Tenure in India, Census of India, 1961, vol. 1,

Leach, Edmund, *Social Anthropology, A Natural Science of Society*, British Academy, 1976.

Leuva, K.K., *The Asur, A Study of Primitive Iron-Smelters*, Bhartiya Adimjati Seva Sangh, New Delhi: 1963.

Lister, E., *District Gazetteer, Hazaribagh*, 1917.

Lyall, Sir Alfred, *Asiatic Studies, Religious and Social*, First Series, London, John Murray, 1907.

Mahadevan, R., "Zeliangrang Naga Uprising of 1930-32: a brief summary", *Proceedings of the Indian History Congress*, Thirty-fifth Session, Calcutta, 1978.

Mahalingam, T.V., "The Nagas in Indian History and Culture", *Journal of Indian History*, vol. xlii, pt. 1, April, 1965.

Maine, Sir Henry Summer, *Village Commuities in the East and West* London, J. Murray, 1890.

Malik, S.C. (ed), *Dissent Protest and Reform in Indian Civilization*, Indian Institute of Advanced Study, Simla 1977,

Maltby, T.J., *The Ganjam District Mannual*, Madras, 1882.

Man in India, Rebellion Number, vol. 25, 1945.

Mangamma, Dr. J., *Alluri Sitarama Raju*, A.P. State Archives, Hyderabad, 1983

Mandelbaum, David G., *Society in India*, Bombay, Popular Prakashan, 1972.

Mann, R.S., "Structure and Role Dynamics among the Bhils of Rajasthan", Singh, K. S. (ed) *Tribal Movements*, Vol. I, Delhi, Manohar, 1983.

Marx, Karl. *Grundrisse*, English trans., with a foreword by Martin Nicolaus, Penguin Books in association with *New Left Revjew*, 1973.

Meharda, B.L., *History and Culture of the Girasias*, Jaipur, Adi Prakashan, 1985.

Misra, Bani, Prasanna, "Kirata Karyokinesis: Modes of Production in Tribal Societies in North-East India", in Arvind N. Das and V. Nilkant (ed), *Agrarian Relations in India*, New Delhi, Manohar, 1979.

Mitra, Kalipad, "Santal Insurrection in Chotanagpur", *Bengal Past and Present*, Vol. VIII, January-June, 1940.

Mukherjee, B., "The Riang", *Bulletin of the Department of the Anthropoligical Survey of India*, vol. 7, January, 1959.

Mukherjee, R., "Economic Structure in Rural Bengal", *American Sociological Review*, December, vol. 14, no. 2, 1948.

——"The Economic Structure and Social Life in Six Villages of Bengal", *American Sociological Review*, vol. 14, no. 3, 1949.

——*The Dynamics of a rural society*, Berlin: Akademic—Verlage, 1957.

——*Six Villages of Bengal*, Calcutta: Asiatic Society of Bengal, 1958.

——"Trends in Indian Sociology", *Current Sociology*, vol. 25, no. 3, 1977.

Munshi, Surendra, "Tribal Absorption and Sanskritisation in Hindu Society", *Contributions to Indian Sociology* (NS), vol. 13, no. 2, 1979.

Murmu, Timothy Tilkai, *The Adibasis, Past and Present, That is a History of the Indian Aborigines from the Earliest Time to the Present Day*, Santal Pargana, 1933.

Nag, A. Kumar, *Rani Gaidinliu: Study of the Jadunang Movement of the Nagas*, Silchar, 1976.

Naik, T.B., "Ramkatha among the primitive tribes of India" Bulletin of the Tribal Research Institute, Chhindwara, M.P., Vol. I, No. 3, Oct. 1957.

Nandi, R.N., "Growth of Rural Economy in Early Feudal India", Presidential Address, Ancient India Section, Indian History Congress, Forty-Fifth Session, 1984.

Nehru, Jawaharlal, *Unity of India*, London, 1948.

——"The Tribal Folk", in *The Tribal People of India*, New Delhi, 1955.

Objections to the missionary work in India considered and answered, speech delivered at a meeting of the SPG in foreign parts, in the Masonic Hall, on November 7, 1881. The Christian Missionary Society, London.

Oldham, C.E.A.W., (ed.), *Journal of Francis Buchanan (kept during the survey of the district of Shahabad*) 1812-13. Patna, 1926.

O'Malley, L.S.S., *District Gazetteer, Santal Pargana*, 1910.

——*District Gazetteer, Sambalpur*, 1909.

Oomen, T.K., "The Concept of Dominant Caste", *Contributions to Indian Sociology* (NS), no. 4 Dec., 1970.

Padma-Purana, published by Hari Narayana Apte. Anandashrama Sanskrit Series, Poona, 1893.

Panda, Daityari, *An interdisciplinary seminar on Mahima Dharma Darshan*, 1972, published for Shamkar Philosophy Association, DAV College, Koraput.

Pandey, Justice Kanhaiya Lal, *Report on the Disturbances which took place at Jagdalpur on the 25th and 26th March, 1966*, Bhopal 1967.

Parulekar, Godavari, *Adivasis Revolt*, Calcutta National Book Agency Private Ltd, 1975.

Parvathamma, C., "The Remembered Village: A Brahminical Odyssey", *Contributions to Indian Sociology* (NS), vol. 12, no. 1, 1978.

Patil, D.P., *Antiquarian Remains In Bihar* Patna, 1968.

Pathy, Jaganath, "Imperialism, Anthropology and the Third World", *Economic and Pollitical Weekly*, April 4, 1981.

———*Tribal Peasantry, Dynamics of Development*, Delhi, Inter-India Publications, 1984.

Pillai, S. Devdas (ed), *Aspects of Changing India, Studies in honour of Professor G. S. Ghurye*, Popular Prakashan, 1976.

Pradhan, H. Prasad and Sengupta, N., "Regional Distribution of Economic benefits arising from a steel plant: Case study of Rourkela Steel Plant (mimeographed).

Pradhan and others (ed), *Anthropology and Archaeology, Essays in Commemoration of Verrier Elwin*, Oxford University Press, 1969.

Prasad, N., and Sahay, A., *Impact of Industrialization on Bihar Tribes*, 1961.

Raghavaiah, V., *Tribal Revolts*, 1971.

Ranga, N. G. and Saraswati, Swami Sahajanand, *Agrarian Revolts* (year not given).

Ray Choudhary, P.C., *Gazetteer of India, Bihar, Shahabad*, 1966.

Reid, J., *Final Report on the Survey and Settlement Operations in the District of Ranchi*, 1902-10, Patna, 1912.

Report of the working group on Tribal Development during the Seventh Five Year Plan 1985-90, Government of India, Ministry of Home Affairs, December, 1984.

Risley, H.H. *Tribes and Castes of Bengal*, vol. I, Calcutta, Bengal Secretariat Press, 1891.

———*The People of India*, Thacker, Spink & Co., 1915.

Roy, A.K., *Jharkhand Aur Lalkhand*, Dhanbad, July, 1981.

Roy, N.B., "New Aspects of the Santal Insurrection of 1855-6", *Indian Historical Records Commission Proceedings*, Vol. XXXV, Part II, February, 1960.

Roy, S.C., *The Mundas and their Country* (Reprint), Asia Publishing House, 1970.

———*The Oraons of Chotanagpur*, Calcutta, 1915.

———*The Birhors* Ranchi, 1925.

———*Oraon Religion and Customs*, Ranchi, 1928.

———*The Kharias*, Vol. I & II, Ranchi, 1937.

———"The Effects on the Aborigines of Chhotanagpur of their contact with western civilization", *Journal of the Bihar and Orissa Research Society*, vol. 17, pt. 4, 1931.

———"The Aborigines and the Depressed Classes in India", *The New Review*, vol. 10, no. 56, Calcutta, August, 1939.

———"The Aborigines of Chotanagpur: their proper status in reformed constitution written in 1936", *Man in India*, Administration Number, vol. 26, nol 2, June, 1946.

Report on the Fifth General Elections to the House of People, India, 1971 vol. II, 1973.

Russell, R. V. (ed), *Central Provinces District Gazetteer, Betul District*, 1907.

Sahay, K.N., *Under the Shadow of the Cross: a study of the nature and processes of Christianization among the Uraon of Central India*, Institute of Social Research and Applied Anthropology, Calcutta, 1976.

———Indigenisation of Christianity, *Man in India*, March 1981.

Sarkar, Jadunath, *A Short History of Aurangzeb* 1611—1707, second edition, 1954.

Sarup, Lakshman (trans.), *Ņighanta and Nirukta*, Oxford, 1921.

Selected Works of Mahatma Gandhi, Ahmedabad, Navajivan Press, 1968.

Sen Gupta, Nirmal, "Class and Tribe in Jharkhand", *Economic and Political Weekly*, 5 April, 1980.

———*Fourth World Dynamics: Jharkahand*, Authors Guild Publication, Oct. 1982.

Sen, Sunil, *Agrarian Struggle in Bengal 1946-47*, 1972.

Sen, T.C., *Tripura in Transition* (1923 tó 57) Agrartala, 1970.

Shah, Ghanshyam, "Socio-Economic Condition of Chodhras: A Restudy", Centre for Social Studies, Surat (unpublished).

Sharma, Dr. Dashrath (ed), *Rajasthan through the Ages*, Vol. I, Rajasthan State Archives, Bikaner, 1966.

Sharma, K.L., "Jharkhand Movement—Bihar", *Economic and Political Weekly*, 10 January, 1972.

Sharma, K.N., "On the word "Varna", For a Sociology of India", *Contributions to Indian Sociology* (NS), vol. 9, no. 2 1975.

Sharma, R.S., *Sudras in Ancient India*, 2nd edn., Delhi, 1980.

———*Indian Feudalism*, Calcutta University, 1965, 2nd edn., 1980.

———*Social Changes in Early Medieval India*, Delhi, People's Publishing House, 1969.

———*Material Culture & Social Formations in Ancient India*, Delhi, Macmillan, 1983.

Sharma, R.S. and Jha, Vivekanand, *Historical Probings, Essays in* memory of D.D. Kosambi, Peoples' Publishing House, 1974.

Sherring, Rev. M. A., *Hindu Castes and Tribes*, Vol. III 1874, London, (Reprint) Delhi Cosmo Publications, 1974.

Shukla, Hiralal, *Bastar Ke Van Vasi Geeton men Gandhi*, Raipur, 1969.

Siddiqui, M.K.A., "Islamization among the Tribes of Western India", *Man in India*, vol. 50, no. 3, July-Sept., 1979.

Singh, Bhupendra, *Planning Strategy for Tribal Development in Retrospect and Prospect, A Mid-Term Appraisal, Occasional Papers on Tribal Development*, 29. Government of India, Ministry of Home Affairs, New Delhi, 1981.

Singh C.S.K., Tribal Movement in Rajasthan 1920-47, Ph.D. thesis, Bhagalpur University 1983.

Singh, Iqbal, *The Andaman Story*, Delhi Vikas 1978.

Singh, K.S., (Same as Suresh Singh) "The Haribaba Movement in Chotanagpur (1931-32)," presented at the Indian History Congress (Ranchi), 1964 and published in *the Journal of the Bihar Research Society*, vol. 9 and 11, Jan-Dec., 1963. (unpublished)

——"Indian tribes in a historical perspective", *National Seminar, Welfare of the Tribes and denotified Communities with reference to the Fourth-Five Year Plan, Souvenir*, Bhopal, Aug. 10-13, 1964.

——*The Dust-Storm and the Hanging Mist—A study of Birsa Munda and his movement in Chhotanagpur* (1874-1901), Calcutta, Firma K.L. Mukhopadhyaya, 1966. Also see the second edn, *Birsa Munda and his movement* 1874-1901, *A study of a millenarian movement in Chotanagpur*, Calcutta, Oxford University Press, 1983.

——"Pattern of agricultural changes in tribal Chhotanagpur", *Trends of Socio-economic change in India* 1871-1961. *Transactions of the Indian Institute of Advanced Study*, vol. VII , Simla, 1969.

——"Tribal Land Organisation in Chhotanagpur and its Development," *Ibid.*

——"Munda Land System and Revenue Reforms in Chotanagpur (1869-1908)" publshed in R.S. Sharma, ed., *Land Revenue in India: Historical Studies*, Delhi Motilal, 1971.

——"State-formation in Tribal Society : Some preliminary observations", *Journal of Indian Anthropological Society*, vol. 6, no. 2, October, 1971, An earlier version of the paper (1967) appeared under the title' 'A Study in State-formation among Tribal Communities' (1967) in R.S. Sharma and V. Jha (eds), *Indian Society: Historical Probings in Memory of D.D. Kosambi*, Delhi, People's Publishing House, 1974.

——(ed.), *Tribal situation in India* The Indian Institute of Advanced Study (IIAS,) Simla, October, 1972.

——"Temples in Ranchi district", *Dr. Satkari Mookerjee Felicitation Volume*, Chowkhamba Publication, 1969.

——"Agrarian Issues in Tribal Chotanagpur (1969)", IIAS, K.S. Singh ed. *Tribal Situation in India*, Simla, 1972.

———"Integration of the tribes and development of tribal economy (1970)", *Tribe*, vol. 6 no. 3 December, 1969, Undaipur.

———"Mahatma Gandhi and the Adivasis", *Man in India*, vol. 50, no. 1, Jan-March, 1970.

———"Tribal Economy in India", Traditional Institutions in the Process of Modernisation of Society: Independent India and Soviet Central Asia, Indo-Soviet Symposium in Social Sciences, Feb. 22-26, 1977, Visva-Bharati, Shantiniketan.

———"From Ethnicity to Regionalism: A Study in tribal politics and movements in Chotanagpur from 1900 to 1975", in S.C. Malik (ed), *Dissent Protest and Reform in Indian Civilisation*, IIAS, Simla, 1977.

———"Tribal Ethnicity in a multi-ethnic society: a study in the processes of conflict and integration in colonial and post-colonial Chotanagpur", *Trends on ethnic group relations in Asia and Oceania, Race and Society*, UNESCO, 1978.

———"The Munda Land System," *The Munda World, Essays in honour of Rev. J. Hoffmann*, Roman Catholic Pressk, 1978.

———"Tribal Development: Problems of Transition, a National Programme", 27 June, 1978, AIR *News Bulletin*, 15, August, 1978.

———"Colonial Transformation of Tribal Society in Middle India", *Economic and Political Weekly*, vol. 13, no. 30, July 29, 1978.

———"John Baptist Hoffmann and the Encyclopaedia Mundarica", *New Republic*, Ranchi, 14 August, 1979.

———"The Economic situation of a Tribal Region", *Vivant Universe*, Belgium, 1979-80.

———"Jawaharlal Nehru, Tribals and their Transformation", Seminar on Nehru and Village, Madras, February, 1980.

———"Chotanagpur Raj—Mythology, Structure and Ramification", Seminar on Tribal Politics and State-Formation in Pre-Colonial Eastern and North-Eastern India, Centre for Studies in Social Sciences, Calcutta, July, 1981.

———"Kol Insurrection", Chittagaon Uprising National Golden Jubilee Committee, August, 1981.

———"Tribal Transformation: Integration, Vs Assimilation" *Economic and Political Weekly* 14/21, Aug., 1982.

———(ed.), *Economies of the Tribes and their transformation*, New Delhi Concept Publishing Company, 1982.

———"Tribal Identity Movement based on Script and Language", *Man in India*, vol. 62, no. 3, 1982.

———"A Temple in a Tribal Village" Seminar on village, Museum of Mankind, Festival of India, London, April, 1982.

———"Tribal Unrest", paper presented at Seminar on Development Aspects of Tribal Areas, November 11-13, 1980, Bhubaneswar, National Commission on Backward Areas, Government of India.

———"A Forest Satyagraha", K. S. Singh (ed), *Tribal Movements*, Vol. II Delhi, Manohar 1983.

———"The Gond Movements", K. S. Singh (ed), *Ibid.*

———*Tribal Movements in India*, vol. 1 (ed), New Delhi, Manohar, 1982.

———*Tribal Movements in India*, vol. II (ed) Delhi Manohar, March, 1983.

———"Tribal Medieval Bihar", *History of Bihar*, vol. 2, Part 1, Medieval period, K.P. Jayaswal Research Institute, 1983.

———*Tribal Laws and Justice: A Report on the Santal by* W.G. Archer (Ed. and Introd.) New Delhi, Concept, 1983.

———"Script Reform and Development: A study of two movements among the Ho tribe in Singhbhum," International Congress of Anthropological and Ethnological Sciences, Quebec-Vancouver, 15-25 August, 1983.

———"Colonialism, Anthropology and Primitive Society", Delhi University, Dec. 7-9. Indo-GDR Seminar on history sponsored by UGC, *Man in India*, Dec., 1984.

———"Varna, Jati and Jana, An Anthropo-historical Perspective", *Proceedings of the Indian History Congress*, Burdwan, 1983.

———"Agrarian Dimension of Tribal Movements", A.R. Desai, Agrarian Struggles in Post Independence India, Oxford University Press (in press).

———The Chero (MS).

———The Tanabhagat (MS).

———"Technology and Acculturation: The Brahmanical Model Reconsidered", *Social Science Probings*, New Delhi, March, 1985.

Singh, Suresh (See K.S. Singh).

Singh, Y., *Social Stratification and Change in India*, New Delhi, Manohar, 1977.

Sinha, Arun, "Bihar's Resurgent Adivasis", *Economic and Political Weekly*, 9 September, 1978.

Sinha, Surajit, "State-formation and Rajput Myth in Central India", *Man in India*, vol. 42, no. 2, 1961.

———"Tribe-Caste and Tribe-Peasant Continua in Central India", *Man in India*, vol. 45, March, 1965.

———"Transformation of Tribal Society in Modern India", Devraj Chanana Memorial Lecture, 1973 (unpublished).

———(ed), "Anthropology of Nirmal Kumar Bose", *Aspects of Indian culture and society: essays in felicitation of Professor Nirmal Kumar Bose.* Calcutta, The Indian Anthropological Soceity, 1972.

Sitaram, Lala, *Ayodhya Ka Itihas* (year not given).

Smith, Clementi "The Bastar Rebellion", *Man in India, Rebellion Number*, December 1945.

Srinivas, M.N., *Religion and society among the Coorgs of South India*, Bombay, Asia Publishing House, 1952, 2nd edn., London, 1965.

———*India's villages*. Bombay, Asia Publishing House, 1955.
———"The Social System of a Mysore village", in McKim Marriott, ed.,
———*Village India: studies in the little community*, Chicago, The University of Chicago Press, 1966.
———*Caste in modern India and other essays*, Bombay, Asia Publishing House, 1966.
———*Social change in modern India*, Berkeley and Los Angelles, 1966.
———"The cohesive role of Sanskritisation", in Philip Mason ed., *India and Ceylon: Unity and diversity*. London, Oxford University Press, 1957.
———"Foreword to Milton Singer", *An Anthropological approach to Indian Civilization, When A Great Tradition Modernizes*, New Delhi Vikas, 1972.

———*The remembered village*, Delhi, Oxford University Press, 1976.
———S. Seshaiah and V.S. Parthasarthy, eds., *Dimensions of social change in India*, New Delhi, Allied Publishers, 1977.
———"The remembered village: reply to criticism", *Contributions to Indian Sociology* (NS), 1978.
Srivastav, S.K., "The Process of Desanskritization in Village India", L.S. Bala Ratnam, (ed), *Anthropology on the March*, Book Centre, 1963.
———*Tharus* [7] *A Study in Culture dynamics*, Agra University, 1958.
Stavenhagen, Rodolfo (ed), *Agrarian and Peasant Movements in Latin America*, 1970.
Swepston, Lee, "Latin American Approaches to the Indian Problem", *International Labour Review*, vol. 117, no. 2, March-April, 1978.

Tarikh-i-Ujjainia, vol II (*date not given*).
Tendulkar, *Mahatma, Life of Mohandas Karamchand Gandhi*, Publication Division, 1952-58,
Thakar, S.V., *Bhilla Sadhu Sri Gula Maharaj Charitra Wa Karya*, Pune, 1938 (in Marathi).
Thakkar, A.V., *Aboriginals' Cry in the Wilderness* (year not given).
———Aborigines of Orissa, *Modern Review*, Sept. 1938.
Thapar, Romila, *Ancient Indian Social History*, Delhi, 1978.
Thusu, K.S., "A Political Movement of the Gonds" K. S. Singh (ed) *Tribal Movements*, Vol II, Delhi, Manohar, 1983.
Trigunayat, Jagdish, *Sosobonga*, 1960 (?) Ranchi.

USSR Academy of Sciences, Editorial Board. *Social Sciences Today, National Relations in the USSR, Theory and Practice Problems of the Contemporary World*, Moscow, 1974.

Vasu, N., N., "Copper-Plate Inscription of Nrsimhadeva II", *Journal of the Asiatic Society of Bengal*, vol. xvi part I-IV, 1869.

Vidyarthi, L.P., *Industrialization in India 'A Case study of Tribal Bihar*, 1970.

Weiner, Myron and John, Osgoodfield, *Electoral Politics in the Indian States: Three Disadvantaged Sectors.* vol. II. Delhi, Manohar 1975.

Wilson, H.H. (trans.), *Vishnu Puran*, 5 volumes, London 1864-70.

Wittfogel. K., *Oriental Despotism*, New Haven, Yale University Press, 1957.

Worsley, Peter, *Trumpet shall sound, study of Cargo cults in Melanesia*, Paladin, 1970.

Yonuo, Asso, ***Rising Nagas***, Delhi, Vivek Publishing House, 1974.

(ii) *Newspapers*:

The Economics Times

The Indian Express, New Delhi

The Indian Nation, Patna

The Patriot, New Delhi

Sagen Sakam, The Kherwal Jarpa Samiti (1964-67) Rairangpur

The Searchlight, Patna

The Statesman, New Delhi

The Sunday Standard Magazine, New Delhi

The Times of India, New Delhi

(iii) *Periodicals*:

The Adibasi, Tribal Research Institute, Bhubaneshwar

The Adivasi Public Relations Department, Government of Bihar, Ranchi

Adivasi Gujarat, Tribal Training and Research Institute, Gujarat Vidyapeeth, Ahmedabad

Economic and Political Weekly, Bombay

The Indian Historical Review, Indian Council of Historical Research, New Delhi

Man in India, Ranchi

The Organizer, Delhi

Ravivar, New Delhi

ABBREVIATION

EPW	Economic and Political Weekly
ITDA	Integrated Tribal Development Agency
MNC	Multinational Corporation
TDA	Tribal Development Agency

GLOSSARY

Abkari	excise
Abwabs	cesses
Adivasi	tribals, original dwellers
Agrahara	brahmanical settlement
Ahimsa	non-violence
Anchal	a unit of revenue administration
Anna	one sixteenth of a rupee
Anuloma	hypergamy
Ashram	hermitage/institution
Avatar	incarnation
Babul	*acacia arabica*
Bania	trader/shopkeeper/moneylender
Bazar	market
Begar	forced labour
Beth	forced labour
Bhagat	the devout
Bhagatism	religion of the devout
Bhai-bahen	brother-sister
Bhaisur	husband's elder brother
Bhajan	devotional song
Bhakta	devout
Bhaktal	priest/shaman
Bhakti	devotion
Bhuinhari	the region where tenures of *bhuinhars*, original Munda settlers, exist
Bhumakal	Bastar uprising of 1910
Bissoyi	Chief, head of the "district" or of *muttadars*
Bitlaha	institution of collective punishment for those offending Santal norms
Brahmana	a category of Vedic works
Chandi bonga	female goddess/spirit
Chando	Santal god/sun god

Chatai	hamlet
Chatties	small bazars
Chaturvarnya	fourfold varna hierarchy/order
Choudhuri	village headman
Chaurasi	a unit of 84 villages
Chowkidari	tax for the chowkidar, village police
Cowrie	shell
Dacoity	brigandage
Dasa	slave
Dasyu	slave/robber
De-Ko	the others
Dhakar	outsider
Dhangar	lowly/servant
Diku	the aliens
Diwan	chief minister
Durbar	court
Dora	leader
Firman	royal, official order
Fituri	tribal uprising or disturbance in south Orissa and north Andhra
Gadi	throne
Ganga mai	mother Ganges
Gameti	village headman
Gamit	village headman
Gaontia	village headman
Garibi hatao	removing poverty
Garh	fort
Ghatwal	guardians of passes and wardens of marches
Gherao	to besiege
Gola	depot
Gotra	'cow pen', exogamous clan unit
Guru	teacher
Harijan	scheduled caste
Hat	fair
Hul	Santal insurrection of 1855-56
Ijara	lease of *khas* village
Ishta devi	chief female deity (of family)
Jagir	a service tenure
Jagirdar	holder of jagir
Jah-era	the sacred grove or its female deity
Jajmani	patron-client relationship
Jana	tribe
Janapada	region
Jati	caste/sub-caste

Jeth	husband's elder brother
Jhum	shifting cultivation
Kali	mother goddess
Kali paraj	"black people", tribals in Gujarat
Kaliyuga	dark age
Kangal	destitute
Karma	deed
Khaddar/Khadi	handspun cotton
Khas or *Khalisa*	own cultivation/self-proprietorship
Khuntkatti	the tenure of the original
Khuntkattidar	holder of the *khuntkatti*
Kisan	peasants
Lat	a unit of villages
Lalkhand	red land
Laraka	militant
Mahaant	haunted/deserted village
Mahajan	moneylender
Mahaashtmi	eighth day of the Dusserah
Mahto	village headman
Mahua	*bassia latifolia*
Majaar	shrine
Malguzar	revenue collector
Mallika	village deity
Mama	maternal uncle
Mandli	local church bodies
Manjhi	village headman
Manki	head of the pir/patti
Mansabdar	head of the *muttadars*/a chief holding a rank conferred by the government
Maund/mound	a unit of weight, thirty seven and half kilos
Meli	tribal disturbances in Orissa
Meriah	human sacrifice
Mudud	Customary assistance
Munda	village headman
Munshi	clerk
Mutta	a union of villages, a fort, a small district of a sub-division of a country
Muttadar	chief of the *mutta*
Nag	Serpent
Naga	hill people
Naik	headman, leader
Pal	a settlement, a congregation of hamlets
Panda	priest
Pardeshi	outsider

Parwana	notice
Pariadari	a form of assessment
Pargana	a unit/division of fiscal administration
Parganait	chief of a pargana
Parha	inter-village/clan council
Patti	a group of villages under a Manki, chief of Munda village leaders
Pawa	a unit of *paria*
Pir	division/saint
Patmanjhi	chief *manjhi*
Pratiloma	hypogamy
Puja	worship
Puran	old traditional history
Puya	chronicle
Raiyat/Ryot	cultivator or owner cultivator
Raj	kingdom/ruler
Raja	ruler
Ram nama	God's name
Ram rajya	the age of righteousness
Rakshasas	demons
Rani	queen
Rashtra devata	god of a region
Risaldar	officer of the cavalry
Rishi	sage
Ryotwari	cultivators' tenure/state's direct relationship with raiyat
Rudraksha	bead
Sabar mantra	black magic
Sadan	non-tribal speaking Sadani language
Sadani	language of the Sadans (non-tribals)
Saheb	Europeans
Sal	*shorea robusta*
Salami	a present, an offering
Sanad	grant
Sapha Hor	clean people
Sari	truth
Sari dharam	the old tribal religion centred on "truth"
Sarkar	government
Sarnaik	chief leader
Sarna dharam	the tribal religion of the 'sacred grove'
Sasan diri	burial ground
Satyagraha	struggle for truth/civil disobedience
Sena	army
Shakti	mother goddess
Sindur	vermilion ?

Singbahini	mother goddess riding a lion
Singbonga	Supreme God
Smriti	Law book
Sud	the Sadan, non-tribal
Suryabhedi	a type of tank
Swami	saint
Swaraj	self rule/freedom
Thakur	god
Thanedar	head of a police station
Taluq	a sub-division
Taluqdar	head of a taluq
Tantra	a mode of union (*yoga*) of self with, and of Shiva with Shakti through mystical (and magical) practices
Tappa	a territorial subdivision
Tilka/Tilak	a mark of investiture
Ulgulan	Munda rebellion of 1895-1901
Vais	outsider
Vanaspati	plant
Varna	colour, fourfold classification based on birth and occupation
Yajnya	sacrifice
Zamindar	owner of an estate
Zamindari	estate of the zamindar

INDEX